The Belt and Road Strategy in International Business and Administration

Wei Liu
University of Sydney, Australia

Zhe Zhang
University of Sydney, Australia

Jin-Xiong Chen
Wuyi University, China

Sang-Bing Tsai
University of Electronic Science and Technology of China Zhongshan Institute, China & Capital University of Economics and Business, China & Wuyi University, China

A volume in the Advances in Business Strategy and Competitive Advantage (ABSCA) Book Series

IGI Global
DISSEMINATOR OF KNOWLEDGE

Published in the United States of America by
IGI Global
Business Science Reference (an imprint of IGI Global)
701 E. Chocolate Avenue
Hershey PA, USA 17033
Tel: 717-533-8845
Fax: 717-533-8661
E-mail: cust@igi-global.com
Web site: http://www.igi-global.com

Library of Congress Cataloging-in-Publication Data

Names: Liu, Wei, 1993- editor.
Title: The Belt and Road strategy in international business and administration / Wei Liu [and three others], editors.
Description: Hershey, PA : Business Science Reference, [2020]
Identifiers: LCCN 2018054603| ISBN 9781522584407 (hardcover) | ISBN 9781522584414 (ebook) | ISBN 9781522584995 (softcover)
Subjects: LCSH: China--Commercial policy. | China--Commerce. | China--Foreign economic relations. | Economic development. | International trade.
Classification: LCC HF1604 .B4586 2020 | DDC 382/.30951--dc23 LC record available at https://lccn.loc.gov/2018054603

This book is published in the IGI Global book series Advances in Business Strategy and Competitive Advantage (ABSCA) (ISSN: 2327-3429; eISSN: 2327-3437)

British Cataloguing in Publication Data
A Cataloguing in Publication record for this book is available from the British Library.

All work contributed to this book is new, previously-unpublished material.
The views expressed in this book are those of the authors, but not necessarily of the publisher.

For electronic access to this publication, please contact: eresources@igi-global.com.

Advances in Business Strategy and Competitive Advantage (ABSCA) Book Series

ISSN:2327-3429
EISSN:2327-3437

Editor-in-Chief: Patricia Ordóñez de Pablos, Universidad de Oviedo, Spain

MISSION

Business entities are constantly seeking new ways through which to gain advantage over their competitors and strengthen their position within the business environment. With competition at an all-time high due to technological advancements allowing for competition on a global scale, firms continue to seek new ways through which to improve and strengthen their business processes, procedures, and profitability.

The **Advances in Business Strategy and Competitive Advantage (ABSCA) Book Series** is a timely series responding to the high demand for state-of-the-art research on how business strategies are created, implemented and re-designed to meet the demands of globalized competitive markets. With a focus on local and global challenges, business opportunities and the needs of society, the **ABSCA** encourages scientific discourse on doing business and managing information technologies for the creation of sustainable competitive advantage.

COVERAGE

- Business Models
- Small and Medium Enterprises
- Strategic alliances
- Entrepreneurship & Innovation
- Joint Ventures
- Value Creation
- Strategy Performance Management
- Outsourcing
- Innovation Strategy
- Strategic Management

IGI Global is currently accepting manuscripts for publication within this series. To submit a proposal for a volume in this series, please contact our Acquisition Editors at Acquisitions@igi-global.com or visit: http://www.igi-global.com/publish/.

The Advances in Business Strategy and Competitive Advantage (ABSCA) Book Series (ISSN 2327-3429) is published by IGI Global, 701 E. Chocolate Avenue, Hershey, PA 17033-1240, USA, www.igi-global.com. This series is composed of titles available for purchase individually; each title is edited to be contextually exclusive from any other title within the series. For pricing and ordering information please visit http://www.igi-global.com/book-series/advances-business-strategy-competitive-advantage/73672. Postmaster: Send all address changes to above address.

Titles in this Series

For a list of additional titles in this series, please visit:
https://www.igi-global.com/book-series/advances-business-strategy-competitive-advantage/73672

Cases on Corporate Social Responsibility and Contemporary Issues in Organizations
Alexandros Antonaras (University of Nicosia, Cyprus) and Paraskevi Dekoulou (University of Nicosia, Cyprus)
Business Science Reference • ©2019 • 402pp • H/C (ISBN: 9781522577157) • US $225.00

Women Entrepreneurs and Strategic Decision Making in the Global Economy
Florica Tomos (University of South Wales, UK) Naresh Kumar (Universiti Malaysia Kelantan, Malaysia) Nick Clifton (Cardiff Metropolitan University, UK) and Denis Hyams-Ssekasi (University of Bolton, UK)
Business Science Reference • ©2019 • 411pp • H/C (ISBN: 9781522574798) • US $215.00

Linking Cultural Dimensions and CSR Communication Emerging Research and...
Maria Palazzo (University of Salerno, Italy)
Business Science Reference • ©2019 • 169pp • H/C (ISBN: 9781522579465) • US $165.00

Evidence-Based Initiatives for Organizational Change and Development
Robert G. Hamlin (University of Wolverhampton, UK) Andrea D. Ellinger (The University of Texas at Tyler, USA) and Jenni Jones (University of Wolverhampton, UK)
Business Science Reference • ©2019 • 850pp • H/C (ISBN: 9781522561552) • US $495.00

Environmental, Health, and Business Opportunities in the New Meat Alternatives Market
Diana Bogueva (Curtin University, Australia) Dora Marinova (Curtin University, Australia) Talia Raphaely (Curtin University, Australia) and Kurt Schmidinger (University of Vienna, Austria)
Business Science Reference • ©2019 • 395pp • H/C (ISBN: 9781522573500) • US $225.00

Handbook of Research on Business Models in Modern Competitive Scenarios
George Leal Jamil (Informações em Rede e Consultoria Ltda., Brazil) Liliane Carvalho Jamil (Independent Researcher, Brazil) Cláudio Roberto Magalhães Pessoa (FUMEC University, Brazil) and Werner Silveira (Philharmonic Orchestra of Minas Gerais, Brazil)
Business Science Reference • ©2019 • 537pp • H/C (ISBN: 9781522572657) • US $295.00

For an entire list of titles in this series, please visit:
https://www.igi-global.com/book-series/advances-business-strategy-competitive-advantage/73672

IGI Global
DISSEMINATOR OF KNOWLEDGE

701 East Chocolate Avenue, Hershey, PA 17033, USA
Tel: 717-533-8845 x100 • Fax: 717-533-8661
E-Mail: cust@igi-global.com • www.igi-global.com

Table of Contents

Section 3
Regional Case Studies Under the Belt and Road Strategy

Detailed Table of Contents

cooperatively issued the "Vision and Action for Promoting the Construction of the Silk Road Economic Belt and the 21st Century Maritime Silk Road" on March 28, 2015. The "One Belt One Road" countries were key areas of cooperation in the context of China's policy in communication, road connectivity, smooth trade, currency circulation, people's mutual understanding, strategic coordination to strengthen bilateral and multilateral teamwork, and corresponding development.

With the continuous upgrading of the economical industry structure and the gradual optimization of the excess capacity, China has begun to get rid of the name "world factory" of "processing with imported materials." However, there are problems still existing, such as the contradiction between enterprises' poor independent innovation ability and consumers' increasing demands on product quality. Enterprises in China have the great opportunity to "go out" because of "The Belt and Road" strategy, but it is extremely complicated in legal system, customs, and social culture, which means how to use of intellectual property in China coexists risks and opportunities for enterprises. This chapter focuses on analyzing problems of intellectual property rights in China and the importance of the protection and development of intellectual property. In addition, this chapter studies strategies that can be provided for the protection and development of intellectual property in China from the perspective of "The Belt and Road."

After the belt and road initiative was put forward, the relevant domestic regions responded positively and carried out research work in succession, making suggestions for the implementation and planning of the belt and road initiative. However, the relevant research work mainly focuses on the political, economic, and cultural problems existing in the implementation of the belt and road initiative. The research on intellectual property protection issues has rarely been reported. By analyzing the intellectual property environment both of domestic and international in which the belt and road initiative located, this chapter focuses on the intellectual property protection strategy in the implementation of the belt and road initiative, aiming at providing reference for intellectual property research under the belt and road initiative.

Section 2
Industrial and Trade Development Studies Under the Belt and Road Strategy

factors on the sharing rate of railway transportation market. Finally, the chapter puts forward corresponding measures to improve the competitiveness of railway transportation market.

Innovation ability is the key to enterprise development. China's electrolytic aluminum enterprises have maintained a high growth rate for many years and have become one of the industries with the highest social contribution rate in the non-ferrous metal industry. However, a prominent problem in the development process of the industry is to put less emphasis on innovation and investment. Excessive production capacity due to blind investment has become a common disease of enterprises, which has seriously affected their performance. This chapter tries to explore cooperative motivation, innovation, and development of the electrolytic aluminum enterprise. The aim is for the enterprise to find source sex power basis, combined with the strategy of "area," all the way to the electrolytic aluminum enterprise value influence, understand all kinds of system to the importance of the synergy of electrolytic aluminum enterprises, in order to further promote collaborative innovation measures to provide adequate basis.

The "One Belt One Road" strategy has been fully implemented since 2016, and the unlimited potential of Macau needs to be developed. The excellent geographic location enables Macau to be a significant geographic node on the maritime silk route; the internalized business regulation and advantages in talent enables Macau to be a significant regulation node of system ensuring the operation of the policy "One Belt One Road"; the advantages in political aspect enables Macau to be a significant financial node of the process of "One Belt One Road" financing and management.

Preface

The Belt and Road Strategy is a development strategy unveiled by the Chinese president Xi in 2013 and officially proposed by the Chinese government in 2015. This strategy aims to connect countries along the routes in Asia, Europe, Africa, strengthen the partnerships, and construct a comprehensive and multilevel interconnected network to achieve pluralistic, independent, balanced and sustainable development. Through mapping a clear road map for development, this strategy focuses on economic and trade cooperation, business development, and infrastructure investment in the current stage.

The role of the Belt and Road Strategy could be reflected in two aspects: (1) International Business context. Multinational Enterprises gain benefits from the strategy and enhance the foreign markets based on policy guidance. (2) Regional governance and management. Infrastructure construction such as transportation and services will be invested in less development countries and this will play its role in different fields and the level of regional administration needs to be identified. Thus, international business and regional administration under the Belt and Road Strategy should be a value research issue.

With the emergence of the information and communication age, international business activities have made extraordinary progress. However, the unstable environment of internationalization in recent years just brought challenges to the sustainable development of corporate internationalization strategies, which is reflected in two aspects: First, the "Brexit" (Britain off Europe) and the U.S. anti-globalization trade policy have hindered enterprises' stability and development through free trade; Second, China-led emerging powers are promoting active international development strategies, such as "The Belt and Road Strategy" which is interpreted as the new "Marshall Plan" by some Western politicians.

Since the Belt and Road Strategy has become one of most important programs embodying economic, regional and political demands in Asian and European environment, it attracts the strong interest of the governments, enterprises and research scholars around most countries. However, as the Belt and Road Strategy is more likely to be pictured as a mostly geopolitical project with obvious political intentions, it attracts less attention from scholars in management field, specifically international business and regional administration.

Therefore, this book is expected to cause wider and divergent concern on program investment and political support reflecting new theoretical and practical mechanism of international business and regional administration from professionals, researchers students and professors working in the topic of the Belt and Road Strategy and the relative studies in international business and regional administration.

This book contains three sections. Section 1, "International Business Studies Under the Belt and Road Strategy," has a total of six chapters. All the chapters in this section are studied and reviewed through the perspective of international business such as corporate internationalization and global strategy. Specifically, Chapter 1 discusses the Chinese development model under the new global situation. Chapter 2 discusses the corporate social responsibility of Chinese firms and its development, risk and strategic decision-making under the Belt and Road Strategy. Chapter 3 discusses how Chinese firms improve the competitiveness to adapt to the international market. Chapters 4, 5, and 6 are a series of studies focusing on intellectual property. The chapters discuss the importance of intellectual property protection, aiming to provide the strategies for intellectual property under the belt and road strategy.

Section 2, "Industrial and Trade Development Studies Under the Belt and Road Strategy," has a total of three chapters. Chapter 7 established a multimodal transport cost model to analyze the cost and time components of shipping trade under the belt and road strategy. Chapter 8 discusses the competitiveness of coal railway transportation in the core area of the belt and road strategy. Chapter 9 explores the motivation and development of the Chinese electrolytic aluminum industry, aiming to promote the collaborative innovation combined with the regionalization strategy.

Section 3, "Regional Case Studies Under the Belt and Road Strategy," has a total of three chapters, in order to provide more specific cases to enrich the study of the belt and road strategy. Chapter 10 introduces the Macau as an important geographic node on the belt and road and discusses how Macau enhances its advantages to contribute to the belt and road strategy. Chapter 11 uses the case of Malaysia to discuss the synergistic development effect of the belt and road strategy to promote cooperation and development of economy, trade, politics and human resources. Chapter 12 analyzes the Mongolian tourism, pointing out the new opportunities for tourism which bring by the belt and road strategy.

To conclude, attempts have been made in this book not just to explore the relationship between international business and sustainable development, providing a practical and comprehensive forum for exchanging novel research ideas or empirical practices in this topic, and also to contribute to developing theoretical, analytical, empirical research, comprehensive reviews of relevant research, conceptual frameworks and case studies of effective applications in this area.

Wei Liu
University of Sydney, Australia

Zhe Zhang
University of Sydney, Australia

Jin-Xiong Chen
Wuyi University, China

Sang-Bing Tsai
University of Electronic Science and Technology of China Zhongshan Institute, China, & Capital University of Economics and Business, China & Wuyi University, China

Acknowledgment

We acknowledge IGI Global for their professional assistance in the publication of this book, as well as all the chapter authors for their contributions to this book. We are very grateful to all anonymous referees for their helpful reviewing work. Most importantly, we acknowledge the financial supports by the National Social Science Foundation of China (Grant No.17CGJ002), and resource supports by the Wuyi University and Macau 'One Belt One Road' Research Centre at the City University of Macau and University of Electronic Science and Technology of China Zhongshan Institute, China and Environment and Sustainable Development Center of China Civil Aviation University, China and Capital University of Economics and Business, China and China Academy of Corporate Governance, Nankai University, China.

Section 1

International Business Studies Under the Belt and Road Strategy

Chapter 1
The China Model in the Global Economy

Bahar Baysal Kar
Kırklareli University, Turkey

Taha Eğri
Kırklareli University, Turkey

ABSTRACT

The purpose of this chapter is to stand against the claim that the same neo-liberal model emerges in all countries as a result of the competitive pressures arising from globalization. Countries can experience a globalization pattern that improves their growth performance and living standards with different policy preferences in the fields of finance, trade, and investment. The variety of Chinese capitalism is a case of this situation. In the first section, this Chinese development model with its illiberal policies first is examined. In the second section, the new development initiatives and institutional arrangements and their potential effects are discussed. In addition, the implications of these new development initiatives are argued in terms of global governance systems.

INTRODUCTION

The dominant power of post-communist world order is US free market capitalism. With the global financial crisis, new varieties of capitalism has emerged and the world order has begun to change in favor of the new capitalism models. "Refurbished state capitalism" (McNally, 2013a), "state-permeated capitalism" (Nölke & Claar, 2013), "strategic capitalism" (Şenses, Öniş & Bakır, 2013) or "state capitalism"

DOI: 10.4018/978-1-5225-8440-7.ch001

(Bremmer, 2010) represented by emerging market economies such as China, India, Russia and Brazil is an example of these new models. While these countries managed to overcome the global crisis quickly, they also became the pioneers of global growth (McNally, 2013, p.33). Chinese capitalism alone is also portrayed as a rival to US capitalism. It is frequently discussed in the literature as the rising power of the global system (Wolf, 2014). Today China's economy is the second largest economy in the world and it is even significantly larger than the sum of Brazillin, Indian and Russian economies. On the other hand, it is also an important resource for world economy with commodity demand (Wolf, 2014, p. 147). In fact, the debate on China's rise in the global system has begun before the global crisis. In these discussions, Beijing Consensus[1] is exemplified[2] which reflects the experience of China's economic development for the southern countries against liberalization, privatization and stabilization based on the Washington Consensus (Yağcı, 2016). On the other hand, China is positioned separately within Asian economies and is regarded as the pioneer of commercial and economic expansion in East Asia and other regions. Thus, there are arguments that China replaced the United States (Arrighi, 2008).

In this study, Chinese capitalism model will be examined as an alternative capitalism to the liberal economic model and as an alternative specific development model. Firstly, the characteristics of the Chinese capitalism model will be defined. Secondly, its different policy preferences in trade and finance will be discussed. Finally, the reforms which are introduced in recent years as a response to the structural problems and their consequences in terms of international political economy will be presented. For this purpose, the "second image" perspective, which underlies that domestic structures play a critical role in explaining the government's preferences for international politics (Ten Brink, 2014; Nölke, Ten Brink, Claar & May, 2015). In other words, this approach emphasizes domestic socio-economic institutions and their political affiliation, questioning the externalization of domestic structures and effectively blending comparative and international political economy approaches. By looking at the preferences of policy makers in the context of China's national development model, it is possible to develop an understanding of how China has risen within the global capitalist system (Ten Brink, 2014; Nölke et al, 2015).

In this study, China model is analyzed as a variety of capitalism pioneered by the state, as seen in the types of capitalism such as "refurbished state capitalism (McNally, 2013a)", "state-permeated capitalism" (Nölke & Claar, 2013), "strategic capitalism" (Şenses et al. 2013) or state capitalism (Bremmer, 2010). The main purpose is to stand against the claim that the same neoliberal model will emerge in all countries as a result of the competitive pressures arising from globalization. Countries can experience a globalization pattern that will improve their life standards and growth performances, with different policy preferences, particularly in the fields of finance and foreign trade (Chang & Grabel, 2004). China is a successful model of economic development with non-liberal trade and financial strategies and bilateral and reciprocal agreements with certain countries instead of multilateral agreements (May & Nölke, 2014). In recent years, the reforms it has developed against certain problems stemming from the export and investment-side growth model have continued to exist in the form of state control and non-liberal policies consistent with its own form of capitalism. In response to these problems, the Chinese government is in an effort to pursue statist solutions, including efforts to recentralize, standardize and better regulate various aspects of the political economy without showing a one-sided dependence on measures of liberalization. These solutions are in line with China's balanced follow-up measures of liberalization and policies that are a combination of efforts to strengthen and maintain state control (McNally, 2013c, p. 48).

STATE CAPITALISM IN CHINA

It is difficult to examine the capitalism emerged in China within firm-centered capitalism models (Hall & Soskice, 2001) because of its extremely parsimonious nature (Nölke & Claar, 2013: 34). Witt (2010) analyzed China's political economy through the "varieties of capitalism (VOC)" approach, which Hall and Soskice (2001) introduced to the literature. This approach presents two types of ideal capitalism in the form of liberal and coordinated market economies. Witt (2010) argues that China does not comply with them but only resembles a liberal market economy due to certain characteristics and also argues that there are more than one variety of capitalism emerged within the national borders of China.

In fact capitalism models focus on the origin and nature of institutional diversity in developed capitalist societies (Pontusson, 2005, p.164). They are inadequate to account for the dynamic institutional structure of emerging market economies that adopt the basic principles of the free market economy model, such as China, where state ownership in key industries and state control at varying degrees in the financial sector still persist (McNally, 2013a; McNally, 2013b). On the other hand, it is not possible to explain differences in the type and degree of neoliberal reforms with VOC approach in countries like China where the role of the state cannot be ignored (Schmidt, 2009). Nölke and Vliegenthart (2009) define an alternative type of capitalism focusing on the interaction of the national political economy and international factors and they criticize the fact that VOC considers national capitalist systems as a closed box. Furthermore they claim that societies are embedded within international economic regulation and global value chain institutions. This criticism becomes more meaningful when the role of foreign investment and especially the importance of global production and information networks in small and medium-sized enterprises are taken into consideration in China. Taking these criticisms into account, it will be a more accurate approach to examine capitalism in China as a rising market economy on the basis of a theoretical structure that integrates state action and international economic relations (Ten Brink, 2014).

Despite the ongoing reform process in China since the late 1970s, a variety of capitalism emerged that could be called state capitalism instead of liberal capitalism. This system does not rely purely on market and economic liberalization but it uses the markets pragmatically. Furthermore it is believed that the government is important in managing and developing the economy (Wang, 2017; McNally, 2013a; McNally, 2013b). The basic characteristics can be summarized as follows.

Firstly, China is a bureaucratic and authoritarian single-party state and for this reason the variety of its capitalism is called "bureaucratic state capitalism" (Buzan & Lawson, 2014). Bureaucratic state capitalism arises when the distinction between economy and politics is blurred and governance is not democratic (Buzan and Lawson, 2014). But this political structure of China, unexpectedly, has created an extremely dynamic and centralized structure that supports economic development (Kroeber, 2016).

In China, the public financial system is dominated by bureaucratic structure too. At the national level, the National Development and Reform Commission and the Ministry of Finance are influential actors in the financial system. The approval of the budget belongs to the National People's Congress and as it is difficult to understand and supervise the budget, the public accountability is almost nonexistent. As an important consequence of this, it creates investment and infrastructure bias in public expenditures. Expenditure on transportation, communication and energy has gone far beyond social expenditure, which increases people's quality of life. In fact, this composition of expenditures is in line with China's growth model based on exports and investments. This is a sign of government's dominance and control in the economy. This has also led to an increase in state savings within national savings. State revenues have turned into savings rather than being spent on social welfare or local governments that are in difficult situations. This leads to an imbalance between savings and consumption in China today (Wang, 2017, p.100-101; McNally, 2013c, p.52).

In addition to this political and financial structure of China, it constantly organizes state economic enterprises (SOEs) in its management structure. Thus, although the share of private enterprises is constantly increasing, the share of the public sector in the economy is still high. The largest corporations in the economy are in public ownership and the most strategic and profitable sectors of the economy are state-controlled. In addition, many seemingly private companies are wholly or largely under state control and are operated by government investments (Balding, 2018; Wang, 2017; Kroeber, 2016). More specifically state-owned enterprises have a total asset base equal to 208% of nominal GDP in 2016. There are also 174,000 SOEs in the industry, transport and wholesale sector according to the data of the same year. According to Balding, *"there is effectively no sector a Chinese SOE does not dominate"* (Balding, 2018, p. 64-65).

Since the 1980s, there has been an intensive de facto privatization process in Chinese industry. Village and town initiatives have emerged in the form of private entrepreneurship and today they are almost entirely private. Private companies dominate competitive sectors in cities[3]. However state ownership is dominant in non-competitive sectors (public services, transportation, telecommunications, oil and gas, defense industry, etc.) and plays a supporting and subsidary role in all other sectors. Thus China's industrial system seems like a mixed economy (Naughton, 2010, p.442). On the other hand the role of companies with foreign capital is also important. Therefore Naughton (2010, p. 441) conceives China's industrial system as a three-tier system consisting of large central government companies, hybrid local and foreign companies, and small-scale companies.

The weight of state ownership and investment causes China to differentiate from East Asian neighbors. For example, in the post-World War II period most of the companies and banks are private companies in Japan. State ownership and state investments are not as common as in China. State's responsibility is limited to the regulation and control of the flow of resources. Again, although the financial system in South Korea is state-owned, entrepreneurship is carried out by the private sector and large family companies are attracting attention (Kroeber, 2016).

China's top-down, state-led development is accompanied by economic development mediated by medium and small-sized companies. These companies use entrepreneurial strategies by creating highly flexible production and information networks and their efforts mediate the formation of "entrepreneurial network capitalism". But this type of capitalism is also based on informal relations between the state and the entrepreneurs themselves (McNally, 2012; 2013a).

CHINESE ECONOMY IN THE PROCESS OF NEOLIBERAL GLOBALIZATION

The purpose of this study is to present that neoliberal globalization is only a form of globalization. When examined in the case of China, it has been argued that different policy choices, especially in foreign trade, investment and finance, can reveal an alternative economic development model and globalization pattern (Chang & Grabel, 2004). The period in which China is integrated with global capitalism is a time when neoliberal globalization gains speed and dominance. On one hand, with the collapse of the Soviet bloc, the involvement of India, Latin America and a part of Africa in the global trade and investment network, China has become part of a wider trade and investment network of global dynamism of capital accumulation. On the other hand, China has gained the opportunity to benefit from increased high-tech investments in the US in this period and new information, initiatives and business models that have accelerated in this period (McNally, 2008; McNally, 2012). China is actually a more open society than the first industrialized countries like Japan, South Korea and Taiwan. However, for strategic industries, China has benefited from similar methods used by these countries, such as subsidized investment programs, export-led growth strategy, stimulating high savings and investment rates, suppressing domestic consumption, exchange rate and capital controls. In this chapter, these illiberal policies of Chinese economy and bilateral and reciprocal relations rather than multilateral agreements with other countries will be examined within the global trade and financial system. In the face of the threats to the sustainability of these policies and strategies, efforts to rebalance China's political economy will be also be analyzed in recent years.

Trade Strategy

One of the most important determinant that have contributed to the rise of China in the global economy is undoubtedly export-oriented production. China has become the "factory of the world" with the labor supply provided by the crowded population and the production with low cost inputs and it has directed this production to export. Total trade volume exceeded 3.7 trillion dolar in 2017 and this trade volume is 200 times higher than at 1978 level[4]. It is the world's largest exporter and the second largest importer with 12% and 10% of world merchandise exports and imports respectively (Amighini, 2018, p. 17) and the largest competitor of the United States today.

Since the early 1980s, integration into the global system has been largely managed and gradual. Exports began at a few authorized private export-processing[5] zones along the southern coast of China. By the mid-1980s, export processing became widespread and a two-stage export regime became evident: Processing export segment which is open to outside and benefiting from duty free imports and a domestic export sector that gets high levels of protection through tariffs and non-tariff barriers (Kowalski, 2010, p. 206).

The export zones that specialize in specific areas (labor intensive, capital intensive or information technology etc.) to support export-oriented industrialization form an example of the strategy of promoting industries of state aiming to develop high technology without giving up the labor-intensive industries by the division of labor that they set out. Especially in the export zone where information-intensive industries are located, the government directly intervenes to provide cooperation of universities, firms and state-owned banks for the development of information technology (Arrighi, 2010, p. 358-359).

In the 1990s, China's reforms towards the transition to the market economy accelerated. China has announced and implemented numerous policy reforms to create the institutional foundations of better functioning commodity, labor and capital markets in order to become a WTO member. China adopted a number of economic institutions, such as minimum standards of intellectual property rights and sanction procedures; mandatory tariff rates, as required by the WTO, and became a member of the WTO in 2001 (Edmonds, Croix & Li, 2006:3).

China has fully integrate into the global markets and attain a market power especially depend on low wage costs with the membership in the WTO. The trade has increased dramatically since 2001. However, despite many policy commitments to liberalization before membership, some important sectors such as agriculture and food products, banking, and finance, remained closed to foreign investment and protected from competition until now (Amighini, 2018, p. 17-18).

The period 2003-2012 has been a statist period and the market reforms have slowed down considerably (Hilbert, 2014, p.17). The main purpose of the government in this period was to facilitate the taking back of market share held by foreign investors in China over the previous ten years (Kroeber, 2016). The liberalization process has begun to reverse, while foreign investors and importers face barriers to entry into the market, privileged domestic investors have been supported and protected by taxes, subsidies and public contracts, and also discriminatory policies against foreign investors have begun to be implemented (Hilpert, 2014, p.18).

The average tariff rates are still high in China compared to the developed countries. According to the WTO's data, the average tariff rates in the US are 3.4%, 5% in EU countries, and 10% in China in 2017. Compared to developed countries such as India (48.5%) and Brazil (31.4%), the relatively lower average tariff levels of China are not a sign of free trade commitments but on the contrary it is interpreted as the likelihood that the Chinese capitalists will leave the emerging middle class market to foreign competitors in the coming years is very low (May & Nölke, 2014, p. 10).

The exchange rate policy[6] in China is an important indicator of trade protectionism (Rodrik, 2013; Amighini, 2018, p. 17-18)[7]. Chinese leaders see the exchange rate not as a price, set in the market but as a tool for a comprehensive development strategy (McNally, 2015, p. 716). The government intervenes in the exchange rate to protect the producers' profitability, and this policy causes trade surplus in China (Rodrik, 2013). The essence of this policy is to artificially lower the value of Renminbi, China's national currency, and gain an unfair advantage in global markets (Wang, 2017). In a way, China creates a current account surplus by subsidizing its exports and causing imports to be more expensive. In that way, it contributes to global imbalances (Hilbert, 2014, p.18; Wang, 2017).

The pilot free trade zones established for the facilitation of trade in China also provide insight into the way the reforms are implemented and their process. These regions do not aim to liberalize trade with other countries, but point to new reform methods. For Chinese government, they are also unilateral policy trial areas (Yao & Whalley, 2016).

China's attitude towards protectionism can also be understood from its attitude toward various areas of global liberalization in the Doha Round negotiations, which continue under the WTO framework. "Singapore Issues" designed by developed countries as the next step for global multilateral trade liberalization in 1996 are measures of deep integration (Stephen & Parizek, 2015; May & Nölke, 2014). These measures target four different areas. The first is about the protection of investments against the discretionary behavior of the host country government and the relationship between trade and investments. The second deals with the competition policy and aims to restrict governments from arbitrarily supporting their local companies. The third aims at restricting the government from giving priority to local or national producers in the supply of public investments and government spending in relation to government procurement while the fourth area aims at facilitating trade in the sense of removing bureaucratic obstacles in trade such as customs procedures. The first three have been deducted from the agenda of the Doha Round negotiations in favor of emerging economies, including China, and only the facilitation of trade has been able to remain on the agenda (Stephen & Parizek, 2015). Stephen and Parizek (2015, p. 22-23) aimed to measure countries' support for trade liberalization by scaling between 0 and 4, while China's trade liberalization was found to be attitude 2, while the G7 countries' pro-liberal attitude was 2.8. This attitude of China is interpreted by the authors as a result of seeking to harmonize their domestic structures with international agreements (p.3).

After the global crisis, China has lowered expectations for growth rates to 6.5% per annum and realized the need to shift from an investment and export-oriented growth model to a more sustainable and consumption-oriented growth model. For China, it is the time to move from a low-cost factory to a high-value-added economy. This is the aim of "Made in China 2025". (Magri, 2018). However, the Chinese government still seeks to shape and manage the economy through state-owned enterprises and other enterprises subsidies and directives. Despite the WTO rules' aim to limit subsidies, the Chinese trading system will continue to maintain these constraints (Eichengreen, 2018).

Bilateral and Regional Trade Agreements

Compared with post-World War II practices, China seems to prefer bilateral and regional trade agreements rather than multilateral trade agreements. This behaviour means a declining role for the World Trade Organization (WTO) (Eichengreen, 2018).

The Chinese government considers free trade agreements both as a method for opening the country out and as a means of being proactive in the process of developing emerging global trade rules. China's free trade negotiations started with the WTO membership in 2001. China, which signed 13 FTAs by April 2018, signed six of them after 2013 in Xi Jinping administration period (Tiezzi, 2018, p. 40). When the signed agreements are examined, China appears to have signed the FTAs, especially with developing countries. One of those agreements is the multilateral agreement with ASEAN countries, which only accounts for 2.5% of China's total trade. Trade agreements with countries such as Pakistan, Peru and Maldives are more political for China than for economic reasons. Negotiations with developed countries are conducted in a wide area including the environment and labor, which make them difficult to conclude. On the other hand, negotiations from developing countries give China the power to determine rules and provide a kind of education for economy bureaucrats (Tiezzi, 2018, p. 45).

Free trade agreements have become increasingly prevalent in China's economic and foreign policy. President Xi describes the FTAs in an explanation he made in 2014 as a "*necessary choice for comprehensively deepening reform and constructing a new system of open-style economy*" and an "*important method for China to proactively handle foreign relations and achieve external strategic goals*" (Tiezzi, 2018, p. 45). It is clear that in the plans and programs published by the Chinese government at different levels after 2012, explicit referrals were made to the FTAs. In this context, diplomatic as well as economic goals are emphasized. It is aimed that China will be active in determining the rules of global trade by becoming active in free trade agreements by connecting countries in the region.

Dependency of the Chinese economy to trade is making it vulnerable to global fluctuations. The decrease in global trade or the increase in protectionism is damaging to the Chinese economy. New policies need to be developed to reduce this fragility. This was mentioned in a report prepared by the Ministry of Commerce in 2010. As the second largest economy, it is emphasized that China should be an active leading country, not a passive country that follows the existing rules both in trade and in investment. The concept of "strong trading power" (maoyi qiangguo) was used to describe this vision (Heath, 2016, p. 175).

Investment Strategies

In addition to international trade, foreign direct investment is also a component of global economic integration in China. However Chinese international regime is less open to inflows and outflows foreign direct investment and it has been applied a "selective openness" (Eichengreen, 2018; Amighini, 2018, p. 31).

In China, investment strategies of companies are driven by the macroeconomic preferences of state units. For this reason, the state acts as an intermediary for large amount of credits, with development banks controlled by the government or ministries. With such credit support, companies have become more competitive against foreign companies. The state can also act as a major consumer of goods and services, particularly through infrastructure and public procurement. Foreign companies are thus excluded from the market (May &Nölke, 2014)

The inflows of foreign investment is seen as a modernizing factor as long as it does not harm the superiority of the national capital in China's mercantilist model and serves the interests of the society (Nölke & Claar, 2013, p. 42; Arrighi, 2010, p. 357). In the economic development model of China, foreign direct investment has played a more important role than societies like Japan and South Korea. Since the early 1990s, more than one third of exports have been made by foreign companies. Reached the highest level in 2005 with 58%. Moreover, the share of foreign companies in the exports of China's high-tech products is quite high. Over the period 2000-2012, more than 80% and almost three quarters today are exported by foreign companies[8] (Kroeber, 2016).

Using the attractiveness of market size and the bargaining power associated with it, the government regulates foreign capital inflows. Medical institutions, automotive manufacturing, higher education institutions, brokerage companies, shipping agencies, airline companies, telecommunication companies and security companies are among the leading companies exposed to certain constraints by various investment instruments (Huang, 2017: 59; Lee, Jee & Eun, 2011:493). The main purpose is to protect certain industries or domestic companies. In this respect, the Chinese government restricts or prohibits the foreign direct investments in some strategic sectors or industries that may jeopardize national economy. For this reason, foreign investors are not subject to equal treatment in accessing or doing business in these specific areas (Chen, 2011:95).

Strategically the most important expectation from foreign investments enter the country is technology transfer. The government actively adopts the principle of trading the market for technology, introducing conditions such as technology transfer and joint venture to the multinational corporations. As a matter of fact, since 1978 more than 80% of foreign capital investments, particularly in the automobile, chemical and electronics industries, have been accepted as based on this principle and the government puts pressure on technology transfer to local partners in these industries (Lee, Jee & Eun, 2011, p. 493). Thus, foreign direct investment companies contribute to the spread of knowledge and qualified workforce, while companies in China learn from them. This process is called parallel learning (Lee, Jee & Eun, 2011, p. 493). However, the weak legal structures and sanctions for the protection of intellectual property rights not only deter the entry of foreign capital with high technology, but also affect the decisions of foreign investors to bring technology. This is one of the main reasons for the low foreign investment from the industrialized countries (Chen, 2011).

The central authorities hindered the outflows of foreign investments in China during the 1990s. However since the adoption of the "Go Global Strategy" initiative, there has been a significant increase in foreign investments made abroad. "*The Government, together with the China Council for the Promotion of International Trade (CCPIT), has introduced several schemes to assist domestic companies in developing a global strategy to exploit opportunities in the expanding local and international markets*" (Amighini, 2018, p. 32). The determinants like high savings rates, global financial imbalances and the reduction of investment demand within the country, have been influental in increasing outward investments. China has reduced tight controls on its reserves against the increase in foreign reserves. Funds have begun to be encouraged for overseas investments and the creation of world-class companies and brands has started to be frequently spoken as part of this policy change (Lee, Jee & Eun, 2011, p. 496; Zhang, 2015, p. 124).

It is possible to observe illiberal characteristics even when direct overseas investments are made, similar to foreign investment in the country. First of all, an important part of China's foreign investments was made by state-owned enterprises (Sauvant & Nolan, 2015, p.3). Foreign direct investment made by China, on the other hand, is promoted by using specific tools. Various financial support, priority access to financial resources, accelerated approval, tax return, and investment advice are just a few of these incentives.

A New Trade and Investmet Strategy: 'One Belt, One Road' Initiative (OBOR)

In the years following the global crisis, the slowdown in the Chinese economy has led to the need to shift from an investment-based economy model to a consumption-based economy model. In addition, a large external market requirement has emerged in which the accumulation of excess industrial capital in the past periods will be exported. These are internal and external factors that cause China's economic development model and foreign policy to change (Zhang, 2015). 'One Belt, One Road (OBOR)' initiative, is China's external response against these changing growth dynamics (Dollar, 2015, p.163), a new trade strategy (Eichengreen, 2018) and a signature for international economic policy (Zhang, 2015, p. 123).

OBOR' initiative is the name of two new trade routes called 'Silk Road Economic Belt' and 'Maritime Silk Road of the Twenty-First Century'. "Silk Road Economic Belt" and "Maritime Silk Road of the Twenty-First Century" which are among the most ambitious initiatives in the international arena are the project of modern times to establish land and sea silk roads. This project, linking Central Asia and Europe by land, North, Southeast and South Asia by sea, is a new trade and economic order proposal for developing countries under China's leadership. According to Eichengreen (2018) as "*a hub-and-spoke system, with China the hub and countries on its periphery the spokes*" it is sign of "*re-shaping the global trading system*" for China. The OBOR initiative has drawn attention to the economic magnitude that it has proposed and the new political implications it will bring. In this context, it seems that China, in particular, has made great efforts to realize the project by taking serious steps both in the political arena and in other fields (Yu, 2017, p. 354).

President Xi Jinping explained the idea of Silk Road in his speech in Kazakhstan in September 2013, while Maritime Silk Road project was announced in Indonesia in October 213. A year later, at the Asia-Pacific Economic Cooperation (APEC) meeting in November 2014, China announced it had created a $ 40 billion Silk Road fund (Aoyama, 2016, p. 5). China embodied this idea in a short span of time like one year, and although many countries are involved in the project, China has proven itself to be the driving force behind the project with the financial resources it allocates. Lin ve Wang (2015, p. 20), claims that the OBOR project reflects China's vision of expanding trade, reform and economic development and is an important solution to crises by increasing total demand through infrastructure investments and raising productivity in the long run. On the other hand, it is possible to read the OBOR project as a new form of globalization:

China's Belt and Road Initiative (BRI) is designed to lay some of the foundations for a new inclusive phase of globalization. The proposal has already received a great deal of support, leading Fukuyama to argue that it is part of 'an historic contest . . . over competing development models . . . between China . . . and the United States (US) and other Western countries . . . [whose] outcome will determine the fate of Eurasia for decades to come'

The Chinese vision differs in significant ways from neoliberal/Washington Consensus globalization and some other recent international initiatives in that it is inclusive. China's emphasis is on strategic international economic partnerships and multilateral credit to address investment, infrastructure, employment and economic development (Liu & Dunford, 2016, p. 325).

The OBOR initiative is the largest project of the last century in terms of area covered and economic magnitude. *The basic principle of OBOR is to enhance connectivity through multi-model transport corridors weather on 'land' or through 'Sea' that lead to economic integration, free flow of goods and services that enhances trade, commerce, economic activity including promotion of people to people exchanges* (Minghong, 2017, p. 7). It covers all the Eurasian geography from East Asia to Western Europe. It aims to merge the South Chinese Sea and the Indian Ocean with the West Pacific coasts. Thus, it concerns about 63% of the world population that is 4.5 billion people. This initiative, which encompasses 64 countries, combines a third of the world's GDP (Zhang, 2015, p. 123). Moreover, in the official action plan prepared in March 2015, OBOR was declared open to all countries thus a globally inclusive and ambitious plan was put forward:

The Initiative is open for cooperation. It covers, but is not limited to, the area of the ancient Silk Road. It is open to all countries, and international and regional organizations for engagement, so that the results of the concerted efforts will benefit wider areas.

The OBOR project has not started as a "plan" or "strategy" but as "initiative" by the Chinese government. The vision aims to encourage all countries that wish to be included in this movement as stakeholders, rather than being a project of the Chinese state. It also aims to be a pluralistic structure without recommending a single model and policy proposal. In this way, OBOR also includes the use of existing bilateral relations, multilateral agreements and cultural differences without establishing a new mechanism and a uniform corporate entity. OBOR, which advocates common interests on the path of economic development and advocates a win-win strategy, is trying to cover the characteristics and interests of all countries (Minghong, 2017, p. 8).

OBOR's most comprehensive purpose is to create a globally free trade system. This aim is contrary to the current system of China, although it reflects the West's liberal internationalist economic doctrine. As a matter of fact, China has never had a liberal internationalist tradition in its history and it would be an irony to think it will be at this point (Zhang, 2015, p. 123-124).

The Belt and Road Initiative has recently helped to consolidate Beijing's image as a net direct and financial foreign investor, working to establish what has been labeled "globalisation with Chinese characteristics", which seems more an outward expansion of Chinese influence abroad than a step towards a truly multilateral approach (Magri, 2018, p. 10). Certainly, the Chinese government has both internal and external priorities in the OBOR initiative. The first goal is to transfer the excess capacity to developing countries resulting from high economic growth performance. It is thought that the capacity surplus of sectors such as cement, steel and railways will be used as a result of increasing infrastructure investments. Secondly, it is aimed to generate more income in the long run by directing the accumulation of Chinese capital to infrastructure projects instead of treasury bills. Thirdly, energy supply security will be ensured through the established secure trade network. Energy flow is highly important for China, which is dependent on oil and natural gas imports. Regional development differences, poverty in the interior and western regions, despite the development of coastal cities, remain as a major problem for China. As the fourth objective of the OBOR initiative, the Chinese government seeks development by providing economic vitality in poor regions. Finally, this project will ensure that China is an authority globally. It is a response to the free trade agreements that the US try to do with Europe and other Asian countries (Zhang, 2015, p.124–125).

In the Barack Obama period, the US government initiated free trade agreements with the Pacific countries and the European Union. The Trans-Pacific Partnership (TPP) and the Transatlantic Trade and Investment Partnership (TTIP) negotiations foresee the adoption of a number of rules, such as development of multilateral free trade and patent rights. Even if these agreements were aimed at improving trade, they included a number of negotiations. The parties were strictly tied to the rules of the agreements and the third parties' participation was based on deals and negotiations. However, the OBOR initiative has become a serious competitor to the TPP and TTIP, by recognizing the participation of all countries openly, foreseeing equal participation of the countries, and beyond all of that, with its infrastructure investments which were promising especially to the developing countries (Du, 2016, p. 39).

OBOR's vision and proposed working structure offers a new cooperation and integration proposal. OBOR is a different globalization proposal in the 21st Century, that provide countries an option to choose the areas they are willing to cooperate with, enabling participation voluntarily in the project, making infrastructure investments that will contribute to the development of their countries, and operating with both bilateral or multilateral agreements, inclusive and open relationship proposals. (Tang, Liu, & Xie, 2017, p. 387). The model of trade and international economic relations that OBOR has proposed offers considerable ambiguities besides providing an opportunity for everyone to gain. The problem of coordination, the ambiguity of countries' loyalties, the lack of a strong leading state perception, and, most importantly, the question of who finances infrastructure investments stay as a problem. In addition to that, Chinese companies' lack of overseas experience, distrust to the Chinese technology, and the economic and political pressures of the US and other western countries can be added to these problems (Nataraj & Sekhani, 2016; Tang et al., 2017).

Asian Infrastructure Investment Bank (AIBB)

The establishment of the Asian Infrastructure Investment Bank (AIIB) is based on the Asia-Pacific Economic Cooperation Summit held in Bali in October 2013. At this meeting, China proposed the establishment of a new multilateral development bank. It has been declared that the bank will give priority to the financing of infrastructure projects, especially in Asian countries and neighboring countries. With the agreement signed in Beijing in June 2015, the Bank was established with 57 founder members and started its activities as of December 25, 2015. However, the membership of the bank has been left open to other countries. AIIB's Articles of Agreement create two classes of membership: regional and non-regional members. According to the AIIB Articles, regional members hold 75% of the total voting power in the Bank (Weiss, 2017, p. 1). In the management structure, the voting rights are distributed according to the capital structure. Accordingly, India has a share of 7.51%, Russia 5.93% and Germany 4.15%, while China has a share of 26.06%, which is well above the others. This structural status gives China more power than the US has in the World Bank or Japan has in the Asian Development Bank. In addition to that, China has the right to veto decisions in the following areas; increasing the bank's capital, increasing the capital subscription of a member, expanding the operations of the bank, changing the size of the board of directors, changing the structure of the board, appointing or removing the president, suspending a member, terminating the bank and distributing its assets, and amending the Articles. At the project level decisions, although China does not have an official veto right, it has the power to decline automatically, due to its voting share since decisions must be taken with 75% of the vote (Callaghan & Hubbard, 2016, p. 129). China has pioneered both the establishment and the execution processes of this bank, as it is in the OBOR initiative. China has pledged to pay half of the $ 100 billion of the bank's founding capital.

The United States is not a member of this bank while England and France are members. The United States is openly opposed to the AIIB, which will compete against the World Bank and the IMF, the cornerstones of the global financial architecture. A New York Times report had alleged that the American administration tried to prevent the AIIB's foundation and tried to persuade the allied countries not to become members (Perlez, 2014).

The establishment of a multilateral development bank has claim with two sides. While one side opposes the US's global economic leadership, the other side reveals the will to change the global financial architecture. The current system, led by the World Bank and the IMF, is leading the international economic system and the US administration is in its captain's corner. The American government holds significant powers with its veto rights. China, which wants to have more voice in the global system with its growing economy, demands more votes in the IMF and the World Bank. Although a positive response was given to this demand in 2010, the US Congress resisted to this decision and it took longer to implement. This prolongation became a source of motivation for China's search for an alternative (Layne, 2018, p. 103). This initiative, which China has done, has created a new formation in which China is at the center against the Bretton Woods Institutions. China, which wants to transfer its economic achievements to the global scene, wants the center of gravity to change to its own advantage. The US administration claims that new financial institutions will not be as successful as existing ones: *"Washington said that its opposition to the AIIB was based on US doubts that the new institution would adhere to the same environmental, governance, lending, transparency, labour and human rights standards as the IMF, World Bank and Asian Development Bank"* (Layne, 2018, p. 103). On the other hand the treasury minister Jack Lew argued that US international credibility and influence are threatened by congressional delays in IMF reforms and that reforms must be approved to sustain the IMF leadership (Donnan & Dyer, 2015).

As mentioned earlier, the OBOR initiative is important for China's political and economic interests. However, the revival of the historical silk road requires a serious political coordination and investment (Callaghan & Hubbard, 2016, p.120). In this context, the Chinese government closely linked the AIIB with the OBOR initiative during the foundation period. AIIB has been put forward for the financing of the OBOR initiative, which envisages commercial cooperation in a vast geographical area from Europe to China and envisages high levels of infrastructure investments. However, with the inclusion of Western countries such as the United Kingdom during the preliminary negotiations, the Chinese government has begun to differentiate the AIIB from the OBOR initiative. As a result of US rivalry and opposition, China has moved AIIB into a complementary position to being an alternative to the World Bank and Asian Development:

In November 2014, shortly after China signed the MOU to begin negotiations, Chinese President Xi said that "China's inception and joint establishment of the AIIB with some countries is aimed at providing financial support for infrastructure development in countries along the 'One Belt, One Road' and promoting economic cooperation." This view of the AIIB's role was reinforced by the spokesperson for the National People's Congress in March 2015, "AIIB and the Silk Road Fund are both created for the better implementation of 'One Belt, One Road.'" Beginning in mid-2015, Chinese officials created more distance between the rapidly expanding AIIB and China's OBOR strategy. In June 2016, during a meeting with global executives, the AIIB President Jin Liqun clarified China's position, saying that while the Bank would support OBOR projects, the AIIB was not created exclusively for this initiative. Speaking in Washington, DC alongside the World Bank's spring 2016 meetings, President Xi said "We would finance infrastructure projects in all emerging market economies even though they don't belong to the Belt and Road initiative." (Weiss, 2017, p. 6)

Financial System

The financial system in China is a system in which banks are dominant and the vast majority of these banks are directly audited by the state (Prasad, 2016). Although the banking system (Kroeber, 2016), which accounts for 80% of the financial resources, is stated to have evolved into a competitive market in recent years, the market share of fully owned state banks in the market is 8% and the "equitized" commercial bank share is 49.2% in which the largest shareholder is the central government. The market share of these banks is close to 60%, with clear evidence that these banks are under government control in China (Martin, 2012; Allen, Qian & Gu, 2017)[9]. Because the global financial markets do not play an important role in financing new investments, the Chinese model differs greatly from the liberal market economies and is more like market economies in coordination with East Asian economies (May & Nölke, 2014; Koeber, 2016).

The central bank, which is at the center of the banking system, actively seeks stability in foreign financial relationships through the accumulation of reserves to prevent exchange rate volatility (Ten Brink, 2014; May & Nölke, 2014). Reserve accumulation is a by-product of policies aimed at preventing the appreciation of national currency (Wang, 2017), as well as the assurance of national strength and security in China. As a part of China's export-based development strategy, it has tightly limited its currency appreciation by accumulating reserves. Despite regulations restricting the entry of foreign capital, speculative capital entered the country with the expectation that the Renminbi would gain value in the future, and led to an excessive increase in reserves (Krugman, Obstfeld & Melitz, 2017:690).

The "financial repression" created by keeping deposit rates at or below inflation level is a key tool for maximizing the government's control over financial resources (Kroeber, 2016), and this policy, combined with the characteristics of the financial system in China, has made a significant contribution to the increase of investments. One of the other two important deteminants contributing to the increase in tendency of investments is the large-scale supervision of the capital account (Prasad, 2016). For this reason, households in China cannot invest in foreign currency shares, bonds or other financial assets. Investments are limited to assets in the country. On the other hand, there are various violations in China such as insider trading, front running. Therefore, investors do not see domestic stocks as an investment instrument (Lardy, 2012, p. 236).

Financial pressure is also a way for the government to transfer funds from the savings owners to the companies (Wang, 2017; Kroeber, 2016). The fact that the government has a considerable power in the functioning of all kinds of banks makes it easier for the financial resources to be channeled to the areas preferred by the government. The government's priority in this sense is the SOEs. The government's interest policy has caused resource transfers from households to companies. According to estimates of a study done, this transfer is between 5-7% of the GDP and gives a great advantage to the SOEs. This intervention of the state's financial institutions is also the main reason for the high investments of the SOEs and the extraordinary profits (Wang, 2017, p.100).

The Chinese government provides subsidized credits not only to state-owned SOEs through the banking system but also to companies preferred as part of the central government strategy. These loans, which are given to increase the competitive power of companies, are seriously controversial due to the accusation of China's unfair competition in world trade (Martin, 2012, p. 37).

Although it has taken selective and prudent measures to remove state control, China still has a comprehensive capital control regime. Although restrictions on capital inflows and outflows have been loosened, they have not been removed (Prasad, 2016), and financial asset and company equity asset sales are limited. In the Chinese stock market, over 60% of the existing assets are held by the state (Allen, Chakrabati, De, Qian & Qian, 2010:156). Therefore, the Chinese stock market is designed to provide capital for a few private companies controlled by state block-holders (May & Nölke, 2014).

Renminbi as an International Currency

China strives to transform Renminbi into international currency. Especially since the 2008-2009 crisis, it has increased its efforts towards this purpose. The most important motivation behind these efforts is to reduce dollar dependency. Rumors about the US's efforts to reduce the debt burden by suppressing the value of the dollar have also raised concerns about the value of China's excess reserves. On the other hand, dependency on the dollar in trade worries authorities. Because of the 2008 crisis, the decline in China's exports was not only due to the contraction in total demand, the restrictions on the access of importers to trade financing and the freezing of loans also paused exports (Bottelier & Dadush, 2011). Therefore, the transformation of Renminbi into a currency of trade agreement will reduce the potential impacts of such shocks on China, reduce exchange rate risk in exports, reduce or eliminate the costs of protection against this risk. On the other hand, making the investments in this currency will reduce the risk of exchange rate for Chinese investors seeking funds for international investments. Moreover, the internationalization of Renminbi will help to reduce China's excessive reserves (Bottelier & Dadush, 2011).

In line with these goals and based on the model of economic development, China has undertaken the supervised internationalization of Renminbi without liberalizing the capital account as a whole (McCauley, 2011; McNally, 2015; Kirshner, 2017). A paper published by the president of the Peoples Bank of China suggests that *"the definition of convertibility of the capital account is open to debate and that flexibility must be provided as to how the standards should be set"*, which is consistent with the aforementioned trend (Kirshner, 2017, p. 190). China tends to be an alternative to the US model by maintaining state control over its policies, domestic financial system, capital flows and exchange rate. This tendency shows that China's capital account control will continue and that the country's financial reforms will proceed cautiously (McNally, 2015, p. 717). Kirshner (2017, p.190) summarizes this pursuit that challenges in a way the current monetary system and the US model: *"To build the infrastructure that will increase the internationalization of the Yuan, spread its use as a tool, and encourage other central banks to keep reserves in the Renminbi and in the meantime, to protect some capital controls and other restraint devices over other markets. China intends to encourage it through bilateral exchange agreements that it has actively engaged in"*. Renminbi's internationalization regenerates some aspects of the internal reforms of Chinese capitalism, such as policy experimentation and institutional hybridization (McNally, 2015, p. 717).

CONCLUSION

The purpose of this paper is to introduce the "globalization with Chinese characteristics" (Eichengreen, 2008). In accordance with the Chinese capitalism model, it is an alternative and successful development model with different policy choices in the fields of trade, investment and finance. Although the willingness to continue globalization is often expressed in policies and expressions, it constantly applies protectionist measures. The Chinese economy is controlled by the state. He also prefers regional and bilateral agreements rather than multilateral negotiating rounds. In recent years, as a response to the changing growth dynamics and some structural problems, China has adopted a new trade initiative and institutional arrangements. These changes have fueled the debate over China's new hegemon of the international order. Especially the attitude of the US administration towards protectionism puts China on the foreground with these new strategies in the international arena.

REFERENCES

Allen, F., Qian, J., & Gu, X. (2017). An overview of China's financial system. *Annual Review of Financial Economics, 9*(1), 191–231. doi:10.1146/annurev-financial-112116-025652

Amighini, A. (2018). China's new economic powerhouse. In A. Amighini & P. Magri (Eds.), *China Champion of (Which) Globalisation* (pp. 13–37). Milano, İtaly: ISPI.

Aoyama, R. (2016). One belt, one road: China's new global strategy. *Journal of Contemporary East Asia Studies, 5*(2), 3–22. doi:10.1080/24761028.2016.11869094

Arrighi, G. (2008). *Adam Smith Pekin'de: 21. yüzyılın soy kütüğü*. İstanbul: Yordam Kitap.

Balding, C. (2018). Is China a market economy? In A. Amighini & P. Magri (Eds.), *China Champion of (Which) Globalisation* (pp. 61–79). Milano, İtaly: ISPI.

Bottelier, P., & Dadush, U. (2011). *The future of Renminbi as an international currency*. Retrieved from https://carnegieendowment.org/2011/06/02/future-of-renminbi-as-international-currency-pub-44338

Bremmer, I. (2010). *The end of the free market: Who wins the war between states and corporations?* New York: Portfolio.

Buzan, B., & Lawson, G. (2014). Capitalism and the emergent world order. *International Affairs, 90*(1), 71–91. doi:10.1111/1468-2346.12096

Callaghan, M., & Hubbard, P. (2016). The Asian infrastructure investment bank: Multilateralism on the Silk Road. *China Economic Journal, 9*(2), 116–139. doi:10.1080/17538963.2016.1162970

Chang, H., & Grabel, I. (2005). *Kalkınma yeniden: Alternatif iktisat politikaları elkitabı*. Ankara: İmge Kitabevi.

Chen, C. (2011) The Development of China's FDI laws and policies after WTO accession. In J. Golley & L. Song (Eds.), Rising China: Global challenges and opportunities (pp. 85-97). ANU Press. doi:10.22459/RC.06.2011.06

Corden, W. (2009). China's exchange rate policy, its current account surplus and the global imbalances. *Economic Journal (London), 119*(541), 430–441. doi:10.1111/j.1468-0297.2009.02319.x

Dollar, D. (2015). China's rise as a regional and global power: The AIIB and the 'One Belt, One Road'. *Horizons,* (4), 162-172. Retrieved from https://www.brookings.edu/wp-content/uploads/2016/06/China-rise-as-regional-and-global-power.pdf

Donnan, S., & Dyer, G. (2015). US warns of loss of influence over China bank. *Financial Times*. Retrieved from https://www.ft.com/content/71e33aea-ccaf-11e4-b94f-00144feab7de

Du, M. M. (2016). China's "One Belt, One Road" Initiative: Context, focus, institutions, and implications. *The Chinese Journal of Global Governance*, *2*(1), 30–43. doi:10.1163/23525207-12340014

Edmonds, C., Croix, S. L., & Li, Y. (2006). *The China's rise as an international trading power*. Economics Study Area Working Papers 88, East-West Center.

Eichengreen, B. (2018). *Globalization with Chinese characteristics*. Retrieved from https://www.project-syndicate.org/commentary/globalization-chinese-characteristics-by-barry-eichengreen-2018-08

Hall, P. A., & Soskice, D. (2001). *Varieties of capitalism: The Institutional Foundations of Comparative Advantage*. Oxford, UK: Oxford University Press. doi:10.1093/0199247757.001.0001

Hilpert, H. G. (2011). *China's trade policy*. SWP Research Paper.

Huang, J. (2017) China. In Foreign Investment Regulatıon Review (pp. 54-66). UN: Law Business Research.

Jiang, Y. (2011). Rethinking the Beijing Consensus: How China responds to crises. *The Pacific Review*, *24*(3), 337–356. doi:10.1080/09512748.2011.577234

Kirshner, J. (2017). Bölgesel hegemonya ve bir RMB bölgesinin doğuşu. In E. Helleiner & J. Kirshner (Eds.), Yeni Çin Seddi: Çin'in uluslararası para ilişkilerinde güç ve siyaset (pp. 173-192). İstanbul: Koç Üniversitesi Yayınları.

Kowalski, P. (2010). China and India: A tale of two trade integration approaches. In B. Eichengreen, P. Gupta, & R. Kumar (Eds.), Emerging giants: China and India in the World Economy (pp. 184-224). Oxford, UK: Oxford Scholarship.

Kroeber, A. R. (2016). *China's economy: What everyone needs to know*. Oxford, UK: Oxford University Press.

Lardy, N. (2012). *Sustaining China's economic growth after the Global Financial Crisis*. Retrieved from https://www.frbsf.org/economic-research/files/Lardy.pdf

Layne, C. (2018). The US–Chinese power shift and the end of the Pax Americana. *International Affairs*, *94*(1), 89–111. doi:10.1093/ia/iix249

Lee, K., Jee, M., & Eun, J. (2011). Assessing China's economic catch-up at the firm level and beyond: Washington Consensus, East Asian Consensus and the Beijing Model. *Industry and Innovation*, *18*(5), 487–507. doi:10.1080/13662716.2011.583463

Lin, J. Y., & Wang, Y. (2015). *China's contribution to development cooperation: Ideas, opportunities and finances*. Working Papers P119. FERDI. Retrieved from http://www.ferdi.fr/sites/www.ferdi.fr/files/publication/fichiers/wp119_lin-wang_paper_for_ferdi_web_1.pdf

Liu, W., & Dunford, M. (2016). Inclusive globalization: Unpacking China's Belt and Road Initiative. *Area Development and Policy*, *1*(3), 323–340. doi:10.1080/23792949.2016.1232598

Magri, P. (2018). Introduction. In A. Amighini & P. Magri (Eds.), *China Champion of (Which) Globalisation* (pp. 7–12). Milano, İtaly: ISPI.

Martin, M. F. (2012). *China's banking system: Issues for congress*. Retrieved from https://fas.org/sgp/crs/row/R42380.pdf

May, C., & Nölke, A. (2014). Capitalism in large emerging economies and the new global trade order. In D. Desse (Ed.), *Handbook of the International Political Economy of Trade*. Cheltenham, UK: Edward Elgar. doi:10.4337/9781781954997.00028

McNally, C. (2012). Sino-Capitalism: China's reemergence and the international political economy. *World Politics*, *64*(4), 741–776. doi:10.1017/S0043887112000202

McNally, C. A. (2013a). The Challenge of refurbished state capitalism: Implications for the global political economic order. *Recht and Management*, *6*, 33–48.

McNally, C. A. (2013b). How emerging forms of capitalism are changing the global economic order. *East-West Center*, (107), 1-8. Retrieved from https://www.eastwestcenter.org/sites/default/files/private/api107.pdf

McNally, C. A. (2013c). Refurbishing state capitalism: A policy analysis of efforts to rebalance China's political economy. *Journal of Current Chinese Affairs*, *42*(4), 45–71. doi:10.1177/186810261304200403

McNally, C. A. (2015). The political economic logic of RMB Internationalization: A study in Sino-capitalism. *International Politics, 52*(6), 704–723. doi:10.1057/ip.2015.15

Minghong, Y. (2017). Understanding the One Belt One Road Initiative: China's perspective. In B. K. Sharma & D. N. D. Kundu (Eds.), *China's One Belt One Road: Initiative, Challenges and Prospects* (pp. 7–26). Vij Books.

Nataraj, G., & Sekhani, R. (2016). *China's One Belt One Road initiative: Analysis from an Indian perspective (HKTDC Research).* Retrieved from http://china-trade-research.hktdc.com/business-news/article/The-Belt-and-Road-Initiative/"China'sOne-Belt-One-Road-Initiative"--Analysis-from-an-Indian Perspective/obor/en/1/1X000000/1X0A5J3C.htm

Naughton, B. (2010). China's distinctive system: Can it be a model for others? *Journal of Contemporary China, 19*(65), 437–460. doi:10.1080/10670561003666079

Nölke, A., & Claar, S. (2013). Varieties of capitalism in emerging countries. *Transformation, 81/82*(1), 33–54. doi:10.1353/trn.2013.0001

Nölke, A., Ten Brink, T., Claar, T., & May, C. (2015). Domestic structures, foreign economic policies and global economic order: Implications from the rise of large emerging economies. *European Journal of International Relations, 21*(3), 538–567. doi:10.1177/1354066114553682

Nölke, A., & Vliegenthart, A. (2009). Enlarging the varieties of capitalism: The emergence of dependent market economies is East Central Europe. *World Politics, 61*(4), 670–702. doi:10.1017/S0043887109990098

Perlez, J. (2014). U.S. opposing China's answer to World Bank. *The New York Times.* Retrieved from https://www.nytimes.com/2014/10/10/world/asia/chinas-plan-for-regional-development-bank-runs-into-us-opposition.html

Pontusson, J. (2005). Varieties and commonalities of capitalism. In D. Coates (Ed.), Varieties of capitalism, varieties of approaches (pp. 163-188). Palgrave Macmillian. doi:10.1057/9780230522725_9

Prasad, E. S. (2016). *China`s economy and financial markets: Reforms and markets, U.S–China economic and security review commission, Hearing on China`s 13th Five Year Plan.* Retrieved from https://www.brookings.edu/wp-content/uploads/2016/07/USCESRCTestimony27Apr16.pdf

Ramo, J. C. (2004). *The Beijing Consensus*. The Foreign Policy Centre. Retrieved from http://www.chinaelections.org/uploadfile/200909/20090918021638239.pdf

Rodrik, D. (2013). *The new mercantilist challenge*. Project Syndicate. Retrieved from http://www.fabricedefever.com/pdf/Rodrik%20%20The%20new%20mercantilist%20 challenge.pdf

Schmidt, V. A. (2009). Putting the political back into political economy. *World Politics*, 1–28.

Şenses, F., Öniş, Z., & Bakır, C. (2013). *Ülke deneyimleri ışığında küresel kriz ve yeni ekonomik düzen*. İstanbul: İletişim Yayınları.

Stephen, M., & Parizek, M. (2015). *New pressures on the WTO: The Rise of illiberal trading states*. Retrieved from https://statecapitalist.wordpress.com/2015/01/15/stephen-parizek-new-pressures-on-the-wto-the-rise-of-illiberal-trading-states/

Tang, S., Liu, D., & Xie, X. (2017). The Analysis of the "One Belt and One Road" for the game between China and the United States. In *Proceedings of the 3rd International Conference on Social Science and Management*. DEStech Publications, Inc.

Ten Brink, T. (2014). The challenges of China's non-liberal capitalism for the liberal global economic order. *Harvard Asia Quarterly*, *16*(2), 36-44.

Tiezzi, S. (2018). Free trade with Chinese characteristics. In A. Amighini & P. Magri (Eds.), *China Champion of (Which) Globalisation* (pp. 39–60). Milano, İtaly: ISPI.

Wang, H. (2017). Küresel dengesizlikler ve döviz kuru silahının gücünün sınırları. In E. Helleiner & J. Kirshner (Eds.), Yeni Çin Seddi: Çin'in Uluslararası Para İlişkilerinde Güç ve Siyaset (pp. 97-106). İstanbul: Koç Üniversitesi Yayınları.

Weiss, M. A. (2017). Asian Infrastructure Investment Bank (AIIB) (Congressional Research Service No. 7–5700). Washington, DC: Government Printing Service.

Witt, M. A. (2010). *China: What variety of capitalism?* INSEAD Working Paper No. 2010/88/EPS. Retrieved from https://ssrn.com/abstract=1695940

Wolf, M. (2014). *The shifts and the shocks: What we have learned-and have still to learn-from the financial crisis*. Penguin Books.

Yağcı, M. (2016). A Beijing Consensus in the making: The rise of Chinese initiatives in the international political economy and implications for developing countries. *Perceptions: Journal of International Affairs*, *21*(2), 29–56.

Yao, D., & Whalley, J. (2016). The China (Shanghai) Pilot Free Trade Zone: Background, Developments and Preliminary Assessment of Initial Impacts. *World Economy*, *39*(1), 2–15. doi:10.1111/twec.12364

Yu, H. (2017). Motivation behind China's 'One Belt, One Road' Initiatives and Establishment of the Asian Infrastructure Investment Bank. *Journal of Contemporary China*, *26*(105), 353–368. doi:10.1080/10670564.2016.1245894

Zhang, F. (2015). China as a global Force. *Asia & the Pacific Policy Studies*, *3*(1), 120–128. doi:10.1002/app5.115

ENDNOTES

1 Beijing Consensus is a concept that is proposed by the Time editor, Joshua Cooper Ramo, against the Washington Consensus and it is a term that is sometimes used instead of the term China Model (Jiang, 2011, p.339). Ramo (2004, p.3-4) defines the Beijing Consensus as follows: *China is marking a path for other nations around the world who are trying to figure out not simply how to develop their countries, but also how to fit into the international order in a way that allows them to be truly independent, to protect their way of life and political choices in a world with a single massively powerful centre of gravity.* Unlike the Washington Consensus, it does not offer a uniform solution for every situation. Economic development can vary from country to county and it is pointless to expect similar results by presenting the same policy prescriptions. It is innovative and experimental. Furthermore "*the Beijing Consensus still holds tightly to his pragmatic idea that the best path for modernisation is one of "groping for stones to cross the river," instead of trying to make one-big, shock-therapy leap. Most important, it is both the product of and defined by a society that is changing so fast that few people, even those inside China, can keep up with it*" (Ramo, 2004, p.4).

2 According to Naughton (2010, p. 437) The Beijing Consensus does not accurately convey China's economic development process and does not represent a compromise between economists and policy makers in China. Moreover, although there are lessons to be drawn from China's economic development experience, these are not features that can easily be copied by other countries and there are specific characteristics related to the institutional structure of the country.

3 *New institutional approaches*, examining the emergence of capitalism in China, are against a state-centered interpretation. They underline the importance of the reform coming from the base, which was one of the two different reform processes started from the late 1970s. According to them, China is not a project that the government has previously designed and conducted. The first reform was made under the leadership of the state with targets such as agricultural development, heavy industrial transition to light industry, decentralization of the economy and greater autonomy of local actors, development of state-owned enterprises. The second reform has emerged spontaneously and has evolved through the influence of various elements, such as self-employed, town and village initiatives, Special Economic Zones. It is this second reform that has led to a capitalist transition in China, which brought a dynamic private sector and a strong resistive market forces to the Chinese economy without much change in the state sector (Coase & Wang, 2015, p. 293-324).

4 Deng Xiaoping has started the country's policy of reform and openness in 1978.

5 Processing export is based on the export of finished products by processing imported and intermediate products (Wang, 2017, p. 89).

6 The question of why exchange rate policy creates global imbalances by creating surplus is a controversial issue in the literature. Wang (2017, p. 88) claims that China's increasing surplus against the United States and the EU is a result of the collective contribution of East Asian economies. He also thinks that it is wrong to focus only on exchange rate policy in China to reduce the current account deficit. Because the exchange rate policy is part of China's export-oriented development policy and the exporting impulse is explained by the high saving and low consumption tendency of the society. Corden (2009) argues that the exchange rate policy alone does not explain China's current account surplus and that the current account surplus in this country has little effect on the emergence of the global crisis. Kroeber (2016) shows with numerical data that artificially undervalued exchange rate is a lesser determinant of export growth. In the period of 2001-2010, when the exchange rate was extremely undervalued, the share of China's global exports rose by 1.1%, but rose from 5% to 15% despite the increase in labor costs during the period 2010-2013, when foreign exchange was left to fluctuate.

7 China's approach to exchange rate policy is experimental and gradual as it is in other strategies. In 1997-2005 period, Renminbi was fixed to dollar and beginning from 2005, a gradual transition to flexible exchange rate system was foreseen (McNally, 2015; Prasad, 2016). The advantages gained from the gradual exchange rate policy under state control are not limited to the increase

in exports. It contributed to the control of inflation in the country and to the stability and predictability of exchange rate (McNally, 2015, p. 715).

8 China's strategy for foreign capital investments has been achieved through the interaction of existing conditions in the international system and political preferences. The period when the Chinese economy was integrated into the global system was not a period in which conditions would allow the establishment of large powerful corporations that would lead the export similar to the situation created in East Asian countries by protectionism. The period when the US sees East Asian countries as ally, and thus, unlike its privileged position in accessing US markets and technology, China's opening up to world markets is a period of accelerated neoliberal globalization. It is a necessity for China to release the access to its own market in a global trading system where the US and Europe dominate world trade (Kroeber, 2016; McNally, 2012).

9 Although the capital markets have started to play a bigger role in financing investments since 2010, the political pressures of both central and local governments on banks have been continuing while the credit decisions are being made (Kroeber, 2016).

Chapter 2
The Belt and Road Strategy in International Business and Administration:
Corporate Social Responsibility

Jianyu Chen
Dong-A University, South Korea

Wei Liu
University of Sydney, Australia

ABSTRACT

Along with the acceleration of "One Belt and One Road" CSR progress, more Chinese companies possess adequate CSR performance capacity and conditions. In this chapter, first, the basic concept of CSR has been briefly introduced and the overviews are mainly stated including the concept, development, and current situation under the Chinese backdrop. Second, the current development of CSR, risk of the CSR, and CSR strategies of Chinese enterprises under the backdrop of Belt and Road Initiative will be introduced. Third, the responsibility of CSR of state-owned enterprises under the backdrop of Belt and Road Initiatives will be mentioned with main reference of the social responsibility reports of state-owned enterprises as well as news reports. Fourth, classic case (China Communications Construction) will be used to analyze the CSR of Chinese enterprises under the backdrop of Belt and Road Initiatives.

DOI: 10.4018/978-1-5225-8440-7.ch002

Figure 1. The pyramid of corporate social responsibility

CORPORATE SOCIAL RESPONSIBILITY(CSR) AND CSR IN CHINA

Corporate Social Responsibility (CSR)

Despite the fact Corporate social responsibility (CSR) is one of the most prominent concepts, it is still difficult to give a commonly accepted definition (Turker, 2009). Indeed, researchers have proposed a plethora of expressions to refer to CSR. Such as corporate citizenship, business ethics, sustainability, etc.

Carroll (1979) is an early pioneer in this area, has recognized four dimensions of CSR and developed the Corporate social Performance Model. As proposed by him, CSR specifically consists of four types of corporate social responsibilities in economics, law, ethics and philanthropy. he also elaborately explained the four responsibilities in a pyramid structure. (Figure 1) Besides, he found that a company has four stakeholders (including society, employees, customers, government) or interest groups.

In addition, there exist many other definitions on CSR given by authoritative international organizations. For instance, as stipulated by ten principles and requirements in "the UN Global Compact", companies should make efforts and perform internationally acknowledged norms to defend human rights, labor standards, environment and prevent corruption. CSR regulated by OECD "aims to make contributions to the development of economics, society and environment with the goal of sustainability".

As a result, in combination with mainstream stakeholder theories, CSR demands companies to assume legal responsibilities for shareholders and employees while earning profits, and in the meantime bear responsibilities for consumers, communities and environment. CSR compulsorily requests companies to surpass the traditional philosophy of taking profitability as the sole goal and pay attention to human values as well as contributions to environment, consumers and society in the production process.

CSR in China

The study on CSR in China started in the 1990s. In the very beginning, scholars mostly introduced the general theoretical results and practical experience in the west and further attempted to establish a theoretical system with Chinese characteristics. Due to the high congruity between CSR and the harmony and sustainable development philosophy of China, there is few controversy about CSR in China. Scholars generally consider that companies ought to positively perform social responsibilities.

Yuan (1990) took the lead in domestic academic circle to think over CSR. In the book *CSR*, he defined CSR as corporate current responsibilities assumed by companies to deal with all sorts of social demands and problems and seek development and living space based on the preservation of international, social and human fundamental rights and interests in combination with relatively mature stakeholder concepts in overseas countries.

Zhang, et al. (2012) explained the definition of CSR based on stakeholder theory, insisting that except as economic responsibilities for shareholders and creditors, companies should also establish a set of formal or informal rights protection responsibility mechanisms for employees, cooperative partners, government and communities, natural environment and other stakeholders (Liu et al., 2017).

China Enterprise Management Annual defines CSR as "the responsibility necessarily concerned and performed by companies for sake of long-term development, including coercive legal responsibility and self-conscious moral responsibility".

Pursuant to relevant documents and reports in China, the development stage of CSR in China could be generally divided to the following *three stages*:

Stage I: From the mid-90s to early 21st century, under the efforts of international sellers and brand owners, the society paid great attention to CSR and established CSR implementation criteria, standards and systems in international procurement. Chinese companies started to accept CSR factory audit enforced by trans-national companies.

Stage II: From the early 21st century to 2006, CSR started to obtain wide attention. Academic institutions and non-government organizations of China and international organizations in China started to systematically introduce and extensively study and discuss CSR report system. Government departments also stressed CSR construction work. For instance, Ministry of Labor and Ministry of Commerce investigated CSR construction conditions of Chinese companies and systematically introduced and profoundly observed CSR report system.
Stage III.

The Chinese Government Gradually Guaranteed the Development of CSR in China at the Level of System

1. Subject to Article 5 of *Company Law of the People's Republic of China*, companies shall abide by laws and regulations, observe social morality and commercial morality, keep honest and trustworthy, accept supervision from the government and social public, bear social responsibility, guarantee the legal protection of corporate legitimate interests free from infringement while engaging in business operation activities. Article 219 took effect on January 1st 2006;
2. On September 25th 2006, Shenzhen Stock Exchange formally enacted and executed *CSR Instruction for Listed Companies*;
3. In January 2008, SASAC issued *Guidance for CSR Performance in Central Companies* to urge central companies to reinforce sense of social responsibility and positively perform social responsibilities;
4. On May 15th 2008, Shanghai Stock Exchange issued *Notice on Strengthening CSR and Issuing Guidance for Environmental Information Disclosure of Listed Companies* to disclose CSR report and environmental protection information;
5. On August 3rd 2009, Shenzhen Stock Exchange price database formally compiled and issued CSR index and real-time index.

Government and Third-Party Corporates Reinforce the Disclosure and Supervision Concerning CSR

1. **China CSR Compilation Guide Issued by Chinese Academy of Social Sciences China:** *CSR Report Compilation Guide* (CASS-CSR1.0) issued in 2009 has been successively upgraded to 3.0 Version for twice. In the past three years, CSR report practice takes place drastic changes. In response to new situations and new requirements, for further increasing the applicability and explanatory ability of the guide and exerting the values of CSR report in China to a large extent, CASS-CSR4.0 was officially issued on November 8th

2017 based on full research and discussion. The positioning of existing CASS-CSR4.0 has been transformed from a "report compilation guide" to "report integrated guide" and accordingly, it turns to be a comprehensive guide which fully integrates report flow, report management and report value management system. CASS-CSR4.0 advocates CSR report value management for the first time so that the report could internally reinforce management and externally boost brand effects. In the future, CASS-CSR 4.0 will continually construct 1 (basic framework) + N (industry-classified guide) + M (topic guide) guide series and build up an entire system to further promote guide systematicness and applicability;

2. **China CSR Report rating standards issued by Chinese Academy of Social Sciences:** Since 2009, Chinese Academy of Social Sciences would regularly issue *CSR Blue Book* per year which systematically studies the CSR development index of top 100 state-owned companies, top 100 private companies, top 100 foreign-funded companies and 16 key industries in electricity, household appliance and real estate, aiming to discriminate the stage characteristics about CSR development in Chinese companies and provide benchmarks for the promotion of policy formation and relevant studies;
3. **Third-party CSR report rating agencies come into being:** Run Ling Global CSR (Ranking CSR Rating, RKS) established since 2009, it has provided a professional rating for corporate social responsibility reports of Chinese A-share listed companies every year. It is an authoritative rating agency for third parties in China. To issue the most just corporate responsibility rating report for investors, consumers and the social people. Run Ling Global CSR report rating system actively refers to the latest international authoritative standards of social responsibility ISO26000, and takes into account the industry differences of listed companies in China, based on Macrocosm-M, Content-C, Technique-T, Industry-I four aspects of evaluation. Fifteen first-level indicators and 63 second-level indicators including strategy, stakeholders, labor and human rights, and fair operation were set up to evaluate the CSR report. The scoring system used structured expert scoring method, and the total score is 100 points. Among them, the integral evaluation accounted for 30%; content type evaluation accounted for 45%; technical evaluation accounted for 15 points; industry evaluation accounted for 15%. The fraction of 0 ~ (100) was divided into nine grades of AAA, AA, A, BBB, BB, B, CCC, CC, and C.

In general, current situation concerning the performance of CSR in Chinese companies remains in the start-up stage. In spite of progressive progress and general low development level, there also exist many prominent CSR cases. According to the latest 2017 *CSR Blue Book on Annual Meeting of Chinese Companies* issued by

CSR Research Center of Chinese Academy of Social Sciences, CSR development index of top 300 companies in China totaled 37.4 points in 2017 generally in the start-up stage, increasing by 2.2 points than that in 2016. Throughout the past nine years, CSR continues to develop in depth and make improvement in China. In 2009, CSR development index of top 300 companies in China totaled 15.2 points generally in the "bystander" stage. In 2012, CSR development index increased to 23.1 points, transiting from the "bystander" stage to the "start-up" stage. In 2017, CSR development index of top 300 companies in China totaled 37.4 points.

In 2017, facing up to the changes in economic and social environment at home and abroad and the growing focus on companies, CSR development index points of Chinese companies presented sustained growth tendency and stably picked up. In spite of the overt differentiation of CSR development index among state-owned companies, private companies and foreign-funded companies in 2017, state-owned companies obtained maximum points (58.7 points), successively followed by private companies (29.7 points) and foreign-funded companies (23.9 points). Additionally, as for rating, around 44% companies had reached the "bystander" development stage and first-star level in 2017.

CSR of Chinese Enterprises Under the Backdrop of the Belt and Road Initiative

The Chinese government places much emphasis on CSR problems in "One Belt and One Road" construction process. As highlighted by The Vision and Action to Push Forward the Construction of Silk Road Economic Belt and 21st Maritime Silk Road (abbreviated for Vision and Action) issued in March 2013, Chinese companies ought to develop local economy, increase local employment opportunities, elevate local living standards, perform corporate social responsibility and protect local species diversity and ecological environment in countries alongside the "One Belt and One Road". While financial institutions such as Asian Infrastructure and Investment Bank (AIIB), Silk Road Foundation, New Development Bank in BRICS further point out in guideline and investment guide that companies must strictly perform CSR in the "One Belt and One Road" construction process.

In general, "going global" Chinese enterprises have become, to some extent, a contributing part of the socio-economic development in host countries. Internationalization of enterprises by far represents China's economic integration into the global economy. In this process, enterprises have come to understand international market rules and embrace diverse cultures and values. Their support for well-balanced development of economy, society and the environment in host countries has honored their commitment to sustainable development, while further efforts are still desirable. To address these issues, all UN Member States adopted

Table 1. Summary of Chinese companies' achievements and challenges in sustainable overseas development (corporate governance)

Corporate Governance		
	Achievements	**Challenges**
Overseas Risk Management	The majority of Chinese companies have established a relatively comprehensive overseas risk management framework.	• Companies' risk prevention practices still fall short of their policies, especially with regard to setting up special risk prevention funds and conducting third-party social and environmental impact assessments
Overseas CSR	An increasing number of Chinese companies have come to acknowledge the concept and value of "corporate social responsibilities", and are gradually turning it into actions. Nearly 90% of them have established or plan to establish an overseas CSR management system, and most of them have appointed special personnel or designated special departments for this work.	• Chinese companies' knowledge on the specific international standards and guidelines on sustainable development needs to be enhanced. • Chinese companies need to be motivated more by such external factors as expectations of their business partners, stakeholders and local communities. • The effective connection between CSR management system and their overseas CSR implementation departments needs to be enhanced. • Overseas CSR reports need to be released at higher frequencies. • Lack of professionals, financial support and incentive/punishment system are the major factors affecting the implementation of CSR initiatives.
Overseas Stake-holders	Chinese companies attach great importance to stakeholders who are highly relevant to their core business (including customers, shareholders, local governments, the Chinese government, and suppliers), and most companies have established a set of approaches for interacting with stakeholders.	• Chinese companies' understanding and appreciation of the role and function of indirect interested parties (local communities, trade associations, news media, international organizations and NGOs) need to be improved. • The existing mechanism for interacting with stake-holders needs better implementation in practice.

Note: Report on the Sustainable Development of Chinese Enterprises Overseas 2015, p.103

"Transforming our World: the 2030 Agenda for Sustainable Development" (the 2030 Agenda) at the United Nations Sustainable Development Summit held in New York from 25 to 27 September 2015. As a programmatic document toguide global sustainable development over the next 15 years, the 2030 Agenda encompasses 17 Sustainable Development Goals and 169 targets to complete what the Millennium Development Goals did not achieve.

The essence of CSR in Multinational Enterprises could be understood as the responsibility assumed by companies for the host country in overseas operation, including local economic development responsibility, environment responsibility and staff rights and interests protection responsibility, etc.

The "One Belt and One Road" strategy is inseparable from the performance of CSR in overseas companies. In the "One Belt and One Road" strategy, "policy communication, road connection, trade smoothness, currency circulation and public

Table 2. Summary of Chinese companies' achievements and challenges in sustainable overseas development (economic performance)

Economic Performance		
	Achievements	**Challenges**
Overseas Business Operations	Most Chinese companies run successful business operations overseas. Most companies believe they have a leading or above-average innovation and R&D capabilities in host countries. The national strategies, policies and planning of host countries are becoming important factors that influence Chinese companies' overseas investments.	• Some companies have yet to achieve profitability in their overseas operations, with 24% of the companies operating at a loss for the time being. • Most companies only have limited financing channels. They mainly work with domestic financial institutions and are not yet adept at working with overseas financial institutions.
Local Procurement	Most Chinese companies assent to the principle of prioritizing local procurement.	• In practice, most companies purchase predominantly from China due to various constraints, including culture and language differences, excessive costs, inexperience at managing local procurement, and quality of host country's suppliers.
Transfer of Technologies and Management Experiences	Most companies believe that they have had a positive spillover effect on local companies by helping local suppliers and sub-contractors improve their technologies and management.	• Some companies are not confident about the effectiveness of such technology and experience transfers. • The system for evaluating the sustainability of suppliers needs improvement.
Compliance and Market Competition	Most companies believe that they can run a compliant and fair overseas business. "Business integrity" is named by most companies as one of their core values for overseas operations.	• The exists competition among Chinese companies overseas.

Note: Report on the Sustainable Development of Chinese Enterprises Overseas 2015, p.104

empathy" (short for "five principles") incorporate some past cooperative proposals and existing cooperative mechanisms into the strategy. This decides that under the "One Belt and One Road" strategy, companies should not merely aim at their own rights and interests, but also need to form cooperative and win-win relation with the host country as a community in responsibility, make contributions to the realization of the five principles and eventually promote the stable implementation of the "One Belt and One Road" strategy. In addition, it is also necessary for companies to have favorable communication with local society, public, community and other stakeholders.

Specifically speaking, when Chinese countries perform social responsibility in overseas countries, they would create development and employment opportunities for local residents, improve skills and solve difficulties in daily life by implementing

Table 3. Summary of Chinese companies' achievements and challenges in sustainable overseas development (environmental protection)

Environmental Protection		
	Achievements	**Challenges**
Compliance	Most Chinese companies represent that they are knowledgeable about the host country's environmental laws and regulations, that they have conducted third-party environmental impact assessment on overseas projects, and that they have adopted certain measures (installing pollution control equipment, investing in environmentally friendly products, and conducting regular assessments, etc.) to reduce the environmental impacts on the host country.	• Although most companies have conducted third party environmental impact assessment, greater effort is needed for follow-up implementation and improvement. • Greater transparency regarding information on the environmental impact is required.
Energy Consumption, Emission and Wastewater Discharge	Most companies have established rules governing energy efficiency, energy conservation, emission control and wastewater discharge.	Companies have limited understanding of energy efficiency management and emission and wastewater management. • The gathering and analysis of relevant information and data need to be improved.
Biodiversity Conservation	Most companies believe that they have not negatively impacted the biodiversity conservation of host countries.	• Industries that have major impacts on biodiversity conservation should attach more importance to understanding and implementing the relevant protective measures.

Note: Report on the Sustainable Development of Chinese Enterprises Overseas 2015, p.104

localization operation and management, establishing favorable relation with local community and developing community integrated activities, therefore making local residents feel respect and favor and effectively conveying government messages to the public.

Risk of CSR Under the Backdrop of the Belt and Road Initiative

Frequent change of state ruling party and leaders, severe racial and religious conflicts, unstable domestic political situations and overall investment environment, and legal risks in some countries alongside "One Belt and One Road" all generate huge hidden dangers for overseas investment companies. In addition, here list the latest "One Belt and One Road" national investment security rating results issued by the *Chinese Academy of Social Sciences*.

Thus it can be seen that all walks of life in China still have certain doubts about the investment risks in countries alongside "One Belt and One Road".

Table 4. Summary of Chinese companies' achievements and challenges in sustainable overseas development (social performance)

Social Performance		
Achievements		Challenges
Labor Relations	Most Chinese companies believe that they have established a relatively comprehensive hiring practice that safeguards equal employment, occupational health, safe production, and wage security.	• Cultural differences are the most prominent issue facing overseas labor relations. • Chinese companies should give higher priority to the training and promotion of local employees and to raising the proportion of local managers.
Community Issues and Overseas Social Impact Assessment	Over half of the companies have conducted thirdparty social impact assessment. Additionally, they actively seek to establish harmonious community relations through strengthening communication with stakeholders, weighing community risks when making investment decisions, stepping up interactions with local residents and increasing investment in public welfare projects.	• Nearly half of the companies have not conducted third-party social impact assessment. • Unfamiliarity with local customs, lack of communication, cultural differences and local residents' misperception are the main issues confronting Chinese companies.
Community Issues and Overseas Social Impact Assessment	Over half of the companies have conducted thirdparty social impact assessment. Additionally, they actively seek to establish harmonious community relations through strengthening communication with stakeholders, weighing community risks when making investment decisions, stepping up interactions with local residents and increasing investment in public welfare projects.	• Greater involvement in charity projects is expected of Chinese companies. • Major factors hindering Chinese companies' public welfare programs include lack of influential partners, lack of sustained and systematic public welfare investment, and inexperience at interacting with media to generate positive publicity.
Overseas Public Welfare Investment	Chinese companies give back to the local communities mainly through such means as organizing cultural exchanges, participating in local infrastructure projects, providing vocational training, and running public welfare programs for underprivileged groups	• Greater involvement in charity projects is expected of Chinese companies. • Major factors hindering Chinese companies' public welfare programs include lack of influential partners, lack of sustained and systematic public welfare investment, and inexperience at interacting with media to generate positive publicity.

Note: Report on the Sustainable Development of Chinese Enterprises Overseas 2015, p.105

Investment risks confronted by China-invested companies alongside the "One Belt and One Road" could be grouped to governance risks, economic risks and cultural risks.

Governance risks are measured by global governance index (WGI). As an index used to measure governance quality issued by World Bank, WGI is able to reflect the integrated risk governance conditions of a country. This index could be further grouped to six indicators including political democracy, political stability and non-riot,

Table 5. "One Belt and One Road" national investment security rating (2018)

2018 Ranking	Country	Region	Ratings	2018 Ranking	Country	Region	Ratings
1	Singapore	Southeast Asia	AA	19	Laos	Southeast Asia	
2	UAE	West Asia	A	20	Tajikistan	Central Asia	BBB
3	Israel	West Asia	A	21	Uzbekistan	Central Asia	BBB
4	Poland	Central and Eastern Europe	A	22	India	South Asia	BBB
5	Hungary	Central and Eastern Europe	A	23	Greece	Central and Eastern Europe	BBB
6	Czech Republic	Central and Eastern Europe	A	24	Cambodia	Southeast Asia	BBB
7	Malaysia	Southeast Asia	A	25	Sri Lanka	South Asia	BBB
8	Romania	Central and Eastern Europe	A	26	Vietnam	Southeast Asia	BBB
9	Bulgaria	Central and Eastern Europe	BBB	27	Myanmar	Southeast Asia	BBB
10	Saudi Arabia	West Asia	BBB	28	Iran	West Asia	BBB
11	Kazakhstan	Central Asia	BBB	29	Bangladesh	South Asia	BB
12	Philippines	Southeast Asia	BBB	30	Mongolia	East Asia	BB
13	Russia	CIS	BBB	31	Ukraine	CIS	BB
14	Indonesia	Southeast Asia	BBB	32	Belarus	CIS	BB
15	Thailand	Southeast Asia	BBB	33	Kyrgyzstan	Central Asia	BB
16	Turkey	Central and Eastern Europe	BBB	34	Egypt	Africa	BB
17	Turkmenistan	Central Asia	BBB	35	Iraq	West Asia	B
18	Pakistan	South Asia	BBB				

government efficiency, regulation quality, legitimacy degree and corruption control. Higher scores indicate more perfect systems. As proved by the scores of countries alongside the "One Belt and One Road", China overseas direct investment does not have any overt preference for the risk governance in the host country. This suggests that governance risk might not have drastic influence on the regional decisions of foreign direct investment. Actually, market size, market potential, degree of opening, resource endowment and other factors in the host country might be more important.

Economic risks constitute another major concern in overseas direct investment. The indicator of macroeconomic environment and financial market development could measure the influence of economic risks on overseas investment in China. Specifically, macroeconomic environment indicators include government budget balance, gross national deposits, inflation rate, government debt and national credit rating, while financial market development indicators include financial market efficiency and reliability. In terms of location choice, Chinese overseas direct investment relatively prefers countries with more mature macroeconomic environment and financial market development. Meantime, it also proves that macroeconomic environment and financial market development of the host country are also two key factors concerned by China-invested companies in overseas direct investment.

Cultural risks in overseas direct investment could be measured by the indicator of cultural distance. In general cases, cultural distance refers to the discrepancy between two countries in norms and values, including language, education and religious belief etc. Owing to its influence on the information exchange between domestic country and host country, cultural distance possibly leads to cross-national misunderstanding in the communication process and forms non-conciliatory contradictions, therefore adding corporate overseas direct investment costs. Throughout the comparative analysis on national cultural distance value and national direct investment flow value in countries alongside the "One Belt and One Road", Chinese overseas direct investment is more inclined to choose countries with shorter cultural distance so as to avoid cultural risks.

On the other hand, it is undeniable that some companies in China indeed ignore the performance of social responsibilities out of the blind pursuit for economics interests. In the eyes of overseas consumers and government, these Chinese companies usually plunder resources, make destructive investment, take over resources, devastate the environment, produce forged and fake products, and oppress staff. Such unfavorable impressions pose new challenges to the overseas investment of China and even force overseas consumers and government to boycott the inflow of foreign capital and generate "China threat theory". Indeed, unfavorable impressions such as "The Marshall Plan" will directly affect the smooth development of "One Belt and One Road" construction in China (Huang, Zhen & Wang, 2018).

From the perspective of policy and law, CSR performance evaluation standards in China still do not integrate with the international society. China does not incorporate internationally acknowledged ISO26000 authentication standards nor formulate uniform evaluation standards for the performance of CSR. Additionally, with regard to CSR supervision in overseas companies, relevant legal system remains to be unsound yet and industry association does not enact or implement designated normative documents yet.

Besides, high-standard CSR norms have become the barrier in cross-national corporate operation. Cross-national companies in developed countries have gone through long-term CSR practice and cultivate favorable brand effects and long-term competitive advantages, while in contrast, the social practice of cross-national companies in developing countries remains in the start-up stage which lacks intense sense of social responsibility like peers in developed countries. In international investment competition, developed countries advocate the establishment of social responsibility standards. The "walk-out" companies in developing countries lack speech right in international responsibility system, which places cross-national companies in developing countries at a relatively disadvantageous status and impairs corporate international competitiveness to some degree. When Chinese companies go abroad or march to developed countries, Chinese companies are usually restricted by high-standard CSR norms and encounter barriers in cross-national business operation. Once there arise any discrepancy in investment environment, environment legislation, and social culture, these problems might be amplified by international media and define Chinese companies as irresponsible companies (Zhang, 2016).

CSR Strategies in "One Belt and One Road" Countries

This research considers that CSR risk policy in "One Belt and One Road" countries could start with the perspective of Chinese government and company as follows:

1. Chinese Government:
    a. It is very essential to formulate corresponding overseas investment laws. Apart from relevant policies and opinions enacted by government departments, there still lack any formal laws and regulations concerning overseas investment. Combining with existing regulations and legal documents, Chinese overseas investment takes incentive and management measures, such as simplifying approval procedures, and converting general outbound project approval system to filling system. However, as indicated by overseas investment protection measures, there still have obvious shortcomings and sluggish legislation phenomenon in system design. Therefore, the government should speed up Chinese overseas investment legislation, offer reference to Chinese overseas investment companies and reduce risks in corporate investment;
    b. The government could expand the protection scope of international investment by signing bilateral and muti-lateral investment protection protocol; or reduce potential loss by improving overseas investment insurance system and providing thorough risk aversion measures for companies;
    c. The government should accelerate the construction of CSR authentication institution in China, establish CSR supervision and evaluation system and hint mechanism for companies with low rating scores, and lower

Table 6. 2005-2016 distribution of overseas investment risk cases in Chinese companies alongside "One Belt and One Road"

Country	Case	Loss Amount /US $100 Million	Sum Ratio/%
Iran	4	252	44.6
Philippines	5	64.4	11.4
Myanmar	2	39.1	2.1
Syria	2	37.7	6.7
Afghanistan	1	28.7	5.1
Vietnam	3	26.8	2.6
Russia	1	25	2.3
India	1	15	2.7
Kazakhstan	1	13.9	1.8
Mongolia	2	12.4	2.2
Indonesia	2	7.3	0.8
Saudi Arabia	1	6.2	1.1
Poland	1	4.5	0.8
East Timor	1	3.5	0.6
Pakistan	2	8.7	1.2
Thailand	1	3	0.5
Bulgaria	1	1.9	0.3
Cambodia,	1	1.9	0.3
Uzbekistan	1	1.1	0.2

Data source: *Chinese investment dataset - China Global Investment Tracker* (2016. 7)

overseas investment entrance threshold for companies with high rating scores. Moreover, it connects CSR performance with other corporate indicators by gradually incorporating CSR performance into overseas investment companies;

d. Chinese government needs to boost overseas investment information service level, and provide information service for risk management in Chinese-invested companies, such as building up an entire "One Belt and One Road" database with basic state information such as economics, politics and culture and timely upgrading database information;

e. Government or relevant departments should positively organize all sorts of exhibitions or international conferences, promote the communication between Chinese-invested companies and surrounding countries, constitute a favorable communication platform with the host country and allow

Chinese-invested companies to make appropriate investment decisions. Furthermore, they also need to organize companies to make field visit in surrounding countries so as to learn about local customs and increase cultural exchange;

f. The government should carry out "One Belt and One Road country/district NGO white list work", add officially recognized public welfare organizations in surrounding countries to the catalogue and offer effective cooperative support to the performance of corporate social responsibility and the implementation of public welfare investment strategies;

g. The government should construct and standardize industry association, exert the bridging role of industry association between companies and government departments, convey the latest state legal policies and information to companies and meantime help companies formulate CSR plans;

h. The government should carry out public diplomacy, create a favorable international environment for corporate direct investment. The Chinese government is supposed to deepen the understanding and identity of countries alongside "One Belt and One Road" about China and provide a loose investment environment and political environment for domestic companies.

2. Chinese Company:

a. Companies should give full evaluation and consideration to the politics, economics and cultural background of target countries of investment projects and try to adjust policies to local conditions. Meanwhile, pertinent risk prevention and emergency plans should be released to reduce the blindness of overseas investment. With focus on compliance review, it is also necessary to make risk evaluation;

b. Companies should reinforce localization operation, weaken the localization colors, and execute localization strategy in personnel, capital, product sources, technical development and human resource development. Additionally, attention should be paid to staff legal rights and interests and harmonious labor-capital relationship;

c. As for corporate scale, major companies (especially central companies) ought to take lead to set up examples, invite the participation of small and medium-sized companies, encourage more Chinese-invested companies to perform CSR by learning from major companies' practices;

d. Furthermore, companies are requested to familiarize with the language, culture, law and talent training in host countries;

e. Even if the investment environment is relatively stable, companies had better make preparations for risk aversion;

f. Companies need to focus on the relation with local community. Foreign investment companies should not simply care about the communication with local government, but ignore the communication with other stakeholders, especially surrounding community. In particular, these companies can never violate business ethics and make contact with local government by bribery and other improper means against the pursuits of other numerous stakeholders;

g. Sustainable development strategy should not be illustrated as corporate long-term development objective. CSR never appears alone in single and short-term project, but habitually connects with philanthropy and donation. In this way, such public-welfare donation lacks sustainability. The feasible way is to target at corporate sustainable development and overall development of economics, environment and social responsibility, and win-win objective with the host country;

h. Companies need to boost corporate publicity and establish rational information communication mechanism. In addition to the communication and exchange with local government, companies have to make contact with local social groups and create a favorable public opinion environment;

i. Companies should positively construct CSR strategy, incorporate CSR into corporate strategic management system, reinforce corporate cultural construction and improve corporate integrated management strategy.

Table 7.

Institute of Economics in Zhejiang University has accumulated rich experience in student training of "One Belt and One Road" countries, including students of master's or doctor's degree who have obtained government scholarship and self-supporting students in surrounding countries. Likewise, International Education Institute of Tianjin University of Finance and Economics recruits students of bachelor, master and doctor's degree in finance and economics major from 33 countries alongside "One Belt and One Road" including Uzbekistan, Kazakhstan, Russia, Britain, Hungary, Thailand, Mongolia, South Korea, Congo, popularizes Chinese International Education and promotes Chinese culture.
China Export & Credit Insurance Corporation releases insurance products for the investment projects in "One Belt and One Road" countries. Investors may partially transfer political risks to insurers by buying corresponding overseas investment insurance and accordingly avoid the influence of political risks. Beyond that, partial risks could be transferred to local partners by joint venture with local capital and equity financing in host countries.

The Mainstay of CSR-State-Owned Enterprises Under the Backdrop of the Belt and Road Initiative

In recent years, along with the advancement of "One Belt and One Road" strategy, Chinese overseas investment size continually expands and more and more Chinese companies go out. In this process, central companies become the major force of "One Belt and One Road" construction. According to the news press concerning "One Belt and One Road" construction presided by central companies on May 8th 2017, State-ouned Assets Supervision and Aministration Commission of the State Council disclosed that for past three years, altogether 47 central companies in China made share investment or cooperated with companies in countries and districts alongside "One Belt and One Road" in 1576 projects. Overseas project operation in state-owned companies also keeps constant development and iteration, which well corresponds to the substantial improvement of technical and management abilities of these state-owned companies. These companies greatly make improvement in project technical level and capital intensity. Besides high speed rail, China General Nuclear Power Group (CGN) and other nuclear power construction companies also adopt "Hualong One" self-independent innovation technology to build up the new-generation nuclear power plants in Europe and Britain and similarly, China Communications Construction and other capital construction companies rely on large equipment such as cutter suction dredger.

From the perspective of the property of companies alongside "One Belt and One Road", state-owned companies (especially central companies), possess prominent advantages in size and capital, while most private companies are still small and medium-sized companies with limited size and capital. These companies even confront problems in survival and existence, let alone the performance of CSR. Now that central companies undertake national image and economic burdens, the performance of CSR inevitably affects national image and especially the query about "China threat theory" in recent years. Therefore, when it comes to the discussion about social responsibility alongside "One Belt and One Road", performance of social responsibility in state-owned companies, especially central companies, becomes an inevitable topic.

As instructed by the latest 2018 *Central Company CSR Blue Book*, central companies should assume the post as the bellwether in the implementation of "One Belt and One Road" initiative and the participation of international operation. In particular, central companies undertake considerable water, electricity, and oil shipping infrastructure construction and supply projects in countries alongside "One Belt and One Road" in Africa and Southeast Asia, and make great contributions to resource energy development and heavy chemical industry construction in nearby countries and regions. Additionally, based on CSR management questionnaire survey for 72 central companies, this report points out that on the one hand, central companies generally have overseas CSR performance awareness in overseas operation, behave positively in information disclosure, democratic management, staff vocational health management, environmental protection, sincere operation, and social integration, construct relatively mature systems and achieve outstanding performance results. In the meantime, in the process of CSR performance, central companies also confront restrictions in professional organizations, talent service, theoretical and support practice. Unpredictable political status, remarked cultural discrepancy between China and foreign countries, insufficient communication with local community and resulting local residents' misunderstanding about Chinese companies pose great threats to CSR performance of central companies in overseas operation.

The report comes up with two suggestions. First of all, State Asset Regulatory Commission should instruct the overseas CSR performance of central companies, actively conduct special improvement work, formulate overseas CSR performance appraisal mechanism, set up overseas performance appraisal and reward-punishment mechanism, urge central companies to enhance overseas performance information disclosure flow and guide the training of professional social responsibility talents. On the part of local social groups, what they should do is to positively go abroad, give full play to professional advantage and speciality, and make use of international resources to help central companies improve the practice values of overseas CSR performance activities. It is the responsibility for domestic mainstream media to give voice on behalf of central companies and establish responsible corporate image and state image by virtue of their global influences, pluralistic means of promotion and cooperation with mainstream media in host countries. Secondly, companies should improve overseas CSR performance management mechanism, including overseas CSR management system and management department and talent team construction, and simultaneously reinforce overseas CSR performance information disclosure and promotion, fabricate overseas responsible brands, consummate responsibility practice pattern, positively join in international responsibility exchange and formulation of relevant international standards, and refer to outstanding corporate CSR experience in host countries so as to elevate overseas CSR performance practice proficiency and establish sincere brand image.

Under the background of "One Belt and One Road", central companies successively turn to be the bellwether in the implementation of Chinese "go-out" strategy. CSR of overseas companies alongside "One Belt and One Road" also becomes a key task on the agenda of central companies in recent years. Besides relevant reports and news which frequently introduce CSR in "One Belt and One Road" implementation process, corporate CSR reports also divert attention to the topic in relation to "One Belt and One Road".

Since CSR report gives response to stakeholders' requests on corporate economic, environmental and social information as a significant communication platform between the company and stakeholders, substantial words about "One Belt and One Road" in the report even more highlight corporate focus on CSR strategy under the background of "One Belt and One Road".

According to the latest 2016-2017 Annual CSR Report, most central companies have mentioned "One Belt and One Road"-related overseas CSR contents (such as "One Belt and One Road"-related CSR topic) in their CSR reports and some central companies even start to enact professional overseas investment country-themed CSR reports. China Communications Construction even issued a CSR report in relation to "One Belt and One Road" topic in 2018. This suggests that many central companies actually have listed CSR strategy under the background of "One Belt and One Road" as a component of corporate organization strategy.

In "One Belt and One Road" construction process, numerous central companies have offered manpower, material and fund guarantee to CSR and achieved outstanding overseas CSR performance. For instance, in the development construction and operation management process of Laos-Nanou River Project, POWERCHINA adheres to the mutual benefit and win-win concept, firmly integrates into local area and builds up community of interests and development community. By carrying out "governance localization", "operation localization", "resource localization", "development localization", "responsibility localization" and "culture localization", and constructing the "six-in-one" localization management system, POWERCHINA propels in-depth overseas CSR performance and lays a firm development environment for the healthy operation of projects. China State Construction Group Co., Ltd boosts the overseas influences of Chinese culture with Chinese architecture, provides reference for other investment construction companies in respect of cultural soft power and internationalization operation, as well as offers experience to other companies in humanistic exchange and communication between government and the public. State Development and Investment Corporation has achieved great performance in sustainable development topics such as poverty elimination, social justice and environmental protection while propelling its international operation, which could be proved by the deepening of international friendship and lifting of corporate brand reputation and influence.

Case Study: First "One Belt and One Road" CSR Report- China Communications Construction

Although some central companies have released overseas country CSR reports, or mentioned some topics in relation to "One Belt and One Road" in integrated CSR reports, China Communications Construction published "One Belt and One Road"

CSR Report in Beijing in May 2018. It was the first "One Belt and One Road" CSR report formally released by Chinese companies.

With integrated businesses covering infrastructure investment and financing, consulting and planning, construction design and management operation nationwide, China Communications Construction now ranks in the 103th place in Global 500. As the third largest international contractor, China Communications Construction joined in "One Belt and One Road" construction and signed new contracts worth of $ 17 billion with countries alongside "One Belt and One Road" in 2017 on the top of Chinese-invested company list. Since its report fails to mention referential compilation guide, the thesis takes content analysis method commonly used in CSR report analysis to expound economic-environmental-social responsibility.

Economy

Most parts of the report involve the performance of economic responsibility, which indirectly manifests the stages and characteristics about central companies' overseas CSR performance. Please refer to the following sections for more details (Summary about infrastructure).

Built major infrastructures in countries alongside "One Belt and One Road", including 152 bridges, 10320-kilometer road, 95 deep-water berths, 10 airports, 754 container cranes, and 2980-kilometer railway; made investment in China-Pakistan Economic Corridor, Mongolian Railway and other projects; new contract amount concerning "One Belt and One Road" totaled $ 16.643 billion in 2017.

Infrastructure connection primarily propelled the construction in four key businesses including "Love Bridge", "Fortune Road", "Development Harbour" and "Happiness Town".

Table 8.

1. **Love Bridge:** To draw close the distance between local area and China by crossing estrangement and natural chasm by bridge construction 2. **Fortune Road:** To enrich local residents by investing in road and railway construction 3. **Development Harbour:** To construct portal in host countries and connect with the world to encourage joint development by investment in seaport and airport. 4. **Happiness Town:** To improve general living and development standards by investing to build a group of new industrial parks. (Opening to the outside world with the "special zone and experiment pilot" development mode is the precious experience throughout the development of China. It also provides Chinese urbanization plans for relevant countries and regions alongside "One Belt and One Road". China Communications Construction has over 20 outbound industrial park projects under construction in surrounding countries. Some established projects have created employment opportunities for local residents and driven the growth of local economy.)

Environment

Established HSE management system and completely executed green construction standard management; researched and developed green technology and craft, and maximally preserved resources and cut down negative influences on environment. All international engineering projects undertaken by central companies had passed environmental protection acceptance inspection for fear of major environmental accidents.

Society

1. To be the excellent talent training base in host countries;
2. Cultural integration: to promote cross-cultural management and cultural integration regulations and management systems, respect and learn cultural differences and reinforce overseas employees' cultural identity and sense of belonging;
3. Localization management: to employee plenty of local staff, and go through "teacher-apprentice" system which designated masterly and skillful Chinese staff to teach one or two foreign workers or sent local talents to study in China by scholarship incentive;
4. Emergency rescue team in host countries;
5. Community construction and relevant voluntary activities (such as Montenegro, Mongolia and other companies or projects); and student loan relief (Kibaale and other areas).

Others

1. Quality engineering compliance engineering quality industry promotion;
2. Security product: to pass overseas engineering security production performance appraisal.

Furthermore, one prominent feature of the report is that it fully sets forth the communication with corporate stakeholders, including local government and internal corporate staff. Exactly, contents concerning local government have received the praise and letter of thanks from the President. More importantly, the report also gives voice for staff. A typical example is its focus on ten foreign young staff.

Obviously, as of the proposal of "One Belt and One Road" initiative, China Communications Construction has formed distinctive "smiling-face mode". After clarifying overseas development priority strategy, China Communications

Construction positively and comprehensively advances construction in "Love Bridge", "Fortune Road", "Development Harbour" and "Happiness Town" in response to state initiative, focuses on key channels, key cities and key projects, undertakes a large group of transportation projects consisting of Kenya-Mongolia Railway, Sudan Port, and Sri Lanka Colombo City to build up a composite infrastructure network. *China Communications Construction "One Belt and One Road" CSR Report* published this time systematically summarizes that since the proposal of "One Belt and One Road" initiative, brilliant responsibility practices and outcomes attained by China Communications Construction in building global quality engineering projects, guaranteeing stakeholder rights and interests, encouraging staff growth, seeking win-win situation with partners, fabricating community harmony, and pursuing environmental sustainability potently prove the important contributions made by Chinese companies in the construction of "One Belt and One Road" and human destiny community.

However, CSR report does not clarify its referential compilation standards and it is merely published in Chinese. More seriously, either in length or contents, most parts of CSR report talk about CSR economic responsibility (which could be proved by infrastructure construction, growth of local economy and promotion of employment) and partially involve environmental and social benefits. Whereas, relevant compilation standards have not been explained and interpreted in detail.

Anyhow, it is a beneficial attempt made by China Communications Construction to join in "One Belt and One Road" construction and release the first CSR report among Chinese companies under the background of "One Belt and One Road". To be sure, it also generates positive impacts on the "One Belt and One Road" CSR decisions for other central companies. Furthermore, it is predicted that more and more companies will release "One Belt and One Road" CSR reports in the future and make for the systematic construction of "One Belt and One Road" CSR management mode, thus pushing forward the further development of "One Belt and One Road" construction on the whole.

CONCLUSION

Up to now, CSR topic has become an inevitable topic among Chinese companies. In spite of the great progress made by CSR, an indisputable fact is that CSR in Chinese companies is still in a relatively low level. In view of unsuccessful CSR performance in China, overseas CSR performance naturally confronts more difficulties and setbacks. Frequent change of ruling party and leaders, severe racial and religious conflicts, unstable domestic political situations and overall investment environment, and legal risks in some countries alongside "One Belt and One Road" all produce risks for overseas investment companies and worsen CSR performance. However, now that CSR performance involves national image and corporate image, humanistic concerns and other problems, it has great significance to the weakening of negative images about Chinese companies such as "China threat theory" and "resource plunder theory". Along with the acceleration of "One Belt and One Road" CSR progress, more Chinese companies will go abroad. While in this process, it is state-owned companies (especially central companies) that play the role of bellwether. With relatively high overseas investment proportion and strong strength, these companies possess adequate CSR performance capacity and conditions. While among these companies, some of them have achieved brilliant performance in "One Belt and One Road" construction and well practise CSR in overseas operation. Furthermore, *Chinese Company Overseas CSR Report in 2015*, first-session "One Belt and One Road" overseas CSR management combat dialogue in 2016, *Central Company Overseas CSR Report in 2018* issued by Chinese Academy of Social Sciences and *"One Belt and One Road" CSR Report in 2018* issued by China Communications Construction all prove that both the government and companies have progressively realized the importance of CSR performance in overseas operation, in particular CSR performance of companies in countries alongside "One Belt and One Road". A conclusion can be hereby drawn that more companies will release "One Belt and One Road" CSR report and reinforce CSR performance in overseas operation and the government will continually improve and formulate CSR-related systems and policies and supervise CSR performance to ensure the further development of "One Belt and One Road" strategy. Apart from large companies in China, the government and international environment will raise higher requirements on overseas CSR performance in small and medium-sized companies.

REFERENCES

Carroll, A. B. (1979). Corporate social responsibility: Evolution of a definitional construct. *Business & Society*, *38*(3), 268–295. doi:10.1177/000765039903800303

Carroll, A. B. (1991). The pyramid of corporate social responsibility: Toward the moral management of organizational stakeholders. *Business Horizons*, *34*(4), 42. doi:10.1016/0007-6813(91)90005-G

Huang, L. Y., Zhen, S. F., & Wang, J. (2018). Research on the Win-Win Corporation Mechanism between Multi-national Corporation and Host Country under the Background of One Belt and One Road: Based on the Perspective of Corporate Social Responsibility. *Management Review*, *30*(2), 172–182.

Liu, W., Wei, Q., Huang, S. Q., & Tsai, S. B. (2017). Doing good again? A multilevel institutional perspective on corporate environmental responsibility and philanthropic strategy. *International Journal of Environmental Research and Public Health*, *14*(10), 1283. doi:10.3390/ijerph14101283 PMID:29064451

Turker, D. (2009). Measuring Corporate Social Responsibility: A Scale Development Study. *Journal of Business Ethics*, *85*(4), 411–427. doi:10.100710551-008-9780-6

Wang, Q. Y. (2008). *Corporate social responsibility of Multinational Enterprises*. China Economic Publishing House.

Yuan, J. F. (1990). Corporate social responsibility. *Maritime Press*, *1990*, 46–52.

Zhang, Z.G., Liang, Z. G., & Liang, K. G. (2012). Research on Corporate Social Responsibility from the Stakeholder Perspective. *China Soft Science, 2012*(2), 139-146.

Zhang, Z. Y. (2016). *''The Blet And Road" and construction of Chinese "Going Global" coporate social responsibility and soft power*. Social Sciences Academic Press.

Chapter 3
The "Outgoing Strategy" of Chinese Companies

Ping Zhou
City University of Macau, China

Tim Wong
City University of Macau, China

ABSTRACT

The globalization of economics and China's accession to the World Trade Organization (WTO) have brought new opportunities and challenges to Chinese enterprises. Taking the sense of globalization, China is participating in global resource allocation, expanding and utilizing the market on the global scale, actively participating in international division and cooperation, and implementing international operation are important steps for Chinese enterprises to go abroad and seize the initiative in the global economic competition. In China, the strategy of "going out" is still at the initial stage. Compared with the developed countries, there is still a large gap between China and other developed countries in terms of investment amount, enterprise scale, and internationalization. China enterprises can adapt to the changing environment of international market; the key is to improve the competitiveness of enterprises in the international market, which is a crucial step in expanding Chinese enterprises' international market.

INTRODUCTION

Since the reform and opening up in 1978, Chinese enterprise competitiveness has been greatly improved, even though constrained by the system, business philosophy, management system, management method, management mode and business goals

DOI: 10.4018/978-1-5225-8440-7.ch003

compared to the developed countries. If Chinese enterprises want to continue to be matured in the international market, they should directly encounter the challenges above mentioned to decrease the gaps.

THE CHALLENGE TO THE COMPETITIVENESS OF CHINESE ENTERPRISES BY THE DEEPENING DEVELOPMENT TREND OF INTERNATIONAL LABOR DIVISION OF LABOR

In the 21th century, economic globalization, distribution of information and economic networking has become an irreversible trend in the multi-national company's development (Duanmu, 2012). The international division of labor has broken the individual country as the main body of the division of labor and turned the national characteristics of the traditional division of the relationship to globalization as the characteristics of multinational enterprises and enterprises between the division of labor, among which has changed in the past the kind of single product manufacturing as the boundary division of labor. Countries and multi-national enterprises paid more attention to the product design, development, research management service and a series of related value-added activities in the value chain thus multinational companies as the main body of the company represented the division of labor. The division of labor of the value chain is more inclined to the outsourcing division of business between the co-ops of the global multinational corporation (Wang et al., 2018). Multinational corporations have become the leading factor in deepening the international division of labor. Multinational corporations have established global production networks through direct investment, so that industries, especially modern manufacturing, have globalized characteristics. Facing the international market competition, Chinese enterprises corresponding to the world economy should face more competition in the international market, and strive for more effective resources. They must go to the most effective area of resource allocation to achieve cross border flow of products, technology, finance and human resources (Liu et al., 2018). Though the output of many manufacturing products has become the number one in the world, the credibility and influence of Chinese enterprises and their brands in the international market are still very small. Chinese enterprises are still passively accepting the industrial transfer of MNCs, and there are no products, technologies and brands that have been developed independently. The international competitiveness of China enterprises is still too disadvantage to dominate the extension of the production of processors the global rules of transnational corporation, which demonstrated that Chinese enterprises are only a world processing plant in the international division of labor system (Lall & Albaladejo, 2004).

THE COMPETITIVENESS OF CHINESE ENTERPRISES IN INTERNATIONAL INVESTMENT

The founder of the theory of international investment, the well-known British scholar John Dunning researched and divided a certain nation's investment cycle, namely, when an economy entity was in the initial stage of development, the investment is mainly to attract foreign investment; economic development is in a stable stage, investment activities into two-way choice; economic development to a higher level, or into the stage of development of foreign direct investment than foreign capital (Dunning, 2009). Many experts believed that China has entered the stage of two-way option from the stage of attracting foreign capital. Looking at the history of the development of the world economy, the economic development of a country, can not simply rely on foreign capital investment, and should establish two-way circulation mechanism for actively absorbing foreign capital, but also let the surplus of domestic capital, the ability to go abroad so that domestic enterprises for resources allocation of global market. Over the three decades of reform and opening up, China absorbed a large number of international capital, the introduction of management experience, advanced technology and equipment, domestic production factors and external factors of production and management factors, optimization and integration of organic collection, product structure, enterprises have been adjusted, technical level, market competition ability and marketing levels increase, improve the China competitive advantage, which laid the foundation for the Chinese enterprises abroad. Some advanced and matured Chinese enterprises have taken the initiative to move towards the international market and transfer oversea production capacity. It is the initiative to go to the world, or to go to the market passively, and to participate in the international market competition and global economic activities with a higher degree of marketization, to gain greater profits, which is an important test for the competitiveness of Chinese enterprises.

THE CHALLENGE OF THE INTERNATIONALIZATION OF ENTERPRISES TO THE DECENTRALIZED INDIVIDUAL BUSINESS MODEL OF CHINESE ENTERPRISES

The evolution of western scholars from different angles of enterprise internationalization, the Nordic school scholar Johanson, the Swedish scholar Forsgren, American professor Cavusgil believed that the enterprise internationalization was a gradual process (Björkman & Forsgren, 2000; Cavusgil & Knight, 2015). The internationalization of enterprises experienced the development process of the local market and the competition in the international market. From the product internationalization to the sales internationalization and the brand internationalization, it will finally come out of the country, become a multinational enterprise, and occupy a place in the international market. Whether the transnational operation can be realized is an important sign of the success of the enterprise internationalization.

The principle of gradual development, on the basis of introduction, China realized the introverted internationalization with transnational enterprises. With the enhancement of the strength of the enterprise, the enterprise goes to the international market. The scale of investment of Chinese enterprises going out is still small and medium sized, which mainly takes advantage of labor intensive advantages, and occupied the international market with the products of low cost advantage of single enterprise as well as no advantage of technology intensive and capital intensive. When economic development is based on collaborative commerce, collaborative competition and win-win principal, Chinese enterprises still develop in a difficult and an exploring journey to form the competition, which is no longer suitable for changing situations. Some people attribute China's overseas investment to six features: "single", "small", "scattered", "soft", "poor" and "flee" (Deng, 2004). Chinese enterprises in overseas investment amount and many belong to different administrative level, the administrative system constraints, these enterprises lack of coordination of the organization, not in the business cooperation and exchange, cannot achieve the capital, technology and market information, the coexistence and complementation, but difficult to achieve diversification, fight the enemy separately, strategic alliances the formation of transnational corporations through transnational mergers and acquisitions, which demonstrated that the internationalization of Chinese enterprises was still in the initial stage; on the other hand the downstream manufacturers internationalization of enterprises were still multinational companies in the industry chain and the companies were at a low level position in the international division of labor system with the lack of international competitiveness enterprise anti risk ability is weak, the lack of international competitiveness.

From David Ricardo's "comparative advantage" of free trade theory to Robert's theory of production factor, the exchange of world trade determines the transformation of resource utilization and cost accounting in the world from the emphasis on the use of domestic resources to the world, and the rapid flow of production like water to the lowest production conditions and the lowest production cost (Maneschi, 2004; Ruffin, 2002). Robert said: capital always has a certain liquidity, but in the past it mainly flows in developed countries. The emergence of new political stability in India and China prompted capital flows to start jumping out of the borders of developed countries. Although the international business of our overseas enterprises has developed initially, there is a clear gap between the developed countries and the emerging industrial countries, with the characteristics of the developing countries, namely, the small investment scale, the single product production and the investment enterprises in the form of joint ventures. In order to encourage Chinese enterprises to actively expand the international market and enhance the competitiveness of enterprises, we must have scientific theoretical guidance and the support and guidance of national macro policies.

The Chinese government should strive to create a "going global" environment and encourage and guide our enterprises to go out.

First, the government should guide enterprises to establish the consciousness and concept of "going out", and let Chinese enterprises eliminate the idea that the Chinese domestic market is enough and no need to expand to the overseas market. Secondly, the government should do a good job for all the services prepared for the enterprise "going out", and formulate policies to encourage enterprises to "go out", such as to improve the foreign exchange management, increase the transparency of examination and approval, change the pre-management of some approvals into registration and filing management. Again, the government should improve the service level, actively promote the cooperation with the international, and sign bilateral or multilateral investment agreements with the relevant countries in order to safeguard the legitimate rights and interests of Chinese enterprises to invest abroad.

It is impossible for Chinese enterprises to have global resources allocation and strategic thinking for international management without global strategic thinking, and there can be no action to "go out" to allocate resources. Enterprises should be good at the global perspective, participate in the allocation of international resources, establish a set of scientific strategic management system and management strategy for transnational management, open up the international market actively, and establish their own international market customer network and sales channels. The competition of enterprises in the international market is mainly based on comparative advantage and competitive advantage, so as to cultivate the core competitiveness of enterprises. The investment plants in the host country pay attention to making full use of local resources, technology and services to realize the localization of overseas enterprises, learn to cooperate with overseas enterprises, make up for their strengths and improve their ability. The enterprise of "going out" needs to develop its own core technology as soon as possible through research and development sections to develop its own products, launch its own brand, and set up a good image of the enterprise.

REFERENCES

Björkman, I., & Forsgren, M. (2000). Nordic international business research: A review of its development. *International Studies of Management & Organization*, *30*(1), 6–25. doi:10.1080/00208825.2000.11656780

Cavusgil, S. T., & Knight, G. (2015). The born global firm: An entrepreneurial and capabilities perspective on early and rapid internationalization. *Journal of International Business Studies*, *46*(1), 3–16. doi:10.1057/jibs.2014.62

Deng, P. (2004). Outward investment by Chinese MNCs: Motivations and implications. *Business Horizons*, *47*(3), 8–16. doi:10.1016/S0007-6813(04)00023-0

Duanmu, J. L. (2012). Firm heterogeneity and location choice of Chinese multinational enterprises (MNEs). *Journal of World Business*, *47*(1), 64–72. doi:10.1016/j.jwb.2010.10.021

Dunning, J. H. (2009). Location and the multinational enterprise: John Dunning's thoughts on receiving the Journal of International Business Studies 2008 Decade Award. *Journal of International Business Studies*, *40*(1), 20–34. doi:10.1057/jibs.2008.75

Lall, S., & Albaladejo, M. (2004). China's competitive performance: A threat to East Asian manufactured exports? *World Development*, *32*(9), 1441–1466. doi:10.1016/j.worlddev.2004.03.006

Liu, W., Shi, H. B., Zhang, Z., Tsai, S. B., Zhai, Y., Chen, Q., & Wang, J. (2018). The Development Evaluation of Economic Zones in China. *International Journal of Environmental Research and Public Health*, *15*(1), 56. doi:10.3390/ijerph15010056 PMID:29301304

Maneschi, A. (2004). The true meaning of David Ricardo's four magic numbers. *Journal of International Economics*, *62*(2), 433–443. doi:10.1016/S0022-1996(03)00008-4

Ruffin, R. (2002). David Ricardo's discovery of comparative advantage. *History of Political Economy*, *34*(4), 727–748. doi:10.1215/00182702-34-4-727

Wang, H., Liu, W., Zhu, M., & Wang, Q. (2018). Embrace or Not? An Empirical Study of the Impact of Globalization on the Country's Sustainability in the Case of NAFTA. *Sustainability*, *10*(10), 3436. doi:10.3390u10103436

Chapter 4
The Study of Intellectual Property Protection System:
Under the Context of "One Belt One Road"

Ping Zhou
City University of Macau, China

Dongjuan Lv
City University of Macau, China

Ying Chen
University of Malaya, Malaysia

ABSTRACT

The "One Belt One Road" strategy is the abbreviation of "Silk Road Economic Belt" and "21st Century Maritime Silk Road." In September and October of 2013, Chinese President Xi Jinping proposed to build the cooperation initiative of "New Silk Road Economic Belt" and "The 21st Century Maritime Silk Road." President Xi Jinping projected to establish the "21st Century Maritime Silk Road" during his visit in Indonesia in October 2013. Finally, the National Development and Reform Commission, the Ministry of Foreign Affairs, and the Ministry of Commerce cooperatively issued the "Vision and Action for Promoting the Construction of the Silk Road Economic Belt and the 21st Century Maritime Silk Road" on March 28, 2015. The "One Belt One Road" countries were key areas of cooperation in the context of China's policy in communication, road connectivity, smooth trade, currency circulation, people's mutual understanding, strategic coordination to strengthen bilateral and multilateral teamwork, and corresponding development.

DOI: 10.4018/978-1-5225-8440-7.ch004

INTRODUCTION

The Proposal of the "One Belt One Road" Strategy and its Impact

The "One belt one road" strategy is the abbreviation of "Silk Road Economic Belt" and "21st Century Maritime Silk Road". In September and October of 2013, Chinese President Xi Jinping proposed to build the cooperation initiative of "New Silk Road Economic Belt" and "The 21st Century Maritime Silk Road". In September of the same year, Chinese President Xi Jinping delivered an important speech entitled "Promoting People's Friendship and Creating a Better Future" during his visit in Kazakhstan and proposed to build the "Silk Road Economic Belt" Jointly. President Xi Jinping projected to establish the "21st Century Maritime Silk Road" during his visit in Indonesia in October 2013. Finally, the National Development and Reform Commission, the Ministry of Foreign Affairs, and the Ministry of Commerce cooperatively issued the "Vision and Action for Promoting the Construction of the Silk Road Economic Belt and the 21st Century Maritime Silk Road." on March 28, 2015 (The National Development and Reform Commission, the Ministry of Foreign Affairs, and the Ministry of Commerce, 2018). The "One belt one road" countries were key areas of cooperation in the context of China's policy in communication, road connectivity, smooth trade, currency circulation, and people's mutual understanding, strategic coordination to strengthen bilateral and multilateral teamwork and corresponding development.

"One belt one road" strategy has a significant impact on the global economics. Firstly, the goal of the "One belt one road" is to establish a mutually beneficial interest, destiny and responsibility community covering through Eurasia countries. Secondly, "One belt one road" is the world's most promising, all-around, multi-level economic cooperation strategy, it originated in China, including Central Asia, Southeast Asia, South Asia, West Asia and parts of Europe. The east is connected to the Asia-Pacific economic circle. The west is closely related to the European economic circle. It covers about 4.4 billion people and has an economic aggregate of about 21 trillion dollars, which accounted for 63% and 29% of the world respectively (Gong, Tian & wang, 2018). Finally, the "One belt one road" strategy has created a new regional cooperation model, at the meantime, continuing to deepen cooperation with developed countries will strengthen cooperation with developing countries significantly by emerging powers and enhance the status of China (Luo, 2018).

THE MAIN PROBLEMS OF IMPLEMENTING IPRS STRATEGY IN THE CONTEXT OF "ONE BELT ONE ROAD"

The Necessity of Implementing the IPRs Strategy

In the context of the "One belt one road", establishing and perfecting the national IPRs strategy and continuously strengthening bilateral and multilateral intellectual property strategic cooperation is the ambition and necessity of the IPRs strategy to keep pace with the times.

Implementing an IPRs Strategy is the Need to Safeguard the Company's Own Interests

At this stage, the footprint of Chinese companies' overseas business is spread across all continents, and with the increasing exchanges and cooperation between domestic and foreign companies, how can we reduce intellectual property risks on the basis of maintaining cooperation? IPRs in the new era is a tough issue. Also, it is a problem that enterprises must seriously consider and treat in order to protect their legitimate interests.

On December 6, 2017, "World Intellectual Property Index 2017" reported by the World Intellectual Property Organization in Geneva give the information that, in 2016, the number of Chinese applications for patents, trademarks and industrial designs in the world reached a new high, and proportion is the highest in the world. China's IPRs both in quantity and quality, are rising, and are gradually moving forward as intellectual property superpower. A big amount of Chinese enterprises have gone abroad in the context of the "One belt one road" strategy, however, most of the "One belt one road" regions are developing countries, and economic development is uneven, infringement of IPRs has occurred occasionally. For example, the "Flying Pigeon" bicycle trademark was pre-registered in Indonesia, a large scale of Chinese trademarks was squatted by foreign companies which caused the Chinese companies lost their autonomy in trademark management during the overseas investment process (Zhang, Gao & Cao, 2015). Implementing an intellectual property strategy can reduce the phenomenon of infringement of IPRs and is an important guarantee for safeguarding the legitimate rights and interests of enterprises.

The Implementation of Intellectual Property Strategy is in Line With the Needs of the Intellectual Property Legal Environment in the International Market

In this era, with the continuous development of economic globalization and the development of the knowledge economy, IPRs have increasingly become the core resource of national development's strategic resources and international competitiveness, and have become an important support for building an innovative country and mastering the initiative of development (Wu & Lock, 2013). The intellectual property legal regulation and institutional environment of the international market is constantly developing and improving and put forward higher requirements for the development of intellectual property in various countries and regions, not only to promote the development level of domestic IPRs but also to strengthen international knowledge. The level of development of property rights promotes the development of intellectual property in the world. Therefore, the implementation of the intellectual property strategy is in line with the trend in the world, and further strengthens the requirements for the exchange and cooperation of IPRs in the international market. It is also the requirement of the international intellectual property legal system and environment.

Major Problems in Implementing the IPRs Strategy for Overseas Investment

In the context of "One belt one road", the implementation of overseas investment IPRs strategy has great prospects and important development significance. At the same time, there are also some problems and unfavorable factors.

Foremost, the political and economic development of different countries in the "One belt one road" region is uneven, and there is a big difference in the degree of emphasis on IPRs. The "One belt one road" region includes more than 60 countries and regions. The political and economic development of each country and region is quite different. The degree of awareness and importance of IPRs are also inconsistent. Therefore, it will cause problems for China to implement overseas investment in IPRs. At this stage, the cooperation between China and the countries in the "One belt one road" region has undergone important changes. From the traditional industries to the high-tech industries such as pharmaceutical manufacturing and electronic equipment manufacturing, it has become an important part. In the high-tech industry, the coordination and protection of intellectual property strategies have become a key focus. If some countries and regions do not attach importance to intellectual property protection in the field of high-tech industries, it will have many adverse effects on China's overseas investment intellectual property strategy.

Additionally, there is no relatively uniform intellectual property legal system between countries in the "One belt one road" region. "The purpose of the legal system is to have a very purposeful and rational purpose: to subordinate human behavior to the guidance and control of general rules." In modern society, effective international cooperation cannot be carried out in the absence of a legal system, especially in the field of intellectual property. At this stage, the intellectual property legal system of the "One belt one road" countries differs greatly, and there is no relatively consistent standard and system. At the same time, some countries in different countries have not participated in, or are still affiliated with different IPRs. There are still differences in the systems between international organizations or regional organizations.

"ONE BELT ONE ROAD" EXISTING INTELLECTUAL PROPERTY PROTECTION SYSTEM IN THE BACKGROUND

The International Protection System for IPRs

At this stage, there are two modes for the protection of IPRs in major countries in the world. One is the "monorail system" model of judicial protection, with the court as the core institution for intellectual property protection. The court passed the trial of intellectual property infringement cases and ordered the infringer to assume the protection mode of legal responsibility such as stopping the infringement and compensating for the loss. This model conforms to the concept of intellectual property protection in modern society. Therefore, the monorail system of judicial protection has been widely adopted by countries all over the world, especially in developed countries such as the United Kingdom and the United States. One is the "dual track system" mode in which both administrative protection and judicial protection exist simultaneously and in parallel, and the administrative organs and the courts simultaneously assume the functions of intellectual property protection. After an intellectual property infringement dispute occurs, the right holder can seek administrative protection from the administrative organ. Can also seek judicial protection from the court.

China's Intellectual Property Protection System

In the practice of intellectual property protection, China has formed an intellectual property protection model of "two ways and parallel operation" of administrative protection and judicial protection (Wu, 2009). This model is rooted in the state of China's social and economic development and the reality of intellectual property protection and has also played an important role in the protection of IPRs in China.

Administrative Law Protection of IPRs

The administrative protection mechanism of IPRs in China is formed and developed on the basis of fully considering the basic national conditions and the development of IPRs. Some scholars pointed out that "in the face of severe international challenges and increasingly fierce international competition, China's administrative organs must adopt more effective policy measures and strive to improve the level of intellectual property administrative protection. Administrative protection can only be strengthened and cannot be weakened." (Qu & Zhang, 2011) At this stage, China's intellectual property administrative protection is mainly carried out by the State Intellectual Property Office, the State Administration for Industry and Commerce, the National Copyright Administration, the Ministry of Commerce and other state organs and the local administrative departments under the above-mentioned ministries and commissions.

Judicial Protection of IPRs

In terms of judicial protection, China's current intellectual property judicial system has played an important role in resolving disputes, coordinating contradictions, and cracking down on infringement activities. The Supreme People's Court has a special intellectual property court, which is responsible for hearing relevant intellectual property cases, conducting research, guidance, and supervision of national intellectual property trials. Other people's courts at all levels have also established intellectual property trial organizations. A fully covered intellectual property litigation body has been established from the grassroots court to the Supreme People's Court. In particular, the establishment of intellectual property courts has greatly enhanced the intensity of judicial protection of IPRs in China. On August 31, 2014, the Tenth Session of the Standing Committee of the 12th National People's Congress voted on the "Decision on the Establishment of Intellectual Property Courts in Beijing, Shanghai and Guangzhou", the establishment of the intellectual property court, the jurisdiction of the case, and the appointment of judges. The regulations have provided a legal basis for the establishment and operation of intellectual property courts. The establishment of intellectual property courts in China is to strengthen the use and protection of IPRs and to improve the incentive mechanism for technological innovation.

"ONE BELT ONE ROAD" INTELLECTUAL PROPERTY PROTECTION STRATEGY UNDER THE STRATEGIC BACKGROUND

Strengthening Intellectual Property Communication Among Countries

Strengthen intellectual property dialogue and cooperation between countries and regions in the "One belt one road" region, through the official and folk channels actively carry out dialogue and cooperation and exchange mechanisms. On the one hand, we will continue to strengthen dialogues between China and the national intellectual property management institutions in the "One belt one road" region, establish regular communication and exchange mechanisms, promote bilateral and multilateral cooperation, coordinate and standardize, institutionalize construction, sign intellectual property memorandums of understanding, and establish peace. The intellectual property protection environment that coexists, promotes and develops together (Wang, 2016). On the other hand, it seeks to use civil forces to actively engage in dialogue and consultation. At present, China's large multinational enterprises have made great progress in both quantity and scale, and gradually occupy core positions or gain a dominant position in various fields of the world (Pan, 2015). These large multinational enterprises can seek regional and regional development according to their own advantages. Civil dialogue and exchanges to promote cooperation and win-win.

Strive to Build "One Belt One Road" Regional Intellectual Property Integration System

The unbalanced development of political economy and culture in the "One belt one road" regions and regions has made the level of awareness and importance of IPRs in different countries and regions different. Some countries such as Singapore and Hong Kong have higher levels of protection. However, some countries and regions lack intellectual property protection due to economic backwardness and perennial war. Therefore, promote the integration of regional intellectual property systems, reduce the differentiation of intellectual property standards, adhere to the implementation of the "One belt one road" strategy and the integration of regional intellectual property systems, and integrate regional intellectual property integration rules with international intellectual property rules (Wu, 2016). Strive to integrate regional IPRs and standardization system on the basis of regulatory integration.

Establishing the "One Belt One Road" Intellectual Property Information Platform and Intellectual Property Database

There are three regional intellectual property organizations with a certain scale in the "One belt one road" area, namely the ASEAN Intellectual Property Cooperation Organization, the Eurasian Patent Organization, and the European Patent Organization. These three organizations are established to strengthen knowledge in the region. The construction of property rights protection, drawing on IPRs contradictions and disputes and improving the level of intellectual property development in the region. At this stage, China and ASEAN countries have signed a number of bilateral and multilateral cooperation treaties in the field of intellectual property protection, forming a good cooperative relationship. At the same time, China and Eurasian patent organizations and European patent organizations are also developing and consolidating cooperation. Therefore, we should make full use of the existing cooperative relationship between China and the above three regional intellectual property organizations, establish a "One belt one road" intellectual property information platform and an intellectual property database, and we can adopt regular dissemination of relevant intellectual property data information to strengthen "One belt one road" intellectual property information sharing in the region, reducing information barriers.

Formulating an Effective Intellectual Property Risk Prevention Mechanism

With the continuous advancement of the "One belt one road" strategy, the scale of "going out" of Chinese enterprises has continued to grow, and the number of infringement disputes involving IPRs will increase significantly. Therefore, it is necessary to formulate reasonable and effective risk prevention mechanisms and dispute resolution mechanisms. In the aspect of intellectual property risk prevention, an intellectual property insurance system can be adopted. It is an effective risk management system to reduce the risk of intellectual property infringement through the intellectual property insurance system. The intellectual property insurance system is an effective intellectual property risk management measure with low investment, high return, and a strong guarantee (Zhang, Wang & Li, 2015).

REFERENCES

Hong, W. (2016). Strategic Collaboration between "Belt and Road" and Intellectual Property Rights. *Frontline*, (10), 70.

Luo. (2018). The Belt and Road Initiative and China's Strategic Vision. *Yunmeng Journal*, (4), 63.

Pan. (2015). On the Protection Model of Intellectual Property Internationalization and China's Coping Strategies. *Law Review*, (1), 159.

Qu & Zhang (2011). Research on Administrative Protection of Intellectual Property Rights. *Political and Legal Studies*, (3), 57.

The National Development and Reform Commission. the Ministry of Foreign Affairs, & the Ministry of Commerce. (n.d.). *Vision and Alignment to Promote the Construction of the Silk Road Economic Belt and the 21st Century Maritime Silk Road*. Retrieved from http://www.xinhuanet.com/finance/2015-03/28/c_1114793986.htm

Wen, Junrong, & Wei. (2014, June 30). New Silk Road: Through Common Prosperity. *The People's Daily*.

Wu, H. (2009). Evaluation and Reflection on China's Intellectual Property Legal System Construction. *Chinese Law*, (1), 57.

Wu, H. (2016). "One Belt and One Road" Strategic Conception and Intellectual Property Protection. The Rule of Law Society, (5), 11.

Wu, H., & Futao, L. (2013). The Concept and Policy of China's Intellectual Property Judicial Protection. Contemporary Law, (6), 42.

Zhang, C., Gao, X., & Cao, H. (2015). Research on the Path of China's Overseas Intellectual Property Protection under the Background of the Belt and Road Initiative. Science Management Research, (5), 7.

Zhang, Z., Wang, L., & Shan, L. (2015). Intellectual Property Strategy under the "One Belt, One Road" Strategic Concept. Chinese Inventions and Patents, (6), 111.

Chapter 5
Research on Protection and Development of Intellectual Property in China From the Perspective of "The Belt and Road"

Ping Zhou
City University of Macau, China

Fuda Li
City University of Macau, China

Linling Zhong
University of Nottingham Ningbo China, China

ABSTRACT

With the continuous upgrading of the economical industry structure and the gradual optimization of the excess capacity, China has begun to get rid of the name "world factory" of "processing with imported materials." However, there are problems still existing, such as the contradiction between enterprises' poor independent innovation ability and consumers' increasing demands on product quality. Enterprises in China have the great opportunity to "go out" because of "The Belt and Road" strategy, but it is extremely complicated in legal system, customs, and social culture, which means how to use of intellectual property in China coexists risks and opportunities for enterprises. This chapter focuses on analyzing problems of intellectual property rights in China and the importance of the protection and development of intellectual property. In addition, this chapter studies strategies that can be provided for the protection and development of intellectual property in China from the perspective of "The Belt and Road."

DOI: 10.4018/978-1-5225-8440-7.ch005

CURRENT SITUATION OF PROTECTION AND DEVELOPMENT OF INTELLECTUAL PROPERTY IN CHINA FROM THE PERSPECTIVE OF "THE BELT AND ROAD"

The Change of Industrial Structure in China

In recent years, China's industrial structure is improving day by day, and the optimization of industrial structure has made some progress. Firstly, the primary industry's share of GDP has become more stable. Then, the share of secondary industry has gradually declined, along with little fluctuation, and maintained its due stable share. Finally, the tertiary industry's share of GDP has soared. It can be seen from this data that the industrial structure has reached a relatively ideal situation in the traditional sense.

China's manufacturing industry was severely impacted after the global financial crisis in 2008. So the Chinese government was determined to transform and upgrade the economical industry structure in order to enhance China's ability to resist risks and to sustain economical growth in the future (Fei & Yan, 2007). In this process, there are two problems. Firstly, there is an intellectual property dispute between China and the original owner of the intellectual property when China introduced the technical knowledge. Secondly, China needs to protect the technological knowledge of its independent innovation while "going out". This is the intangible asset, which represents the core competence of China and Chinese enterprises, will help China win a place in the world in the future.

Complex Internal Market in China

The movie Dying to Survive which was released in July 2018, reflects the problem in dealing with intellectual property under a certain circumstance in China. On the one hand, the public authority needs to maintain the dignity of the law,so the behavior of the infringement of intellectual property has to be punished. On the other hand, the normal Chinese patients have to face the contradiction between the desire of survival and the unaffordable medical bills. Pharmaceutical manufacturers invest a lot of money and manpower to develop drugs. In order to retrieve the costs, they can only choose to price the medicine to a very expensive level. The contradiction among the three parties is also reflected in other areas of intellectual property in China. On eighteen October, 2017, on the 19th National Congress of the Communist Party of China, the Chinese President Xi Jinping emphasizes that socialism with Chinese characteristics has crossed the threshold into a new era and the principal contradiction Chinese society has evolved—what we now face is the contradiction between unbalanced and inadequate development and the people's ever-growing needs for a better life (*State Intellectual Property Office, 2015, 2018*). Human-being is born to be rational and draw on the advantages and avoid negative factors. People can be influenced by politics, economics and culture which are corresponding to power, capital and knowledge. Under the highly centralized and unified conditions, people need security most, and individual rationality is up to its potential. The survival of knowledge depends on the free public atmosphere, which is exactly the premise of cultivating public rationality, and it is also the expectation to reach a balance among power, capital and people. However, any public problem is essentially the result of the behavior of the elite class presented at the grassroots level. Without competition and supervision, the strong force is inevitably self-collapse, and there is no normal public sphere to buffer. Accumulated distrust endangers life. So from the perspective of consumers, government and enterprises, consumers need the cheaper medicine to survive, while enterprises need to retrieve costs and pursue profits in order to continue developing new medicine, and the government needs a balance between order and development to maintain its own rules.

Intellectual property in China now is facing a dilemma. The government needs the development of enterprises to promote economic growth and consumers need cheap and fine products and their demand for quality is higher than before. But the reality is that on the one hand, the products based on enterprises' independent research are difficult to meet the requirements, on the other hand, the independent innovation products are susceptible to plagiarize and the development costs are unbearable. Thus, enterprises were forced to plagiarize the intellectual property of other companies in order to achieve profit quickly.

Increase of Friction in the World Economy

Trump, the new president of the United States, maintains its own hegemony to protect the trade interests, and violates principles of World Trade Organization (WTO) regardless of other countries' objection. Plus, he launched a trade war against China and even made trade contradictions and conflicts with American "Allies", which severely damaged free trade order based on the WTO. In the "301 investigation" launched by the United States against China in August 2017, the purpose of the United States is to make sure that the laws, policies and practices related to technology transformation, intellectual property and innovation by the Chinese government are unreasonable or discriminatory, which would constitute a burden or restrict American businesses. [4]Although this is a "war" initiated by the United States, China should also improve its weaknesses when dealing with other "big event". China can better protect intellectual property since the reform and opening-up, but it is undeniable that the current level is difficult to meet the standards of developed countries, because it is related to economical development. In this increasingly competitive world, it is an inevitable choice to strengthen the protection of intellectual property in order to break through China's economic slump and make a difference.

China can take the advantage of the new conditions created by "The Belt and Road" strategy, so that China not only can provide opportunities for optimization of the spatial pattern, but also provide new growth for China's economic development.

The Status of Intellectual Property Protection and Development in Countries Along "The Belt and Road"

There are more than 100 countries along "The Belt and Road"(original 64 countries) and international organizations expressing their active support and participation by 2016. More and more countries are involved. There are differences in political, economical, legal and cultural aspects among countries. On the one hand, some countries have relatively better intellectual property protection, such as developed countries in Europe and Singapore in Southeast Asia. On the other hand, intellectual property protection in some countries is not mature and the system is not perfect, which causes the protection of intellectual property weak. Therefore, the level of intellectual property protection along "The Belt and Road" is in a state of bifurcation, which requires China to implement an appropriate protection strategy based on local conditions (State Intellectual Property Office, 2015).

The Status of Communication About Intellectual Property Between China and Countries Along "The Belt and Road"

At a press conference in Beijing Monday, Spokesperson for China State Intellectual Property Office, Hu Wenhui, said that in 2017, there are 5608 patent applications of China in countries along "The Belt and Road", reported a 16 percent year-on-year rise. While there are 4319 patent applications of the countries along "The Belt and Road" in China, reported a 16.8 percent year-on-year rise. Four new countries have applied for patents in China, bringing the total to 41 countries, indicating that China's "The Belt and Road" has begun to yield results. But there are also problems coexisting.

In China, the distribution of relevant nation's patent applications is uneven, compared with other countries, such as Russia, India, Israel, Turkey and other countries that have early intellectual property legislation, and relatively consummate system. These countries' intellectual property is developing vigorously, which leads to the uneven patent distribution (USTR, 2017). In 2017, patent applications of countries along "The Belt and Road" (not including China) rose 16 percent year-on-year, involving 17 countries (India, Russia, Singapore, Vietnam and Poland account for 91.7%) from the data published by the State Intellectual Property Office.The layout of patent applications is highly centralized. [8] There are two imbalances existing. First of all, the number of countries for patent applications is small, which is only about 25%. Secondly, the number of patent applications is too concentrated, and a few countries almost have a monopoly on patent applications.

According to the statistics of the State Intellectual Property Office, there is still a significant gap between the world intellectual property powerhouse and China. In 2017, the number of patent applications published by the United States, Japan and Germany and the other countries along "The Belt and Road" was higher than that in China: 8.8 times, 2.6 times and 1.6 times respectively (Zhang, Wang & Li, 2015).

Therefore, although the cooperation of intellectual property between China and countries along "The Belt and Road" is progressing steadily, China has not yet reached the dominant position due to two major problems. The first problem is that the number of patent applications which is entirely public is small and highly centralized. The second is that the number of patent applications is obviously lower than that of the world's developed countries, which is difficult to surpass in the short term.

The Status of Communication About Intellectual Property Between China and Countries Along "The Belt and Road"

Before the implementation of "The Belt and Road" strategy, countries along the line have already formed several regional or targeted intellectual property cooperation platforms and organizations, such as ASEAN (the Association of Southeast Asian Nations), and European Patent Organization and Eurasian Patent Organization. The causes and backgrounds of these organizations are different, and the intellectual property issues concerned by member states are also different. Thus, there must be some contradictions in the intellectual property protection system, mainly embodied in the following aspects. First of all, the regional intellectual property organizations and platforms are set up for their own area of conflict resolution, in order to strengthen the regional intellectual property exchanges and promote the development of intellectual property. These organizations have strong provincialism and characteristics, which means it is impossible to suit for any countries. Secondly, every region has to protect their own interests, so they will establish the protection rules against non-regional countries to the maximum extent, which is not conducive to the integration of regional patent system and external patent system. Thirdly, due to the long existing of regional patent organizations, the member states in the region have varying degrees of adaptation. If they are required to accept new intellectual property system and rules, it is very difficult to control the cost and willingness. Anyhow, setting up a suitable intellectual property system under the background of "The Belt and Road" should adjust interests of all aspects, because intellectual property is a legal concept, and it has its own internal unity, which can result its maximum internal advantage trough seeking common ground while reserving differences. Then, it can help establish a fair and universal system. In the initial stage of integration, intellectual property protection system can absorb the advantages of various organizations, and then gradually form a complete and unified system.

THE REASON OF PROTECTING AND DEVELOPING INTELLECTUAL PROPERTY IN THE BACKGROUND OF "THE BELT AND ROAD"

External Reason: A New Chance for China to Adjust its Strategy

A New Chance to Break American Hegemonism

At present, international economic frictions are escalating. There are trade war between China and the United States. Then the United States began to set up trade tariff barriers against the European Union, Canada and other old Allies. This kind of measurement fully embodies the hegemony of the United State. After the president of the United States—Trump came to power, he continuously Implement the policy "Let the United States Return to Greatness", which radically speaking is containment and suppression strategy used to against China—the world's second largest economy and a second country can threaten America's own global economic hegemony. (Japan is the first) All this is based on its overall national interest.

According to Yi Jiming's point of view, a professor from Beijing university, incidents in the south China sea, the Diaoyu islands and the Taiwan issues, China effectively resolve the crisis through the TaiChi Theory, and actively advocate "The Belt and Road" construction and globalization, which made the United States in a passive position (Yi & Li, 2018). Therefore, the United States seizes China's weakness, using trade and intellectual property to force China to yield and to achieve the goal of containing China's development.

In the international economic pattern, the United States adopts the principle of isolation, and Geopolitical blockade China like a letter "C". America also uses its own economic juggernaut status in order to exclude China from Trans -Pacific

Partnership Agreement (TTP) and Transatlantic Trade and Investment Partnership Agreement (TIPP). China's corresponding strategy is establishing "The Belt and Road". Now the United States utilizes the intellectual property and trade friction, so China's response strategy is also based on the development and protection of intellectual property in the context of "The Belt and Road". China has to strengthen its own weaknesses.

A New Chance to Establish China's Core Competitiveness

The world has experienced several industrial revolutions as the economy is developing steadily. However, the world has entered the era of knowledge economy that Innovation is the soul key after the 21st century. From the macroscopic analysis, paying attention to the intellectual property protection is an important foundation for a country to maintain sustainable development and to keep a leading position in the world economy. From microscopic analysis, Intellectual property strategy is an important part of the enterprise development, and enterprises which have the independent innovation ability can maintain their core competitiveness in the market under the brutal elimination, and enterprises which develop through the intellectual property, especially small and medium-sized enterprises, usually accomplish a great task with little effort by clever maneuvers.

According to the statistics released by the State Intellectual Property Office, Main Statistics Report on China's Patent Intensive Industries (2015) pointed out that China's patent labor-intensive industries are capable, and the added value of China's patent labor-intensive industries from 2010 to 2014 amounted to 26.7 trillion yuan, accounted for 11.0% of the total GDP, and the average annual real growth is 16.6%, which is twice the average annual real growth rate (8%). [9]Although the longitudinal data of China's intellectual property industry is very optimistic, the industry is still insufficient if compared horizontally in the world. For example, on 25 October, 2016, the European Patent Office (EPO) and the European Union Intellectual Property Office (EUIPO) released the Labor-Intensive Industry of Intellectual Property and Its Economic Performance in the European Union Report (hereinafter referred to as the "report") and according to the report, the European Union's total GDP during 2011-2013 is about 13.4 trillion euros, and 42.3% generated by labor-intensive intellectual property. [10]The European Union's intellectual property industry contributes far more to GDP than China's. So it can be seen that China's development advantages based on intellectual property in international development is not obvious (see Table 1).

To re-examine the existing countries along "The Belt and Road", most of them still belongs to developing countries, and their economic strength is relatively weak. Using intellectual property index can clearly distinguish the competitiveness of

Table 1. Labor-intensive industry

Labor-Intensive Industry	Added Value/GDP (Millions of Euros	Proportion of EU GDP
Trademark intensive industry	4812310	35.9%
Design intensive industry	1788811	13.4%
Patent intensive industry	2035478	15.2%
Copyright intensive industry	914612	6.8%
Geography intensive industry	18109	0.1%
Plant variety intensive industry	51710	0.4%
All intellectual property intensive industry	5664168	42.3%
Total GDP of EU	13387988	100%

Note Appended: Because of the overlapping use of IP power, the sum of individual industry exceeds the sum of intellectual property labor-intensive industries.

different countries in the field of innovation. The higher of the value, the clearer the property rights. According to 2014 World Intellectual Property Index released by World Intellectual Property Organization(WIPO), Intellectual property index is relatively low in both Central and South Asian countries, but relatively high in Singapore and Malaysia in Southeast Asia. As an advocate "The Belt and Road", China must set an example by advocating the protection of intellectual property, and at the same time set a keynote for its future development direction. Then China can lead the rest of the developing countries in the region to achieve common interests.

Above all, on the one hand, China is not competitive compared to the developed regions and countries in the world in spite of its rapid development of the intellectual property industry. Besides, intellectual property as the core part of the future knowledge economy, must be paid more attention, so under the background of "The Belt and Road" strategy implementation, China strengthens the protection of intellectual property and promote the development, and also to build China's core competitiveness in the severe international economic pattern.

Internal Reason: A New Direction for China to Upgrade Industrial Structure

China's industrial structure has tended to be stable, forming a pattern of taking the primary industry as the foundation, the secondary industry as the pillar and the tertiary industry leading the economy. However, the prominent problem that restricts the transformation and upgrading of making China's secondary industry as the main industrial structure is that there is no manufacturing ecosystem matching the upgrading consumer structure. Small and scattered manufacturing enterprises lack basic capabilities of product quality and product design, and also lack innovative R&D capabilities in key spare parts and high-end production equipment, leading to the serious loss of craftsmanship and professionalism (Zhang, 2016; Zhang, Gao & Cao, 2015). In daily life, the rise of overseas purchases and the popularization of luxury brands are popularized, which can be expressed as "I can't get what I want in China, but I don't want made in China". The structure of Chinese consumer demand is changing from low-end demand to medium-high-end demand. This is also the current situation in China and the direction of optimization in China.

On the one hand, China's market has the greatest consumption potential in the world, on the other hand, China is short of independent innovation ability, and product quality is difficult to upgrade and there are imitation and plagiarism prevailing, so China is gradually eliminated by international market. Since China's accession to the WTO, the market has gradually opened up, and the Chinese government is also steadfastly implementing the policy of reform and opening up, which shows that it is increasingly difficult for enterprises which is short of independent innovation ability to survive only by national coercive force. Enterprises' profits and development based on the "combination of government and business + government preferential policy dependence" must be hit severely.

In short, after the reform and opening up, enterprises, which rely on government support and assistance to develop, has no longer adapted to the increasingly fierce competition in the world. Enterprises must seize the opportunity created "The Belt and Road", improve the capability of independent innovation, and strengthen the development and support of China's intellectual property industry, so they can progress in the industrial structure optimization in the future.

CHINA'S STRATEGIES OF INTELLECTUAL PROPERTY PROTECTION AND DEVELOPMENT UNDER "THE BELT AND ROAD"

China's Domestic Strategies of Intellectual Property Protection and Development Under "The Belt and Road"

Establishment and Improvement of Intellectual Property Courts

China is paying more attention to intellectual property, and gives it judicial protection. Continuous improvement of the judicial level of intellectual property is also an important task in implementing China's judicial reformation. In China's economically developed regions, intellectual property disputes have led to a surge in the number of cases. Conventional civil trials are unable to meet the quantity and professional requirements. That is why in the 2015, special courts for intellectual property come into being in Beijing, Shanghai and Guangzhou, which shows that China's determination to strengthen intellectual property protection and also proves that in the future, China may promote the establishment of intellectual property courts throughout the country to ensure the leading role of judicial protection when it comes to intellectual property, and also effectively protect the incentive role of intellectual property for economic development. So China's independent innovation environment can be well optimized.

To Make the Macroeconomic Regulation and Control at Full Capacity

China's is a developing country and this is based on the basic national conditions. China's reform and opening up has just passed 40 years, while the developed countries in Europe and the United States have gone through hundreds of years on the road of intellectual property development. This will inevitably lead to China's intellectual property protection and development in an imperfect state, so the way of dealing with intellectual property disputes should also be based on specific national conditions. Under the condition that China has entered a new era of social change, the contradictions in the complex economic development are constantly emerging. How to deal with the interests among the government, enterprises and consumers is an unavoidable topic, and the existence of intellectual property will have a considerable impact on some aspects. For example, some companies produce products that infringe intellectual property by copying and imitating, which can benefit consumers in the short term. However, in the long run, once the self-innovative enterprises find that the products they invested in are easy to be "stolen" by others. What is more, the self-innovative enterprises' profits are more difficult to obtain. So they will fall into an embarrassing cycle of "bad money drives out good". Ultimately, it is the consumers themselves who are injured. The key to change this cycle relies on the government: how the government handles it and how to balance the interests of all parties.

Strengthening Judicial Function and Reducing Administrative Interference

After 40 years of reform and opening up, China still has some traces of the planned economy era, such as policy-dependent enterprises, and even some zombie enterprises. Of course, the Chinese government is also trying to transfer from a "management-oriented government" to a "service-oriented government". Under the general circumstance, an important issue in China's judicial reform is to reduce the administrative interference on justice.

China has always adhered to the policy of focusing on economic construction since the reform and opening-up, and has penetrated into the hearts of every administrative official in the administrative region which has always been "caring" for local enterprises and often elected interests of local tax-paying enterprises compared to the interests of intellectual property. So when it comes to intellectual property disputes, local administrative leaders always have various excuses to exert pressure on the local judiciary to ensure that local enterprises can profit from the disputes or not lose too much.

Therefore, in order to protect and develop intellectual property rights in China, we must strengthen the role of justice and reduce administrative interference. Specifically speaking, it can be divided into several steps: firstly, judiciary's property should be independent, and directly be managed by the higher levels of the judiciary; secondly, judiciary should establish the authority, and strengthen the popularization of the law in order to promote the development of the law, so that the concept of intellectual property can come into the hearts of the people; thirdly, government should use a variety of channels for supervision. If power loses supervision, it will inevitably lead to corruption and corruption is also a major obstacle to the development of intellectual property right.

China's International Strategies of Intellectual Property Protection and Development Under "The Belt and Road"

Construction of International Intellectual Property Communication and Cooperation Platform

The politics, economic, culture and other aspects of the countries along "The Belt and Road" are very complex and intellectual property is closely related to the public power of a country. It is a manifestation of the regulatory capability. Governments should cooperate with each other to establish a set of long-term and effective platform for the protection and development of intellectual property. Some scholars believe that on the one hand, China should actively participate in the formulation of the rules of the International Intellectual Property Organization, in order to implement the rules of intellectual property in countries like China in the stage of economic transition. On the other hand, we should strengthen the cooperation with relevant countries on intellectual property, and sign agreements on intellectual property protection, and urge relevant countries to protect intellectual property (Yi & Li, 2018).

China should also cultivate its own legal talents who can handle intellectual property disputes and problems, in order to cope with the future development of

"The Belt and Road". On the basis of communication and international trust, the exclusive intellectual property framework of "The Belt and Road" should be set up to deal with intellectual property competition among countries and regions throughout the world after the completion of the personnel training system.

Exploring and Building an Integrated System of Intellectual Property in "The Belt and Road" Area

With increasingly fierce international competition, "The Belt and Road" has been stimulated by various reasons to break through the US military and economic strategic strike, and now almost all regions in the world have their own regional economic integration system or agreement system. For example, the European Union, the TPP or TIPP, all have their own rules of economic operation. China's "The Belt and Road" should also establish its own integration system, and the most important one is the regional intellectual property integration system.

The construction of the intellectual property integration system in "The Belt and Road" area has the following advantages: firstly, it can reduce the economic frictions between participating countries, and provide a consultative mode for them; secondly, on the basis of meeting the minimum standards of international intellectual property protection, it can also protect the intellectual property of all countries according to their levels of intellectual property protection, so that they can achieve mutual benefit and win-win situation; finally, the integration system can also enable the participating countries to enhance their ability to resist risks, such as the global trade frictions caused by the United States. If the integrate system of intellectual property can be completed in advance, participating countries are strong enough to fight back effectively and to better safeguard their own interests.

The Protection and Development of International Multilateral Intellectual Property Based on the Common Aspiration of the People

On 28 March, 2015, China clearly pointed out that "The Belt and Road" will be strengthened in cooperation management from five aspects, namely, policy communication, facilities interconnection, trade unimpeded, financing and common aspiration of the people. In ancient China, there is an old saying: water can carry a boat, and it can also overturn the boat. If we want to build "The Belt and Road", we will need the support of the participating countries and will need to improve mutual understanding and increase interaction among people. This is the basis for regional cooperation and an important foundation for the formation and development of intellectual property.

Promoting the "common aspiration of the people" is the prerequisite for solving the multidimensional regional problems including customs, habits, and mixed religious beliefs with many nationalities. This is an internal and external problem before implementing "The Belt and Road".

Regional Contradiction

The ASEAN Intellectual Property Cooperation Organization, the European Patent Organization and the Eurasian Patent Organization have already existed before "The Belt and Road". Besides, "The Belt and Road" is an open propose. There will be more countries and regions involved in the future. Therefore, when it comes to the inherent system and rules of regional organizations, the important issue is to discuss how to solve the contradictions among regional organizations, and contradictions between regional organizations and non-regional organizations. The common aspiration of the people will help countries to deepen strategic mutual trust, deepen understanding and eliminate doubts, which will help countries to participate actively in the construction of "The Belt and Road" through multiple channels of communication.

External Influence

Due to historical and realistic reasons, conflicts about the interests of the border and natural resources exist between some countries and China. Some irresponsible media in Europe and the United States continue to brag about the "China Threat Theory", so that the countries and regions along "The Belt and Road" have some doubts about China (Hu, 2017). If China wants to break these false statements from Western countries, it should constantly promote its own values of peaceful development on the basis of promoting the common aspiration of the people. Specifically, in the process of "going out", enterprises should pay attention to their social responsibility. According to the different cultural customs of different countries and regions, enterprises should timely communicate with local people, and strengthen mutual trust. Respecting local intellectual property rules is an important way to safeguard the international image of Chinese enterprises. The starting point is respecting and protection of intellectual property and the basis is the common aspiration of the people, China will, after a certain period of time, accumulate the trust of all parties, and form a multilateral and mutual trust mechanism for the protection and development of intellectual property.

Prospects for Intellectual Property Cooperation Between China and Countries Along "The Belt and Road"

China started relatively late in the field of intellectual property protection. Although it has gone through 40 years of reform and opening up, its intellectual property development history is still pale compared with that of the western developed countries which have been developing for hundreds of years. Besides, due to historical reasons, cooperations of business and politics among China and countries along "The Belt and Road" have started relatively late. However, China, driven by the values of peaceful development, will adhere to the principle of multilateral mutual benefit and win-win situation and gradually establish mutual benefit and mutual trust with the countries along the line on the basis of common aspiration of the people. The cooperation among China and countries along the line needs time to constantly ameliorate the status quo. We believe that differences in religion, customs, legal systems and other aspects will be inclusive and understood through the continuous development of the economy. This is a long-standing process that requires joint efforts from all sides.

REFERENCES

Fei & Yan. (2007). Regional Practice of the Patent's International Protection and Patent's Unification in Europe. *Journal of Dalian Maritime University: Social Science Edition*, (6), 15-18.

Hu. (2017). *China's Patent Applications to "The Belt and Road" Related Countries Show A Favorable Growth Trend.* Academic Press.

State Intellectual Property Office: Main Statistical Data Report on China's patent intensive industries. (2015). State Intellectual Property Office: A review of Intensive Intellectual Property Industries and Its Economical Performance in the European Union.

State Intellectual Property Office: Statistics on Patent of Countries along "The Belt and Road. (2018). Patent Statistics Bulletin, 2018(1).

USTR. (2017). *Announces Initiation of Section 301 Investigation of China.* Retrieved from https://ustr.gov/about-us/policy-offices/press-office/press-releases/2017/august/ustr-announces-initiation-section

Yi & Li. (2018). The United States Launched 301 Investigation into China and China's Countermeasures. *Journal of Northwest University (Philosophy and Social Sciences Edition),* (1), 65-81.

Zhang, Gao, & Cao. (2015). Research on China's Overseas Intellectual Property Protection under the Background of "The Belt and Road". *Scientific Management Research*, (5), 5-9.

Zhang, Z., Wang, L., & Shan, L. (2015). Intellectual Property ProtectionStrategy under the Concept of "The Belt and Road". *China Invention & Patent*, *c*(06), 107–112.

Zhang. (2016). Obstacles, Predicament and Reform Prospects in the Transformation and Upgrading of China's Industrial Structure. *Journal of Renmin University of China*, (5), 29-37

Chapter 6
Intellectual Property Protection Strategy Under the Belt and Road Initiative

Yong Zhang
University of Macau, China

ABSTRACT

After the belt and road initiative was put forward, the relevant domestic regions responded positively and carried out research work in succession, making suggestions for the implementation and planning of the belt and road initiative. However, the relevant research work mainly focuses on the political, economic, and cultural problems existing in the implementation of the belt and road initiative. The research on intellectual property protection issues has rarely been reported. By analyzing the intellectual property environment both of domestic and international in which the belt and road initiative located, this chapter focuses on the intellectual property protection strategy in the implementation of the belt and road initiative, aiming at providing reference for intellectual property research under the belt and road initiative.

INTRODUCTION

The "Belt and Road" is the abbreviation of "Silk Road Economic Belt" and "21st Century Maritime Silk Road". In September 2013, President Xi Jinping first proposed the idea of constructing the "Silk Road Economic Belt". In October 2013, he attended the APEC Leaders' Informal Meeting and proposed the "21st Century Maritime Silk Road" initiative. In November 2013, the belt and road initiative was

DOI: 10.4018/978-1-5225-8440-7.ch006

written in the "Decision of the Central Committee of the Communist Party of China on Several Major Issues Concerning Comprehensive Deepening Reform" and was listed as the one of most important tasks of the main economic work in 2015 at the Central Economic Work Conference held in December 2014.

The belt and road initiative gives the ancient "Silk Road" a new era connotation. It is a national development strategy put forward by China in the new period of deepening reform and opening up. It aims to promote the economic and trade development between China and the countries along the route. On the basis of mutual trust and peaceful cooperation, we will take advantage of geographical proximity and economic complementarity to achieve mutual benefit and win-win. The Belt and Road Initiative benefits many countries and regions along the route, which is conducive to the harmonious development of regional economic integration and economic globalization, improving the imbalance of world economic development, promoting the multi-polar development of international economic and trade, and accelerating the formation of a new pattern of international trade. On the other hand, the belt and road initiative has further optimized the spatial pattern of China's economic development and provided a new growth point for China's economic development. At present, China's economic development has entered a new normal, economic structure and industrial structure have been deeply adjusted, and innovation has become the main driving force for economic development. Innovation is inseparable from intellectual property protection. With the deep integration of intellectual property and economic development, intellectual property has become a key factor in stimulating innovation and supporting the new normal of economic development.

However, since the belt and road initiative involves multiple countries and regions, the intellectual property environment along the belt and road initiative is complex. The differences in domestic intellectual property systems are bound to make conflicts among them. How to properly use the intellectual property strategy to escort the implementation of the belt and road initiative is a problem that deserves the attention of all of us.

STATUS OF CHINA'S INTELLECTUAL PROPERTY RIGHTS

Since the implementation of the national intellectual property strategy in 2008, China's intellectual property legal system has been gradually improved, the level of law enforcement has been continuously improved, the number of intellectual property rights has grown rapidly, international exchanges in the field of intellectual property have increased, and international influence has gradually increased. At the same time, the implementation of the belt and road initiative will lead to the adjustment of the intellectual property order in the international region. As more and more Chinese companies enter the international market, international intellectual property disputes that Chinese companies encounter overseas will grow rapidly.

China's Patent Applications to Countries Along the Route

On the one hand, from the analysis of patent application data, in the past 10 years, China has applied for about 14,000 patents to 27 countries along the route, but only accounted for 0.6% of the total number of patent applications accepted by these countries, and the amount of patent applications is very small compared with other countries (below 3%). It can be seen from the Table 1, the countries that apply for patents in China are mainly regional powers and countries with close economic relationship with us, including India, Russia, Singapore and Israel.

On the other hand, from Figure 1, we can see the trend of patent applications. Since 2013, the amount of China's patent applications in the main target countries that along the belt and road initiative, such as, India, Russia, Singapore, and so on, have continued to grow rapidly.

According to the data released by the Planning and Development Department of the State Intellectual Property Office, in 2016, the number of patent applications filed in India was 3,017 (1.7 times that of 2015), and the number of applications in China's patent applications to countries that along the "Belt and Road" ranked

Table 1. The status of patent applications in major countries along the route and the entry of Chinese patent applications

Countries	Total Amount of Patent Application	Amount of Domestic Application	Amount of Foreign Patent Application Entry	Amount of Chinese Patent Application Entry	The Percentage of Amount of Chinese Patent Application Entry
Russia	71.2	57.1	14.1	0.220	1.6
India	31.5	6.9	24.6	0.650	2.7
Poland	26.1	12.8	13.3	0.010	0.1
Ukraine	12.7	10.6	2.1	0.010	0.5
Hungary	11.6	4.9	6.8	0.003	0.1
Singapore	10.8	0.7	10.1	0.190	1.9
Israel	9.1	1.8	7.3	0.010	0.1
Czekh	7.7	3.8	3.9	0.005	0.1
Roumania	7.0	4.2	2.8	0.001	0.1
Turkey	6.2	3.3	2.9	0.010	0.5

Figure 1. Trends of China's application in the major countries from 2006 to 2016

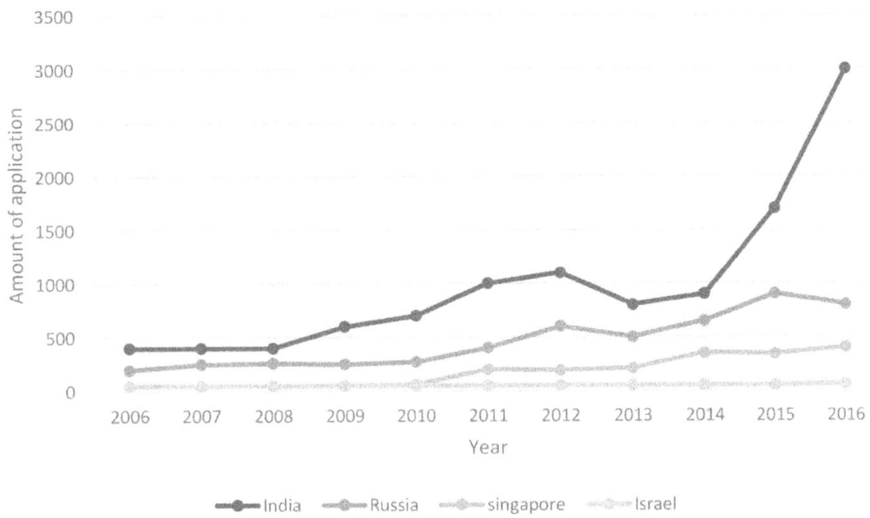

first; the number of patent applications in Russia was 789, ranked second; Singapore (425), Thailand (300) and Vietnam (285) were ranked 3rd, 4th and 5th respectively. The sum of patent applications in India and Russia accounted for 78.7% of the total number of patent applications in China along the "Belt and Road", indicating that China's patent applications in the "Belt and Road" countries are more concentrated, indicating that the patent layout is imperfect.

Domestic IP Enforcement

With the implementation of the national intellectual property strategy, the judicial protection of intellectual property rights has also been given full attention. The courts has continuously strengthened the judicial reform of intellectual property rights, implemented the requirements of judicial protection of intellectual property rights in the national intellectual property strategy, and continuously improved the jurisdiction of intellectual property rights. In 2015, the intellectual property courts in Beijing, Shanghai and Guangzhou began to operate, and the establishment of the special court for intellectual property rights demonstrated China's determination to increase the judicial protection to intellectual property rights.

Figure 2 shows that the trend of the new and concluded intellectual property civil first-instance cases of the National People's Court of the People's Republic of China from 2010 to 2013. It can be seen that the National People's Courts have newly received and intellectual property civil first-instance cases respectively from 2010. 42,931 pieces and 41,718 pieces rose to 88,583 pieces and 88,286 pieces in

Figure 2. Amount of the new and concluded intellectual property civil first-instance cases of the courts

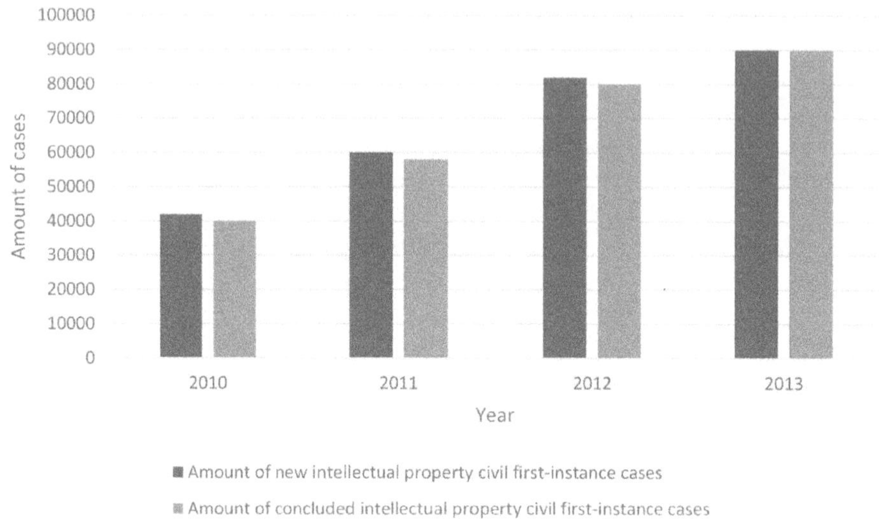

2013. The data show that China's intellectual property judicial trials have achieved remarkable results, and the leading role of intellectual property judicial protection has become increasingly apparent, effectively playing the role of protecting intellectual property rights and stimulating innovation, so that China's intellectual property innovation environment has been well optimized.

International IP Disputes

The higher the output of the industry, the more urgent the requirements for intellectual property protection strategies will be (Wang, 2016). Especially in the high-tech industry, there are many scientific and technological innovations involved, so the requirements for the intellectual property protection strategy are particularly urgent, which can be seen from several typical projects in the overseas aid of intellectual property rights launched by Beijing in recent years.

First, Xiaomi Company was sued by Ericsson in India for patent infringement case. In 2014, shortly after the launch of Xiaomi's mobile phone products in India, Ericsson suddenly launched a patent complaint, claiming that Xiaomi infringed on eight patents. At the request of Ericsson, the Indian court issued a "pre-suit forbidden sale order" to Xiaomi. After Xiaomi's appeal, the court only agreed to sell Xiaomi mobile phones equipped with Qualcomm chips in India, but each mobile phone still needs to pay deposits, while another product equipped with MediaTek chips is still banned to sell. Second, Beijing GUODIANFUTONG SCIENCE AND

DEVELOPMENT Co., Ltd was sued in Italy by the Italian company MAGALDI for patent infringement. In 2009, Beijing GUODIANFUTONG SCIENCE AND DEVELOPMENT Co., Ltd. filed an infringement lawsuit against MAGALDI in India for violating its Indian patents when bidding for a thermal power project in India, demanding that the court issue a temporary injunction prohibiting all violations of GUODIANFUTONG in India; Third, TONGFANGWEISHI Company in Malaysia sued local company named PAT for patent infringement. In 2013, Beijing TONGFANGWEISHI Technology Co., Ltd. discovered that two sets of scanning equipment purchased by PAT from a company in Beijing and sold to Malaysia Customs infringed the patents shared by Tongfang and Tsinghua University in Malaysia. After more than one year of trial, the court's decision basically supported all the claims of TONGFANGWEISHI. However, the follow-up defendant and the third party were dissatisfied with the result of the defeat and appealed separately.

With the gradual high-end export of the industry in the construction of belt and road initiative, similar intellectual property disputes will become more and more frequent. Therefore, breaking the predicament of the intellectual property system and raising the requirements for the intellectual property strategy have become the premise and guarantee for the smooth progress of the construction of belt and road initiative.

DIFFERENCES IN INTELLECTUAL PROPERTY SYSTEMS AMONG COUNTRIES

65 countries and regions were involved in the implementation of the belt and road initiative, and the intellectual property protection systems of different countries are not the same. We can find out lots of reasons, but there are mainly three reasons: different organizations of IP, different international treaties and legal systems. It is precisely because of these differences that some countries such as India, Russia, Singapore and other intellectual property rights protection levels are relatively high, and some countries have very weak intellectual property systems, which makes the phenomenon that the level of intellectual property protection among these countries were polarized.

Different Organizations of IP

Countries with high levels of intellectual property protection actively use their own advantages to promote the integration of intellectual property rights. For the time being, there are three main intellectual property organizations involved in the belt and road initiative, included the ASEAN Intellectual Property Cooperation Organization,

Eurasian Patent Organization and European Patent Organization. Different IP organizations, different background, different questions that they concerned, making the phenomenon that collisions and contradictions are inevitable. The formation of this three-legged situation has also created obstacles to the formation of a unified intellectual property system along the belt and road initiative (Zhang, Wang & Li, 2015).

ASEAN Intellectual Property Cooperation Organization

The ASEAN Intellectual Property Cooperation Organization is a regional intellectual property cooperation platform of the Association of Southeast Asian Nations, covering 630 million people in Southeast Asia. It aims to foster a good intellectual property environment, establish an integrated ASEAN intellectual property system, and promote economic development in Southeast Asia. In 1995, ASEAN countries formulated the Intellectual Property Cooperation Framework Agreement, which made the cooperation of ASEAN countries in the field of intellectual property from theory to reality. After that, ASEAN countries successively formulated the 2004-2010 ASEAN IP Action Plan and 2011-2015 ASEAN IP Action Plan. Under the guidance of the action plan, ASEAN countries actively took measures to coordinate national IP development strategies and promote ASEAN. The integration of intellectual property rights and the strengthening of international cooperation and exchanges in intellectual property rights have significantly improved the ASEAN intellectual property environment (Wang, 2016).

As early as 2004, China signed the Action Plan for the Implementation of the China-ASEAN Joint Declaration on Strategic Partnership for Peace and Prosperity (2005-2010) with ASEAN, and signed the Memorandum of Understanding on China-ASEAN Intellectual Property Cooperation in 2009. These two files made a very solid foundation for the cooperation between the two sides in the field of intellectual property.

Eurasian Patent Organization

The purpose of establishing the Eurasian Patent Organization is to solve the problems left in the patent field between the CIS countries after the disintegration of the Soviet Union. It aims to establish a unified Eurasian patent system and be responsible for the application, review, authorization and management of patents in each member state. In 1995, the Eurasian Patent Office began to operate. After the patent application submitted by the Eurasian Patent Office has been examined and found it meet the authorization conditions, the Eurasian patent right can be obtained, and the Eurasian patent right has uniform effect on each member state.

The establishment of Eurasian patents unifies the effectiveness of each member state in patent application, approval and authorization.

In 2010, the Eurasian Patent Office led a delegation to visit the State Intellectual Property Office of China for the first time. The two sides conducted in-depth discussions on the future direction of cooperation and laid the good foundation for the long-term cooperation between the two offices.

European Patent Organization

The European Patent Organization was born in 1977, it aims to strengthen the cooperation of intellectual property protection among the member states. The European Patent Organization has an Administrative Commission and the European Patent Office. The function of the European Patent Office is to be responsible for the examination, approval and authorization of European patent applications submitted by member states. After a patent application filed by a member state with the European Patent Office under the European Patent Convention is granted a patent right, it can be entered into force in all designated countries, and is equivalent to the patents granted by the designated countries in accordance with the national patent law. The establishment of the European patent system has improved the efficiency of patent examination and approval, and unified the standards for patent examination and approval, which is conducive to promoting the growth of intellectual property protection in member states. Since the European patent system only can be applied to the approval stage of patents, and pay litter attention to the maintenance and protection of European patents in the designated countries, which leads to the lack of legal certainty in European patents. In order to solve the legal certainty of European patents, the European Patent Organization established a European single patent system. The European single patent system is characterized by a European patent application authorized by the European Patent Office, and according to the application of the right holder, it provides uniform protection and uniformity in the member states that participated in the framework of the single patent protection system, thereby fundamentally solving the legal certainty issues of European patent.

In 2011, the bilateral meeting between the Chinese Patent Office (SIPO) and the EPO, held in Chongqing (South West China) last week, was further testimony to the long and fruitful relationship, both of offices have now enjoyed for many years. China and Europe, SIPO and the EPO already became strategic partners in the patent field.

The common point of the above three intellectual property organizations is the purpose that to solve the problem of intellectual property rights in the region, thereby promoting the development of the intellectual property system in the region.

Therefore, the patent systems formulated by different organizations have relatively lots of limitations. They may be targeted at resolution of intellectual property issues in the region and relatively efficient, but it is not conducive to the effective integration of patent systems within and outside the region, which may lead to conflicts in various patent systems. For example, contradictions that happened among regional organizations, between member states and regional organizations, or among member states. The differences among the three organizations are the background of their establishment and the level of intellectual property protection, and the point that they focus on, which has clearly become a hindrance to regional cooperation. Fortunately, China has established a good cooperation relationship with the above three patent cooperation organizations, made full use of the coordination role in the intellectual property protection, and helped solve the contradictions among different countries, all of these helped establish a kind of universal and fair atmosphere. And this kind of intellectual property system that concentrates the advantages of each organization is the key to realizing the protection of overseas intellectual property rights of the belt and road initiative.

Different International Treaties

International treaties refer to written agreements between the subjects of international law governing their rights and obligations under international law. The international intellectual property system was established through the 1883 Paris Convention and the 1886 Berne Convention. The main international treaties that countries along the Belt and Road initiative involved, included, the Convention establishing the World Intellectual Property Organization, the Paris Convention for the Protection of Industrial Property, the Berne Convention for the Protection of Literary and Artistic Works, the Patent Cooperation Treaty, the Patent Law Treaty and the Agreement of establishing the World Trade Organization.

The Convention Establishing the World Intellectual Property Organization

The WIPO Convention, which was formed by the World Intellectual Property Organization (WIPO), was signed in Stockholm on July 14, 1967, entered into force in 1970, and was amended in 1979. WIPO is an intergovernmental organization that became a specialized agency in the United Nations system in 1974. WIPO has two main objectives, one is to promote the protection of intellectual property in the terms of world, and the other is to ensure administrative cooperation between intellectual property alliances established by WIPO-administered treaties.

Paris Convention for the Protection of Industrial Property

The Paris Convention for the Protection of Industrial Property (referred to as the Paris Convention) was signed in Paris on March 20, 1883 and entered into force on July 7, 1884. The object of adjustment of the Paris Convention is industrial property rights, including invention patents, utility models, industrial designs, trademarks, service marks, manufacturer names, goods marks or appellations of origin, and the suppression of unfair competition, and so on. The basic purpose of Paris Convention is to ensure that the industrial property rights of a member state are protected in all other member states. On March 19, 1985, China became a member of the Convention.

Berne Convention for the Protection of Literary and Artistic Works

The Convention came into being on September 9, 1886 and it is the first international copyright convention in the world, and established an international standard for the protection of copyright that is acceptable to most countries. The Convention is administered by the World Intellectual Property Organization. The Convention was signed by 10 countries, including the United Kingdom, France and Germany. It came into effect in 1887 and was revised and supplemented seven times. By 1999, the number of countries and regions participating in the Convention reached 136. In October 1992, the Convention entered into force for China. The current text of the Convention is a revised text in Paris in 1971. It mainly regulates the basic principles of international copyright protection, the scope of protected works, minimum standards of protection, and limited special treatment for developing countries.

Patent Cooperation Treaty

The Patent Cooperation Treaty (referred to as the PCT) is the most important international treaty in the field of patents after the Paris Convention for the Protection of Industrial Property. It was signed by 35 countries in Washington on June 19, 1970. And China officially became the member States of the Patent Cooperation Treaty is on January 1, 1994.The Patent Cooperation Treaty provides an internationally uniform standard for the acceptance and examination of patent applications. Within the scope of a member state, applicants are required to submit an international application in one country in a prescribed language, and specify the patent in the application. The protected countries have the effect of submitting national patent applications to countries respectively. The application procedures stipulated by the treaty and simplify the procedures for applicants to apply for patents in multiple countries for the same invention, and also reduce the duplication of work of national patent offices.

Patent Law Treaty

On May 11, 2000, the Diplomatic Conference for the Adoption of the Patent Law Treaty was held in Geneva, and the General Assembly adopted the Patent Law Treaty by consensus. China and other 103 states and three intergovernmental international organizations, the European Patent Office, the Eurasian Patent Office and the African Regional Industrial Property Organization, signed the final text of the Diplomatic Conference. On April 28, 2005, the Patent Law Treaty entered into force. The purpose of the Patent Law Treaty is to streamline and harmonize the procedural requirements of national and regional patent offices for filing and accepting national and regional patent applications, thereby reducing the burden on applicants, simplifying the procedures of patent offices, and avoiding unnecessary duplication of work.

Agreement of Establishing the World Trade Organization

The Uruguay Round Ministerial Conference of the GATT, held in Marrakesh, Morocco, on April 15, 1994, decided to establish a global World Trade Organization (WTO) to replace the GATT, which was established in 1947 (GATT). The WTO is a permanent international organization independent of the United Nations. The basic principle and purpose of the organization is to achieve the goal of promoting world trade liberalization by implementing the principles of market openness, non-discrimination and fair trade. It officially began to operate on January 1, 1995, and is responsible for managing the world economy and trade order. It is headquartered in the GATT headquarters building which is beside the Lake Geneva in Geneva. On January 1, 1996, it officially replaced the GATT Provisional Institution. Compared with the GATT, the scope of WTO jurisdiction in addition to the traditional trade agreement with the Uruguay Round, also included, intellectual property rights, investment measures and non-goods trade (service trade) that are long-term outside the GATT. The WTO has legal status and it is more authoritative and effective in mediating disputes among member states. On November 11, 2001, Doha, the capital of Qatar, officially signed an agreement on China's accession to the World Trade Organization (WTO). One month later, China officially became a member of the WTO and integrated into the world's multilateral trading system.

As can be seen from Figure 3, among the 65 countries that along the belt and road initiative, although there are only 24 member states of the Patent Law Treaty, the number of other member states of convention exceed two-thirds of the total number. In particular, the number of member states of the Convention on the Establishment of the World Intellectual Property Organization has reached 64. Therefore, although

Figure 3. The number of members of international treaties

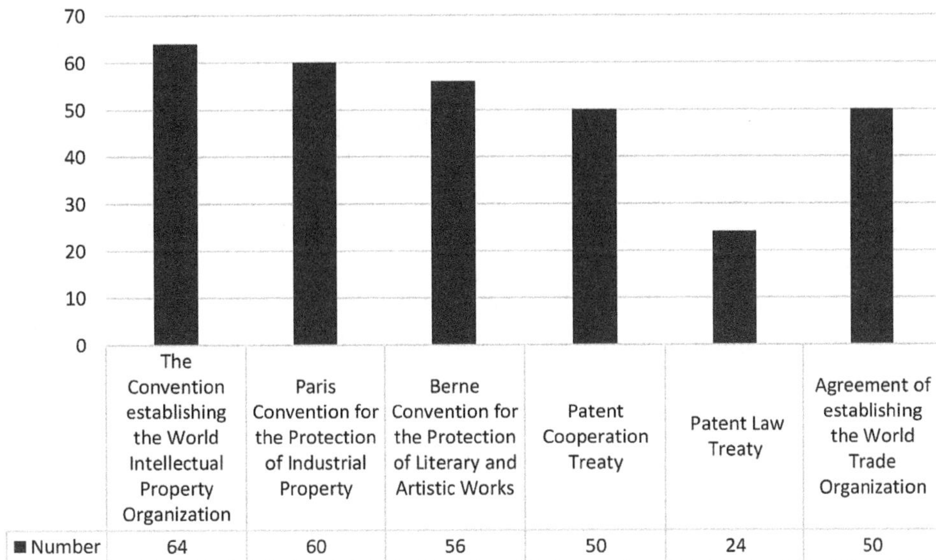

there are many differences in the member states of international treaties, in general, it is very optimistic, which will certainly provide tremendous help for the formation of a unified intellectual property system along the belt and road initiative.

Different Legal Systems

The legal system is the concept used in the comparative law to divide various laws, and refers to the sum of the legal systems of the same or similar traditions, principles, systems, and characteristics. Generally speaking, the legal system in the world can be divided into the common law, the European legal system, the Chinese legal system, the Nordic legal system, the Far East legal system, the socialist legal system, the Islamic legal system, and the Indian legal system. The countries that along the belt and road initiative involves the Common Law, the Civil Law, the Socialist Law, the Islamic Legal System, and the Mixed Legal System. Different legal systems mean that one country may has its own particular systems or rules, and so on. For example, in the intellectual property system, there are differences in the Author's Rights and copyright between the Common Law and Civil Law, from emphasizing the author's rights to emphasizing the author's moral rights, the Civil Law gives a basic feature of the meaning to the author's right; while the Common Law pays more attention to the author's property rights and gives it the meaning of copyright (Zheng, 2003).

Common Law

The Common Law is also known as the Anglo-American Legal System, the British Legal System, and the Case Law. A general term for laws developed on the basis of English common law. It refers to the unique legal system gradually formed by the United Kingdom from the 11th century on the basis of the common law derived from Germanic customary law and the legal system of other countries and regions emulating the United Kingdom. It originated in the United Kingdom and later expanded to many countries and regions that were once British colonies and affiliated countries, including the United States, Canada, India, Pakistan, Bangladesh, Malaysia, Singapore, Australia, New Zealand and individual countries and regions in Africa. It is a long-standing and influential legal system in the Western countries that is juxtaposed with the civil law system. It focuses on the continuity of the code, and based on traditions, jurisprudence and customs (Lu, 2013).

Civil Law

The Civil Law refers to the laws of the European continent that originated from the Roman law and represented by the 1804 French Civil Code. Therefore, the Civil Law is also called the Roman Legal System. In 1896, Germany formulated the German Civil Code which based on the French Civil Code. After the Code was followed by some countries, the Civil Law was also known as the Roman-German Legal System. In addition to France and Germany, there are laws in Austria, Belgium, the Netherlands, Italy, Switzerland, Spain, Japan that after the Meiji Restoration, and some French-speaking countries or regions in Asia, Africa and Latin America (Wu, 2013).

Socialist Law

Socialist Law or Soviet Law denotes a general type of legal system which has been used in socialist and formerly socialist states. It is based on the civil law system, with major modifications and additions from Marxist-Leninist ideology. There is controversy as to whether socialist law ever constituted a separate legal system or not (Quigley, 1989).

Islamic Legal System

The Islamic Legal System also known as the Arabic Legal System. A general term for the laws of the Arab countries and other Muslim countries that believe in Islam in the Middle Ages. The main content is the Qur'an and the Sunnah (Muhammad's words and deeds). During the heyday of the Arab Empire in the 8th and 9th centuries, Islamic law also flourished, from the Indus Valley in the east to the Atlantic Ocean in the west, and Islamic law in countries ranging from the Himalayas to the Mediterranean shore. Following the collapse of the Arab Empire, the influence gradually weakened. To the present, with the development of capitalism and social change in Muslim countries, secular law has largely replaced Islamic law in most countries. However, since Islam is still one of the dominant ideologies, Islamic law still has different degrees of binding on Muslim behavior in various Muslim countries, and it is a legal system with considerable influence (Zou, 1991).

Mixed Legal System

The Mixed Legal System is a combination that some of the above legal systems.

It can be seen from the Figure 4 that the countries along the belt and road initiative are mainly Civil Law countries and Mixed Legal System countries, accounting for 54% and 34% respectively. Although there are still differences in the legal system, as long as the countries along the route strengthen intellectual property communication and solve the conflicts caused by these differences in time, it is also possible to form a unified intellectual property system along the belt and road initiative.

Different National Intellectual Property Legal System

Intellectual property rights refers to the rights that people enjoy the fruits of certain intellectual activities, which are monopolistic and exclusive. According to the Agreement on Trade-Related Aspects of Intellectual Property Rights, there are seven categories of the intellectual property rights will be protected, including Copyright or Author's Rights, Trademark, Patent, Geographical Identification, Design of Exterior, Design of Integrated Circuit Layout, Undisclosed Materials or Trade Secrets (Li, 2008). There are many differences in the intellectual property legal system of countries along the belt and road initiative. This paper will take the Copyright and Trademark as examples.

Different Periods of Copyright Protection

Copyright is composed of the author's moral rights and economic rights. Moral rights refer to the rights of the author in respect of the personality or spirit embodied in the work. It is generally believed that the author's moral rights consist of four parts, namely, the right to publish, the right to authorize, the right to protect the integrity of the work, and the right to withdraw the work; the economic rights of copyright, also known as property rights in Chinese Copyright Law, refer to the

Figure 4. Proportion of legal systems of countries along the belt and road initiative

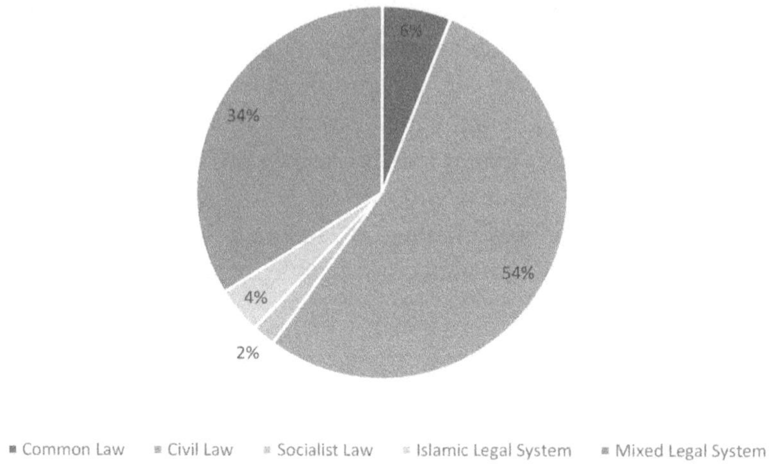

author or the right of other copyright owners to use the work and obtain economic benefits. Generally speaking, economic rights of copyright can be divided into three categories, namely, the right of reproduction, the right of deduction, and the right of public communication.

Countries along the belt and road initiative have different periods of copyright protection. On the one hand, there are two theories of "monism" and "dualism" in the period of copyright protection. According to the theory of "Monism", the moral rights and economic rights produced by the creation of works are an inseparable unity. According to the theory of "dualism", the economic and moral rights generated by the creation of works are separated from each other. Among the civil law countries, Germany and France are typical examples of "monism" and "dualism". According to the French Copyright Law, the period of protection of economic rights is 70 years plus the author's lifetime, or 70 years after the last author die in the case of a cooperative work. The protection of moral rights has no time limit and is inherited by the descendants of the author. According to Germany's "Monism", the protection period of its moral rights is the same as the protection period of economic rights, that is, the author's lifetime plus 70 years.

The Chinese Copyright Law is close to the French "dualism" in the period of copyright protection, that is, the period of economic rights protection is the author's lifetime plus 50 years, and there is no limit of time for the protection of moral rights, the right to authorship, the right to modify and the right to protect the integrity of works, but the protection period for publication rights is 50 years plus the author's lifetime. This is really different. In addition, as can be seen from Figure 4, more than half of the countries along the belt and road initiative are civil law countries. It is conceivable that the number of countries with different copyright protection periods is big. On the other hand, the length of time copyright protection of countries along the belt and road initiative is also different. China is the author's lifetime plus 50 years. The Czech Republic is the author's lifetime plus 70 years. India is the author's lifetime plus 60 years, while Egypt is the author's lifetime plus 50 years, and so on.

Different Ways to Obtain Trademark

Trademark is a mark that distinguishes the goods or services provided by a producer from the same goods or services provided by other producers. Trademark rights are the rights of producers and operators to their trademarks. On the one hand, in the civil law system, trademark rights are usually obtained through registration, while in the Anglo-American legal system, they are mainly obtained through use. It can be seen from Figure 4, the countries along the belt and road initiative are basically the common law and civil law countries, it means that the number of countries along the route have different ways to obtain trademark is large.

On the other hand, even if the same way to obtain trademark that is through registration, this is still very different. Whether a mark can be registered as a trademark in a country along the route depends on the definition of the trademark which is very different in different countries. Such as, according to the China Trademark Law, any sign that can distinguishes goods of natural persons, legal persons or other organizations from those of others, including words, figures, letters, numbers, three-dimensional signs, color combinations and sounds, and combinations of the above elements, can be used as trademark. According to the Czech Republic Trademark Law, any logo that identifies a company's goods or services and other companies' goods and services and can be written or plotted, including text, personal name, design style, letters, numbers, colors, shape or package of the goods, can be used as trademark. According to the India Trademark Law, any mark that can identifies a product or service of a company and that is expressible or can be written down, including the shape or package of goods and combination of color, can be used as trademark.

THE ISSUES AND CHALLENGES OF CHINA'S INTELLECTUAL PROPERTY PROTECTION

The belt and road initiative is a strategy of going out to the world, and going out will inevitably face various problems and risks. The sources of the problem mainly include the enterprise itself and government of China, and the risks come from countries along the route and traditional developed countries.

Enterprises of China

At present, there are two main problems in the intellectual property strategy of Chinese enterprises. On the one hand, enterprises paid insufficient attention to intellectual property rights; on the other hand, the independent innovation capability of enterprises is insufficient. No matter which one is very deadly, it can be said that Chinese enterprises must attach importance to and solve them if they want to catch up with the belt and road initiative and achieve long-term development.

Enterprises Pay Insufficient Attention to Intellectual Property Rights

Subjectively, enterprises in the domestic environment do not pay enough attention to intellectual property rights and lack awareness of the intellectual property layout overseas. Objectively, the national patent system and intellectual property protection level along the belt and road initiative far apart. At the same time, countries are also affiliated with different regional patent organizations, which also brings difficulties for Chinese enterprises to carry out patent layout and formulate intellectual property protection strategies. From the patent data from 2011 to May 2016, Chinese companies have only obtained patent licenses in more than a dozen countries along the belt and road initiative, including Russia, India, Singapore, Malaysia and other countries. There are few patent applications in Eastern Europe, West Asia and Central Asia. Even in countries where there are already patent applications, the number of applications and the number of grants is small, which is not enough to form an effective patent layout.

Insufficient Capacity of Independent Innovation

At present, China is moving from “Made in China” to “Created in China”. The ability of independent innovation is a key factor in the core competitiveness of enterprises and even the whole country. However, from a realistic point of view, the ability of independent innovation of Chinese enterprises is obviously insufficient. In terms of internal factors, in recent years, Chinese enterprises have invested more and more in R&D expenditures. However, it can be seen from the distribution of expenditures that only a small part of the funds are spent on basic research, and most of the expenses are in updating equipment. In terms of hardware investment, the proportion of funds invested in technology research and development is not high. From the external factors, the innovation power of many enterprises in China now comes from the market-driven, market demand is contingent, and the innovation brought by it is not only passive but also poor in continuity, which leads to a large number of intermediate products technology and products still depends on imports.

At the dawn of the sixth scientific and technological revolution in the world, the lack of independent innovation capability makes it difficult to grasp the latest developments in technology development and cannot respond to market demands in a timely manner. In the long run, if we want to take the lead in the process of building the belt and road initiative and remain invincible, we must fundamentally strengthen our ability to innovate independently.

Government of China

There are two main problems in the Chinese government's intellectual property strategy, on the one hand, the intellectual property public services provided by government are not in place; on the other hand, the intellectual property service agencies lack experience in docking countries along the belt and road initiative. The development of Chinese enterprises is inseparable from the government's policy support, and a good government policy environment is more conducive to the rapid development of enterprises (Chen, 2007).

The Intellectual Property Public Services are not in Place

For a long time, the administrative departments of intellectual property at all levels have placed more public resources on the creation, use and protection of domestic patents, and insufficient support for overseas development of enterprises. In the patent application, the funding for domestic patent applications is relatively strong at this stage, and the funding for international patent applications is obviously insufficient. On the other hand, due to the high cost of international patents, it also leads to the enthusiasm of enterprises for their lack of overseas patent applications. In the acquisition of patent information, because there is no corresponding government information platform, it is difficult for enterprises to obtain sufficient patent information in the first time after the occurrence of international intellectual property disputes, and it is impossible to respond quickly. In recent years, the administrative departments of intellectual property at all levels have done a lot of work in supporting enterprises to "going out" in terms of early warning and safeguarding rights assistance. But limited by funds and other aspects, the effect is not obvious. For example, the enterprises in responding to overseas intellectual property disputes is still limited.

Lack of Experience in Docking Countries Along the Route

China's IP service institutions have a good momentum of development in terms of quantity and scale, but there is a lack of understanding of the complex geopolitics and different economic conditions of countries along the belt and road initiative. Most of

China's service organizations mainly stay in single areas. Such as, the agent of patent application, registration of trademark, copyright, and integrated circuit design and registration. They lack experience in conducting high-end comprehensive services such as risk warning, overseas rights protection, and strategic consulting. Also, due to not well understand the political system and the intellectual property system of countries along the belt and road initiative, resulting in a weak international vision and it is difficult to provide effective assistance.

Countries Along the Route and Traditional Developed Countries

Countries along the route and traditional developed countries are both partners and opponents to China. In particular, the latter will more likely to be an opponent to China. The risks they may bring can be divided into two aspects. On the one hand, the attitude of scientific and technological cooperation with China is complicated; on the other hand, the existence of issues such as politics, legal system, and discourse power.

The Attitude of Cooperation With China is Complicated

In the process of implementation of the belt and road initiative, the attitude of science and technology cooperation between countries along the route and China is negatively correlated with their comprehensive strength. The countries that have positive attitudes toward China's scientific and technological cooperation include Mongolia, Myanmar, Thailand, Pakistan, Kazakhstan, etc. These countries generally welcome the belt and road initiative and are more active towards scientific and technological cooperation; countries with strong comprehensive strengths, such as, Russia, India and Korea, have a vague attitude toward the belt and road initiative. They want to share the benefits of the initiative, and they always maintain a certain vigilance, showing a vague attitude toward cooperation, more political statements and slow action; some countries in Africa and the Middle East are politically unstable and have a wait-and-see attitude and skepticism about the belt and road initiative. At the same time, countries with a number of technology exporting, such as, the United States and Japan, have a cold attitude towards cooperation with China and to some extent resist cooperation. Hence, the patent layout along the route of those countries will inevitably restrict and affect the development of China's patent layout and cooperation with other countries. The main risk of "going out" may brought is that the major countries that along the route are not active in cooperation, even worse, hinder joint action and weaken cooperation revenue.

Political, Legal System, and Discourse Power Issues

Based on the belt and road initiative, according to the development needs of China's patent internationalization, it is necessary to establish an international protection system such as the intellectual property community. However, due to differences in laws, regulations, technologies, and standard forms, China faces three major difficulties. Firstly, policy and legal risks of regional intellectual property rights. On the one hand, there are risks of political instability in the Middle East and Africa along the belt and road initiative, which will affect the coherence of intellectual property policies and economic and trade relations. On the other hand, Chinese enterprises have legal risks in overseas intellectual property rights and are more likely to fall into the dispute of infringement and rights protection; Second, differences in the regional intellectual property system. The economic zone of Belt and Road initiative covers three major regions of Asia, Europe and Africa. Countries in each region have great differences in intellectual property-related industries, laws, values, and culture. Last but not least, there is a lack of regional intellectual property rights, and the national science and technology systems vary greatly along the route. The belt and road initiative involves the formation and construction of regional intellectual property rules, while developing countries including China face challenges arising from the lack of experience due to dealing with the technological differences and reducing transaction costs.

COUNTERMEASURES

The proposal of the belt and road initiative is not only an international strategy advocated by the Chinese government for cooperative development, but also a local strategy for the new normal of economic development and innovation. Under the guidance of the belt and road initiative, China needs to actively promote the international strategy for the creation of a regional system for intellectual property rights, as well as the domestic strategy for the continuous development of intellectual property rights. Based on a comprehensive analysis of the domestic and international intellectual property environment, the following suggestions of the intellectual property protection strategy under the belt and road initiative from the domestic and international levels.

Domestic Strategy

In order to improve the influence of China in the technical field along the belt and road initiative as soon as possible, and win the competitive advantage of the international market for enterprises, reduce the international intellectual property disputes that may be encountered in the process of "going out", and reduce the external impact brought by the lock-up of a few technical fields, the following work should be carried out as soon as possible.

Strengthen Intergovernmental Cooperation

The fundamental function of the intellectual property system is to promote economic development, and a good international cooperation mechanism for intellectual property rights is the basic guarantee for realizing this function. On the one hand, it is necessary to strengthen communication between China and the intellectual property management institutions of various countries, establish an intellectual property communication mechanism with countries along the belt and road initiative, and promote various activities. Such as, promoting bilateral or multilateral cooperation, signing the intellectual property memorandums, and so on. Establishing an environment for intellectual property protection for peaceful coexistence and common development. On the other hand, it is necessary to strengthen cooperation with relevant intellectual property organizations and trade zones such as the ASEAN Intellectual Property Cooperation Organization, the Eurasian Patent Organization, the European Patent Organization and the Gulf Cooperation Council, and accelerate the signing of cooperation treaties or agreements. Form a mutual assistance system and promote international review cooperation.

Provide With Strong Public Service for Enterprises

Establish a comprehensive information platform of the belt and road initiative and intellectual property protection, and encourage the social forces to participate in the construction, maintenance and use of the platform, to provide enterprises with the most timely and effective dynamic tracking of intellectual property rights in various countries and industries, and to enhance the convenience of enterprises to obtain intellectual property information in target countries. Strengthen overseas intellectual property risk warning and rights protection assistance, formulate national guidelines on trade investigation and risk prevention and control related to intellectual property rights, and provide timely and effective intellectual property layout recommendations for enterprises. Exploring the establishment of special funds to support enterprises in the whole chain of early warning analysis, patent application, and rights protection assistance. Playing active role of being a bridge between various associations, chambers of commerce and associations, and introduce international advanced intellectual property management experience into the country, use intellectual property as a link to deepen understanding and trust among enterprises, and create a good atmosphere of common development of enterprises in various industrial chains.

Enhance the Independent Innovation Capability of Enterprises

Creating a good policy environment and effective incentive mechanism to protect and encourage inventors and scientific and technological personnel to engage in creative activities, and creating good conditions for researchers to carry out research, invention and technological breakthroughs, and promoting enterprises to enhance their independent innovation capabilities. Increasing publicity, strengthen corporate intellectual property awareness, change the wrong impression that enterprises apply for patents, registered trademarks, etc. as a means of get rewards and benefits, and enhancing awareness of enterprises of the legal meaning and rights behind the patents and trademarks. While enterprises are making strategic plans for intellectual property rights in developed countries in Europe and America, strengthen their awareness and emphasis on the layout of intellectual property rights in countries along the belt and road initiative.

International Strategy

The intellectual property protection under the belt and road initiative facing with many risks, especially in developed countries, which highlights the trend of constructing a new international economic and trade order, weakening the influence of the original World Trade Organization and the Agreement on Trade-Related Aspects of Intellectual Property Rights. To this end, China should advocate the countries that along the belt and road initiative to commit themselves to the construction of a regional intellectual property legal order, and establish a community of intellectual property laws and institutional guarantees as an important supplement and adjustment of the international intellectual property protection system (Yuan, 2014).

Build a Regional Intellectual Property Integration System

The implementation of the belt and road initiative is accompanied by the promotion of regional intellectual property integration. Reasonable regional intellectual property integration rules should be well integrated with international intellectual property rules. On the basis of meeting the minimum international protection standards for intellectual property rights, it is also possible to implement differentiated protection according to the differences in the level of intellectual property protection among countries in the region, so as to achieve mutual benefit and win-win for intellectual property protection among countries in the region. To construct a reasonable regional intellectual property integration rule, we need to consider the differences in the intellectual property status of each country, adhere to the principle of mutual respect, mutual assistance, cooperation and win-win, and allow different countries to implement different protection strategies to ensure fair and reasonable rules. At the same time, it is necessary to fully study the conflicts and contradictions between the international intellectual property system and regional rules, to avoid the phenomenon of closed doors in the region, to keep pace with the times, actively integrate into the international intellectual property system, and to make good foundation for the region's intellectual property achievements come into the world.

Make a Good Patent Layout Along the Belt and Road Initiative

Patent layout is an effective means for enterprises to occupy the technology market, suppress competitors, and defend against patent infringement. Do a good job in patent intelligence analysis, fully exploit the industry information hidden behind patent data, and use patent navigation to make patent layout is the important weapon to enterprise in the technology market to win.

The layout of patents is usually divided into three categories: patent area layout, patent industry layout and patent overseas layout. Different types of patent layouts focus on different points. The patent area layout focuses on the advantages of regional resources, targeted patent layout, and promotes the rapid development of the regional economy. The layout of the patent industry focuses on the development planning of the entire industrial chain, focusing on the development of advantageous industries and maintaining the leading position of advantageous industries. The overseas layout of patents focuses on the competition and expansion of enterprises overseas, and provides protection for enterprises to occupy the market overseas and prevent infringement.

Under the belt and road initiative, we plan the distribution of patents in line with China's national conditions, promote the development of the central and western regions through the domestic regional patent layout, promote the professional upgrading of traditional industries and the development of strategic emerging industries through the industrial layout, and lead the overseas layout. The approval of the dominant enterprises in the belt and road initiative overseas business competition, striving for world-renowned enterprises, and promoting enterprises to take the initiative and the right to speak in the global market. All of those are very important for establishing China's leading position in the belt and road initiative.

Enhance the Communication of Intellectual Property Between Countries

Through the communication of intellectual property, countries along the belt and road initiative can enhance the mutual understanding between countries along the route, conflicts of intellectual property can be coordinated, and losses caused by intellectual property conflicts can be reduced. The two or more parties communicate with each other can handle intellectual property friction by signing a memorandum of understanding, establish a good environment that mutual respect and peaceful coexistence, jointly safeguard the achievements of regional intellectual property protection, and promote the development of intellectual property rights.

CONCLUSION

This paper introduces the basic connotation of the belt and road initiative, and analyzes the intellectual property environment from the view of domestic and abroad. Although the environment of domestic intellectual property has not yet reached the optimal status, the trend of continuous optimization has laid good foundation for the formulation of the intellectual property protection strategy of belt and road initiative. And the complexity of the international intellectual property environment along the belt and road initiative indicates that building a fair and universal intellectual property system is the key to realize the intellectual property protection of belt and road initiative. On the basis of comprehensive analysis of the environment of domestic and international intellectual property, the paper analyzes the intellectual property protection strategy under the belt and road initiative from both domestic and international levels. In terms of domestic, we should strengthen intergovernmental cooperation, provide with strong public service for enterprises, and enterprises should enhance the capability of independent innovation; in terms of international, we should build a regional intellectual property integration system, make a good patent layout along the belt and road initiative, and strengthen the communication of intellectual property between countries. Hope these can provide reference for intellectual property research under the belt and road initiative.

REFERENCES

Chen. (2007). Globalization, Regional Integration and Localization of Intellectual Property Law: Problems, Doctrines and Methods. Journal of Guangxi Normal University: Philosophy and Social Sciences, 43(6), 134.

Hong, W. (2016). The Cooperation between the Belt and Road Initiative and Strategic of Protection Intellectual Property. *Front Journal*, *10*, 20.

Li. (2008). *Intellectual Property Law*. Beijing: Law Press China.

Lu. (2013). *Dictionary ofManagement*. Shanghai: Lexicographical Publishing House.

Quigley, J. (1989). Socialist Law and the Civil Law Tradition. *The American Journal of Comparative Law*, *37*(4), 781.

Wu, Z. (2013). *Legal concept*. Beijing: Law Press China.

Yu, Z. (1991). *Law Dictionary*. Beijing: China University of Political Science & Law Press.

Yuan. (2014). National Strategy Analysis of the Belt and Road Initiative. *Theoretical Monthly, 11*, 6.

Ze, W. (2006). *Association of Southeast Asian Nations*. Beijing: China Legal Publishing House.

Zhang, Z., Wang, L., & Shan, L. (2015). Strategic of Protection Intellectual Property under the Belt and Road Initiative. *Chinese Invention and Patent*, *6*, 30.

Zheng, S. (2003). *Intellectual Property Law*. Beijing: Law Press China.

Section 2

Industrial and Trade Development Studies Under the Belt and Road Strategy

Chapter 7
An Assessment of the Belt and Road Performance:
Based on the Case of Machinery Shipment From Shanghai to Rotterdam

Sedat Baştuğ
https://orcid.org/0000-0002-7121-2882
Iskenderun Technical University, Turkey

Turgay Battal
https://orcid.org/0000-0002-0710-4692
Iskenderun Technical University, Turkey

ABSTRACT

The aim of the chapter is to propose a methodology to illustrate the cost and time components of door-to-door movement by One Belt and One Road (OBOR) and traditional routes alongside with modes. The study is concentrated on a case study and uses established multimodal transport cost model as a research framework. Interviews with industry practitioners and observation from primary methods of data collection. The use of multimodal transport cost model is common in the containerized cargoes. Hence, this study provides an original analysis for OBOR initiative. The volumes of OBOR shipments are large, with a high value-to-volume ratio. The research initially confirms that multimodal transport alternatives and modal combinations may successfully be applied and assess the performance of OBOR initiative.

DOI: 10.4018/978-1-5225-8440-7.ch007

INTRODUCTION

Globalization and trade liberalization have benefitted China by making it the world's largest manufacturing center and the country has emerged as an engine of Asian economic growth (McGregor, 2006). This phenomenon made China has grown to the largest manufacturing and trading country in the world. However, in recent years, China has faced a slowdown of its domestic economy that has affected global and inter-regional trade (Timmer et al., 2016).

More than 2,000 years ago, China's imperial envoy Zhang Qian helped to establish the Silk Road, a network of trade routes that linked China to Central Asia, Middle East and Europe. The name came from one of China's most important exports silk. And the road itself influenced the development of the entire region for hundreds of years (Jinchen, 2016:1). In 2013, president, Xi Jinping proposed establishing the new regional cooperation model and called Silk Road Economic Belt. This proposal contains new maritime silk roads, new railways network, roads, pipelines and utilities that would connected to China, Central Asia, West Asia, parts of South Asia and Europe. The geographical coverage of which is illustrated in Figure 1. This proposal is officially called as the One Belt, One Road initiative (OBOR) or the Belt and Road initiative.

This plan connects China with its neighbors in Asia and beyond, involving more than 60 countries. Among the objectives of OBOR, a key one is to ease the bottlenecks for cross-border trade, especially to investigate how to achieve a well-connected transport infrastructure with effective logistics services (Garca-Herrero and Xu, 2016). One Belt and One Road (OBOR) initiative or New Silk Road consists of two major parts. First part is the Silk Road economic belt which establishes a road stretching from China to Europe and encompassing a host of trade and infrastructure

Figure 1. New Silk Road, One Belt and One Road (OBOR)
Source: Xinhua, 2018

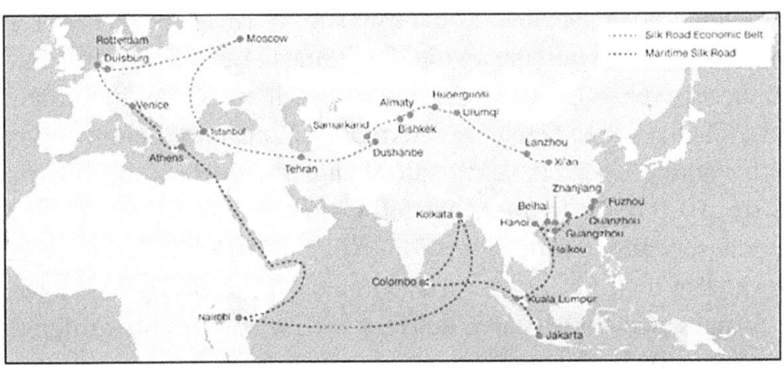

projects and secondly it aims to build maritime Silk Road which is based on sea-based network of shipping lanes and port developments throughout Asia and the Pacific.

In 2014, it has launched the Asian Infrastructure Investment Bank (AIIB) and set up a US$ 40 billion Silk Road Fund. Chinese officials claim that the Belt and Road Initiative (BRI) is also part of the new round of China's opening up. There is certainly a lot of truth in this claim. Firstly, China is facing challenges of overproduction and overcapacity, particularly in the steel and construction materials sectors. This can be addressed by the BRI which will open up foreign markets to many Chinese companies. Secondly, as labor costs rise, China will move its labor-intensive and low value-added manufacturing facilities overseas (Li, M., and 2015:3). After 2008 financial crisis, large supply chain managers realized the problems of offshore production and selling at consumption areas. As well as production cost in offshore is not so low nowadays, mass production does not meet with customer demand. Due to the lack of mass production elasticy and with introduction of new models such as "additive production", the supply chain managers tend to moves the production facilities at near shores in supply chains. Therefore, BRI has to be improved by China because of fear in loss of market. On a macro scale, OBOR countries have accelerate the construction of transport infrastructures to promote cargo freight. Railway Express, for example is able to transport container from China to Europe and other countries along OBOR. In accordance with the goals of the OBOR strategy, cross-border e-commerce is growing rapidly. According to reports from Ali Baba, half of its customers, which are more than 100 million, on the Business-to-Customer (B2C) platform locate within the OBOR region. Therefore, it can be seen that international logistics cooperation is essential to meeting the growing demand (Lui, X. et al. 2018:1).

Following this initiative, there are two important railway systems significantly impacting the current shipping service network from China to Europe. First, as an important part of the OBOR initiative, the railway along New Eurasia Land Bridge has achieved a quick development in recent years. The New Eurasia Land Bridge, also known as the Second Eurasia Land Bridge, is an international railway line connecting China and other Eurasia countries such as Kazakhstan, Russia, Belarus, and Poland. Through capitalizing on the New Eurasia Land Bridge, eleven Chinese cities have successively opened direct railway container services to European cities, for example, Chongqing to Duisburg (Germany), Wuhan to Melnik and Pardubice (Czech), Chengdu to Lodz (Poland), and Zhengzhou to Hamburg (Germany). By October 2015, 1070 trains in total have left China for Europe with cargoes, as the number of trains increased from 17 in 2011 to 623 in 2015. Thus, the cargo delivery service provided by this railway system is continuously increasing, leading to possibly extensive changes on the other cargo delivery services such as liner shipping (Yang, D. and Wang, S., 2017:1).

Second, following the OBOR initiative, the railway system built to connect Southern European hub ports to their hinterland is also changing the current shipping network. In particular, in Fig. 1, Venice and Piraeus (Athens) are highlighted as two gateway ports in Europe. In order to help build these two gateway ports and better utilize them to construct the liner shipping service network, a Chinese liner shipping company, i.e., COSCO, signed a concession agreement to operate Piraeus port with the Piraeus Port Authority in 2016, which provides COSCO with 67% shares of the port. Furthermore, COSCO is expected to invest more than half a billion euros (€552 million) in the Piraeus Port within the next five years and the investment aims "to make Piraeus the biggest transit port in the South Europe" (Brînză, 2016).

With respect to the importance of these gateway ports in Central and Eastern Europe (CEE), besides COSCO's investment on the port construction, China also cooperated with CEE to construct a high-speed rail line (as shown in Figure 2) linking the Piraeus Port of Greece in the south to Budapest of Hungary in the north via Skopje of Macedonia and Belgrade of Serbia.

Upon its completion by 2018, the travel time by train between Southern and Central Europe will be significantly reduced. More importantly, the investment on these hub ports and the railway system linking the hub ports with other inland cities will tremendously reduce the cargo delivery time from China to other inland European cities through these ports and thereafter the railway (Yang, D. and Wang, S., 2017:2). In the other hand, the port of Venice is aiming to transform itself into a Venice Offshore Onshore Port System (VOOPS), preparing for docking megaships of 18,000 TEU and beyond.

In summary, OBOR initiative has land corridors (as shown in Figure 3) which include (Ramasamy, 2017):

Figure 2. Rail connection from Piraeus to Middle Europe
Source: Yang and Wang, 2017

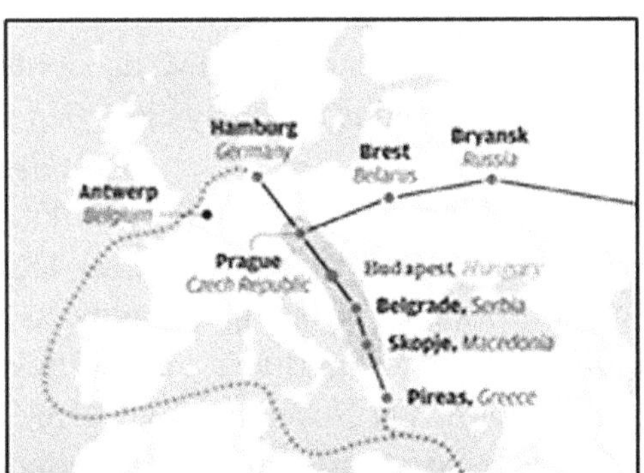

Figure 3. OBOR: Six Economic Corridors Spanning Asia, Europe and Africa
Source: HKTDC Research, 2018

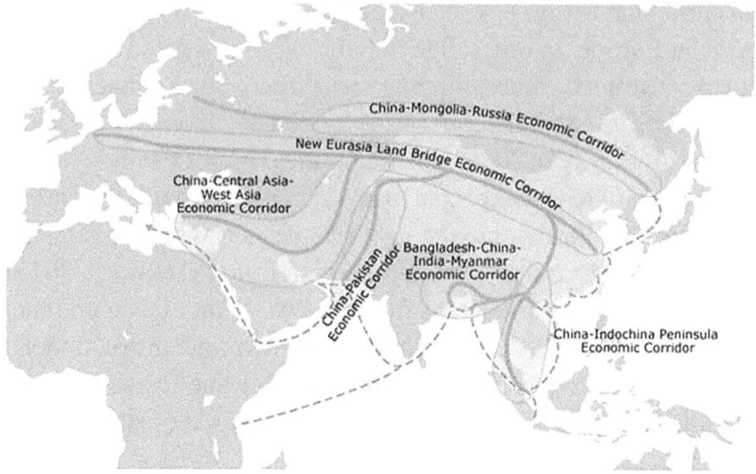

1. The New Eurasian Land Bridge (NELB) runs from Western China to Western Russia through Kazakhstan, and includes the Silk Road Railway through China's Xinjiang Autonomous Region, Kazakhstan, Russia, Belarus, Poland and Germany;
2. The China–Mongolia–Russia Corridor (CMR) will run from Northern China to the Russian Far East. The Russian government established Russian Direct Investment Fund and China Investment Corporation, a Chinese government investment agency, partnered in 2012 to create the Sino-Russian Investment Fund, which concentrates on opportunities in bilateral integration;
3. The China–Central Asia–West Asia Corridor (CAWA) will run from Western China to Turkey;
4. The China–Indochina Peninsula Corridor (ICP) will run from Southern China to Singapore;
5. The Bangladesh-China-India-Myanmar (BCIM) Economic Corridor, runs from southern China to Myanmar and is officially classified as "closely related to the Belt and Road Initiative";
6. The China–Pakistan Economic Corridor (CP) also known by the acronym CPEC, also classified as "closely related to the Belt and Road Initiative," which is a US$62 billion collection of infrastructure projects throughout Pakistan that aims to rapidly modernize Pakistan's transportation networks, energy infrastructure, and economy. On November 13, 2016, CPEC became partly operational when Chinese cargo was transported overland to Gwadar Port for onward maritime shipment to Africa and West Asia.

BACKGROUND

"The Belt and Road" Initiative is a new research field in the logistics industry because of its strategic significance and practical value. It is the new interest area for scholars who works research themes, such as geography including geopolitical studies, foreign direct investment theories, optimization of transcontinental transportation, and so on (Liu, 2015). In addition to the geography, there are several research themes to be examined by scholars. Some relations including government-enterprise and central & local authorities (Liu, 2015) and multiple bilateral partnerships of cross-regional integration (Chu & Gao, 2015) are highlighted in this literature. However, the concept still sounded vague and its content was difficult to interpret. Hence, scholars focus on process of the initiative by examining barriers and costs, such as construction and maintenance (He et all, 2015). Heavy infrastructure and maintenance costs pushed scholars into research about foreign direct investments (Yang & Yan, 2015), industrial upgrading (Dong & Liang, 2015) and industrial transformation (Su, 2015). With regard to supply chain research field, there is a growing body of researches on logistics literature. Sheu and Kundu (2017) proposed the use of Markov chains to forecast time-varying logistic distribution flows for a three-layer supply chain framework. Zeng et al. (2017) modified the gravity prediction model to calculate the changes in transshipment traffic. Yang et al. (2017) explored a bi-level programming model to reconstruct the shipping service network between Asia and Europe. Lee et al. (2017) discussed the research trends on the Belt and Road initiative with a focus on transportation and logistics.

There are also research trends with future agenda in transport, port, and logistics in the context of OBOR. There are fourth possible research agendas for future research trends (Lee et al, 2017). The first agenda is that hinterland size of Shanghai is shrinking because container cargoes are to be diverted alongside the corridors, although the quantity of cargo has not been identified by scholars. The project "CPEC" is not a single road project but it supports Gwadar seaport, airport, road, railway, hydropower plant, pipelines, industrial zones, and free trade zones. It initially aims the carriage of oil/LNG from Iran and Iraq but it may also reduce the traffic flow for tanker fleet passing through the Malacca Strait and may result to diminish port revenues for the Port of Singapore. It also aims that container cargoes in the inland of China heading towards Europe and Africa can be transported by land to Gwadar Port because the "CPEC" project may cause to lower freight costs and save time, thanks to decline in trading distance. The second research agenda is to investigate the impacts of OBOR on regional transport systems, by performing a possible connection test between railway and maritime networks in the region of Euroasia. The third research agenda is closely deal with single window system that may reduce paperwork and logistics costs and promote customs clearance cooperation between container ports and cross-border custom offices. The fourth possible research agenda is that OBOR contributes to promote international trade connectivity, economic development, value-added, and employment during the phase of infrastructure construction. However, infrastructure construction requires huge investments in order to build transportation corridors. That's why, there is a research trend to investigate the values, positioning and routes of seaports to the OBOR. The corridors in association with the development of Kolkata and Colombo ports may draw port capacity issue and inter-port competition in the Indian Ocean (Chen and Yang 2017).

Although a lot of scholars from many aspects investigated OBOR Initiative, there is no empirical study to focus on the cost and time components and the studies were not systematically compare traditional sea route with proposed routes of OBOR initiative between the West Europe and East Asia. On the other hand, majority of the studies (Bulis et al, 2014; Soong, 2016; Nazarko et al, 2017) only include the political and economic development aspects for the specific regions such as Eastern Europe and ASEAN states. This study does not only study specific regions but also investigates the region of Eurasia.

The aim of the study is to propose a methodology to illustrate the cost and time components of door to door movement by OBOR and traditional routes alongside with modes. This study used a case study methodology to investigate the alternative route combinations between Shanghai (China) and Rotterdam (Europe). The study is composed of three main parts. The next part focuses on the multimodal transportation of containerized cargoes between China and Netherlands. Then, the research model and methodology are given. The third part analyses the case study of machinery shipment from Shanghai to Rotterdam.

MULTIMODAL TRANSPORTATION OF CONTAINERIZED CARGOES

Multimodal transport is well established in the general cargo and container shipping market, where the cargo value, number of shippers and the different cargo mix allow for combinations of routes, modes and methods. Besides, the general cargoes and containers can present opportunities for multimodal transportation. China's exports to Netherlands amounted to $93.8 billion or 16.3% of its overall imports in the year of 2017. Machinery parts which have high value commodity and small volumes, are frequently transported by containers. The total import of machinery from China was about $25.7 billion and its share is around 25 percent in overall import.

The principle is that increasing the size of consignment on the shipping leg can reduce unit costs, which provides economies of scale. The consequence of the OBOR initiative that general and containerized cargoes potentially makes the use of several modes in combination including “sea maximizing and land minimizing” principle. The efficient logistics, especially cheap shipping, thus contribute critically to the footloose nature of much of the world’s manufacture, particularly where logistics follow the normally preferred “sea maximizing and land minimizing” transport model (Banomyong and and Bereford, 2001). The cost based approach taken by Beresford (1999) would suggest that, for long supply chains, “sea maximizing and land minimizing” is consistent with the modern manufacturing business models.

MAIN FOCUS OF THE CHAPTER

Cost model of multimodal transport originally proposed by Beresford and Dubey (1990) and developed by Beresford (1999) was used in this study. The model is stand-alone and very flexible enough to be applied to any operational circumtances and to a supply chain at any lenght. The main elements of the model are cost, time, distance, transport mode and intermodal transfer. The cost model which is used here includes (ports, rail and freight terminals, ICD’s) and it makes use of costs, time and distance components. The validity of model is tested against a real case in international freight logistics, namely the export of goods Vientiane in Lao PDR to Singapore, (Banomyong and Beresford, 2001), transport of whisky from Scotland to Greece (Beresford, 1999), flowers from Taiwan to China (Beresford et.al., 2006a), ATMs from Eire to China (Beresford et.al. 2006), home textile from Turkey to UK (Denktaş Şakar and Beresford, 2009), foodstuff from Turkey to Germany (Deveci and Denktaş, 2010), iron ore from Australia and China (Beresford et al., 2011) and fertilizer shipment from Serbia to Turkey (Bastug, et all, 2013). The case studies of articles are representative. Because Peters (1998) says “one very valid reason for doing a case study is to collect information on the topic in question, especially while the case is still in progress”. Examining the OBOR initiative while it is still in progress may be especially valuable in comparative studies, for instance a researchers may be less familiar with comparing alternative routes. This is why this study is also representative case study.

The main assumptions of the multimodal transport cost model are based on the premise that unit costs of carriage vary between transport modes and the stepness of the cost curves highlight that for volume movements, sea transport should be the cheapest per tone-km, rail transport should be transport cost model are based on the premise that unit costs of carriage vary between transport modes and the stepness of the cost curves highlight that for volume movements, sea transport should be the cheapest per tone-km, rail transport should be fairly expensive. Cargo handling charge is levied at ports and terminals, without any progress being made along the overall supply chain and each vertical step in the cost curve represents the costs incurred (Beresford, 1999).

The use of multimodal transport cost model is common in the context of containerized cargoes. Therefore, the objective of this section is to propose a cost/time methodology to illustrate the cost and time components of door-to-door movement by available routes and modes as well as to illustrate the delays at borders or other inspection points up to the point of destination within OBOR Initiatives.

This study used a case study methodology to investigate the alternative route combinations between Shanghai (China) and Rotterdam (Europe). The study only focus two main active corridors (NELB and CEE) for carriage of container cargoes. Yin (2003:23) states that a case study is "an empirical inquiry that investigates a contemporary phenomenon within its real-life context, especially when the boundaries between phenomenon and context are not clear evident". It is a research approach that focuses on understanding the dynamics present within single setting (Eisenhardt, 1989). It is argues that case study method is more suitable to answering "how" and "why" questions and where the researcher has little control or no control over events and subjects (Yin, 2003). The study uses a qualitative technique which may be used to increase reliability. Yin (1994) suggests that the reliability can be provided by assurance of meaningful parallelism of findings across multiple data sources. With regard to multiple data sources, five operation managers are selected from international freight forwarding companies in Turkey. They confirmed the parallelism of the findings with real market.

THE CASE OF MACHINERY SHIPMENT FROM SHANGHAI TO ROTTERDAM

China is currently undertaking what it considers the largest project of the century by building a network of railroads and shipping lanes linking itself with 70 countries across Asia, Africa, Europe, and Ocenia. However, there is a need to compare which routes are actually the cost effective between Asia and Europe. Because, reliance on silk road in international context can create problems for logistics companies. These problems can be ranked from delays at borders, the road restrictions, empty wagon imbalances, interruptions in rail transportation due to heavy traffic on railway network.

The study proposed three main alternative routes currently being used by the logistics operators and shippers in the case study in terms of transportation costs and transit times for OBOR Initiatives. The study is assumed to transport the industrial machinery parts by 40 foot container from Shanghai to Rotterdam by using three different routes.

Table 1. Freight routing alternatives from Shanghai to Rotterdam

Route	Origin	Mode	Transfer	Mode	Transfer	Mode	Destination
1	Shanghai	Railway	Chongqing	Railway	Duisburg	Road	Rotterdam
2	Shanghai	Sea	No Transfer	Sea	Venezia	Road	Rotterdam
3	Shanghai	Sea	No Transfer	Sea	No Transfer	Sea	Rotterdam

Data Source: Compiled from industry sources.

ALL RAILROAD AND ROAD TRANSPORT WITH ROUTE 1

Route 1 begins with Shanghai in China and ends at the destination point of Rotterdam in Holland (See Figure 4).

Table 2 shows the main figures regarding the routes, costs, distance and transit time. The first leg of the route 1 is organized as railway transportation between Shanghai to Chongqing terminals. The 40 foot container transportation with railway is only suggested because of 20 foot container is too risky to be organized. Because, railway weight limit is 23 metric tonnes for 40 foot container.

Loading of container takes very short period of time to railway truck in Shanghai. Then the cargo proceeds to Chongqing from where the distance is 1678 km. Leg 2 of route 1 is organized from Chongqing to Duisburg and its voyage lenght is 8838 km alongside with 456 hours by railway. The container free return deport is Duisburg. Upon completion of leg 2, the cargo dropped off at Duisburg with cost of USD 500. Then it is transported from Duisburg to Rotterdam by road. The voyage distance is 208 km.

Figure 4. Map of Route 1

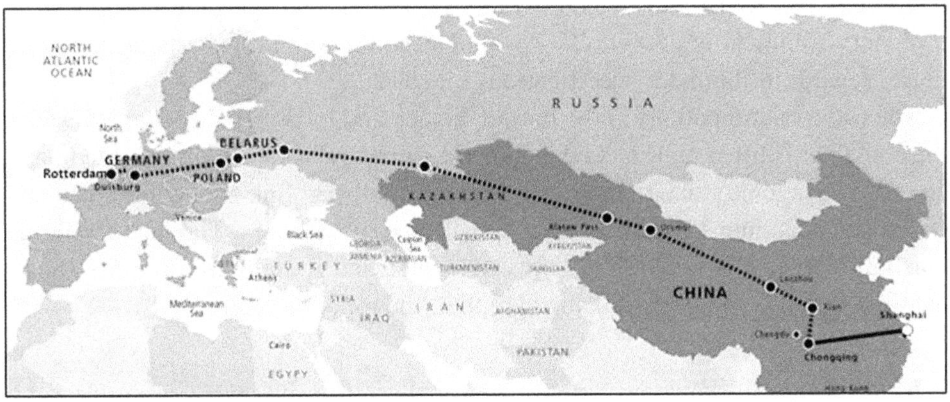

Table 2. All railroad and road transport with Route 1

Step	Legs	Mode	Transit Time	Distance (km)	Cost ($)	Cost per Distance
1	Shipment from Shanghai to Chongqing	Railway Transportation	18 hours	1678	1100	0,72
	Pre-Shipment Formalities		1 hour		100	
	Transferring to other voyage		4 hours		-	
2	Shipment from Chongqing to Duisburg	Railway Transportation	455 hours	8838	2400	0,33
	Container Drop off				500	
3	Shipment from Duisburg to Rotterdam	Road Transportation	2 hours	208	800	3,85

The overall transit time of route 1 is 20 days with average speeds of vehicles with total freight 4.400 dolar alongside with container drop off charge of USD 500. In case of any dead freight, 50% of terminal to terminal freight once upon cancellation within 7 days and 3 days before departure, 100% of terminal to terminal freight once upon cancellation within 3 days before departure. Figure 5 shows that time distance and costs-distance graph of the route 1.

ALL SEAWAY AND RAILWAY TRANSPORT WİTH ROUTE 2

Second route option (as shown in Figure 6) is mostly dominated by sea transport between Shanghai and Venice but railway transport option is included between Venice and Rotterdam.

Main leg of the route by container ship takes 20 days and total lenght of the sea route is 16.243 km (8871 nautical miles). The sea transportation of industrial machinery shipment is 2709 dollar for 40 DC container. Table 3 shows the main figures regarding shipment specifications for route 2.

The cargo is dropped off in the port of Venice and its drop off cost is USD 310. The container is lifted and stacked, handled entirely by machine, until loaded on to the railway wagon to take them away. There is a railroad link between Venice and Rotterdam, spanning 1301 km with a transit time of 13 hours. The leg of railroad transportation cost is USD 2739 between Venice and Rotterdam. Figure 7 shows that time distance and costs-distance graph of the route 1.

Figure 5. Time-distance and costs-distance for all railroad and road transport (Route 1)

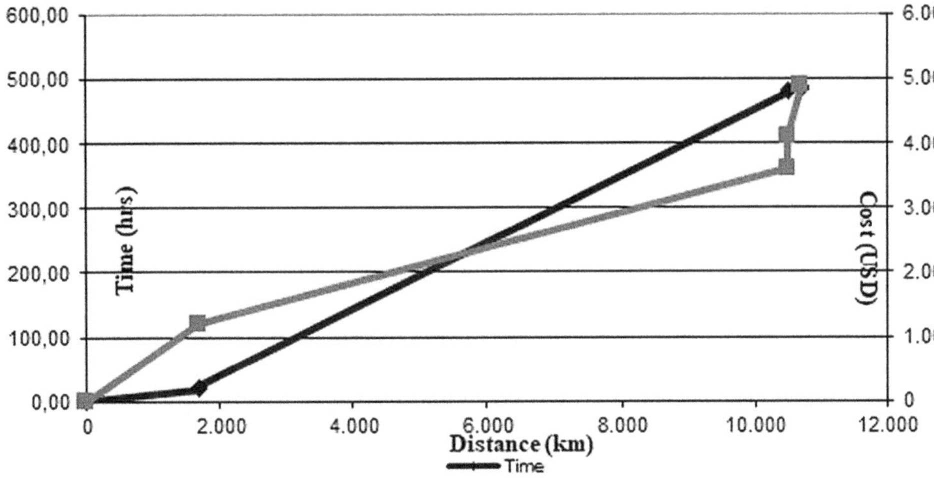

Figure 6. Map of Route 2

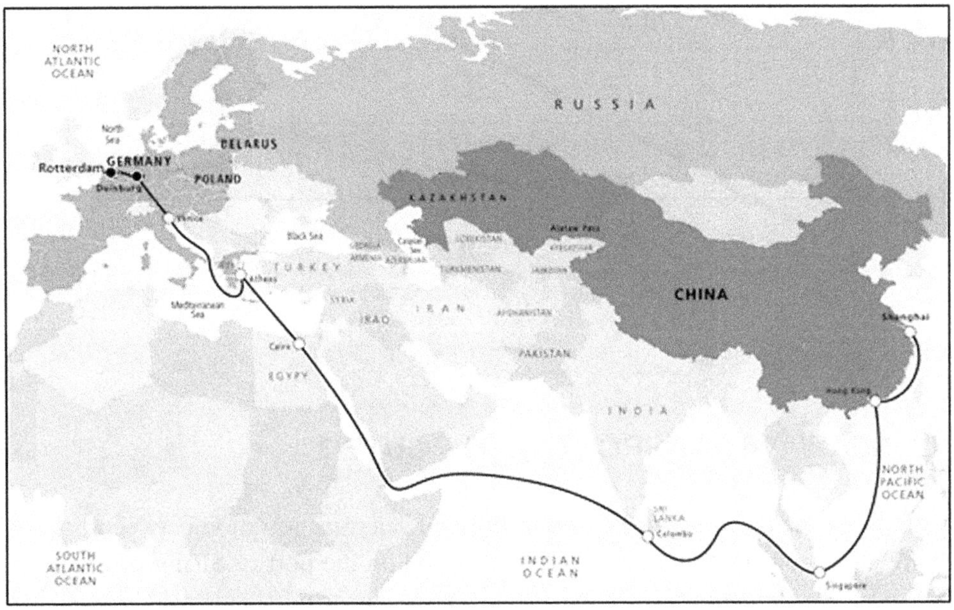

Table 3. All railroad and railroad transport with Route 2

Step	Legs	Mode	Transit Time	Distance (km)	Cost ($)	Cost Per Distance
1	Shipment from Shanghai to Venice	Seaway Transportation	480 hours	16.243	2120	0,16
	Pre-Shipment Formalities (Export Service, Terminal Handling Service, Documentation)		1 hour		279	
	Merchant Haulage Imports, Terminal Handling Service, Documentation		5 hours		310	
2	Shipment from Venice to Rotterdam	Railway Transportation	13 hours	1301	2739	0,47

Figure 7. Time-distance and costs-distance for all seaway and railway transport (Route 2)

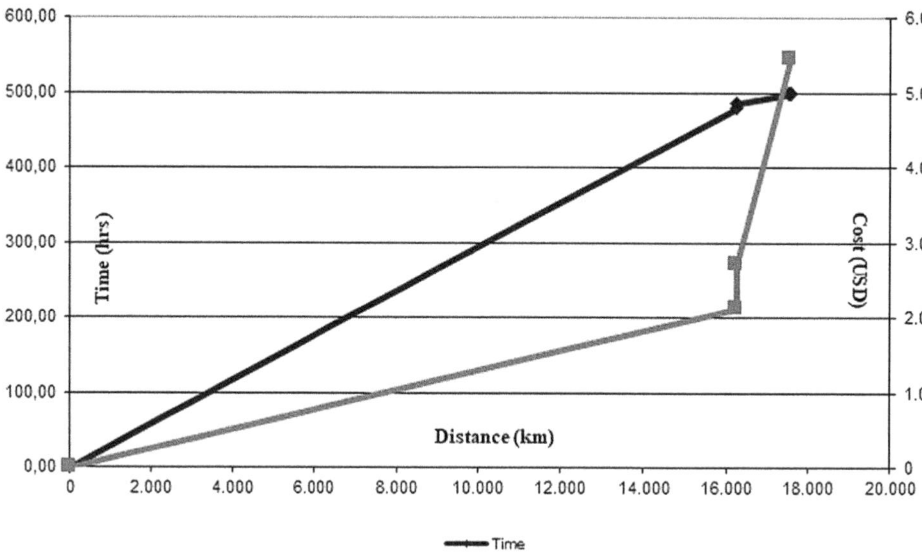

ALL SEAWAY TRANSPORT WITH ROUTE 3

Route 3 (as seen in Figure 8) is the traditional sea transportation between port of Shanghai to port of Rotterdam. Cargo is loaded on the port of Shanghai and then proceed to the next port of call. The distance between the ports is 19.942 km (10.768 nautical miles) and it takes 35 days with 5 stops (Shanghai-China, Yantian-China, Tanjung Pelepas-Malasia, Rotterdam-Netherlands). Yantian and Tanjung Pelepas are the hub ports and they are the part of hub and spoke system. The cargo operations

Figure 8. Map of Route

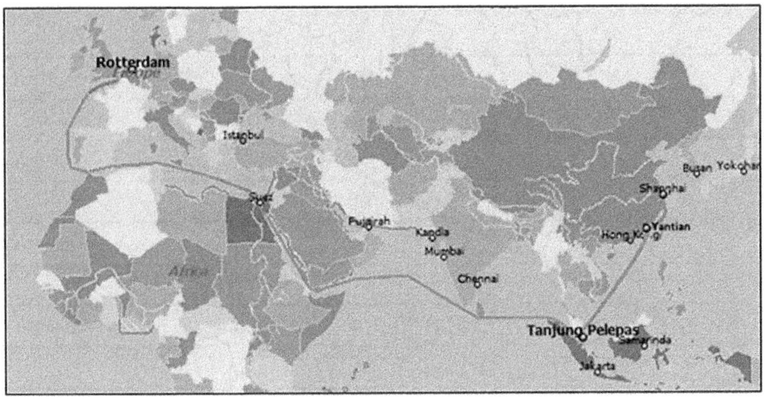

in hub ports take only 1 day and the voyage time between the hub ports is 1 day. The shipment cost is USD 955 alongside with the loading cost of USD 217 and discharging of USD 284.

Table 4 shows the figures (costs, modes, transit times, distances and cost per distance) of traditional sea transport between Shanghai and Rotterdam.

CONCLUSION

Multimodal transport can become more efficient by encouraging the development of alternative routes, not only one transit country but also through different countries. OBOR Iniatives is crucial for the development of multimodal transportation by developing OBOR countries transportation infrastructures and their trades. With

Table 4. Traditional sea transport with Route 3

Step	Legs	Mode	Transit Time	Distance (km)	Cost ($)	Cost per Distance
1	Pre-Shipment Formalities (Export Service, Terminal Handling Service, Documentation)	Seaway Transportation	2 hour	19.942	217	0,07
	Shipment from Shanghai to Rotterdam		768 hours		955	
	Merchant Haulage Imports, Terminal Handling Service, Documentation at Destination		5 hours		284	

Figure 9. Time-distance and costs-distance for sea transportation (Route 3)

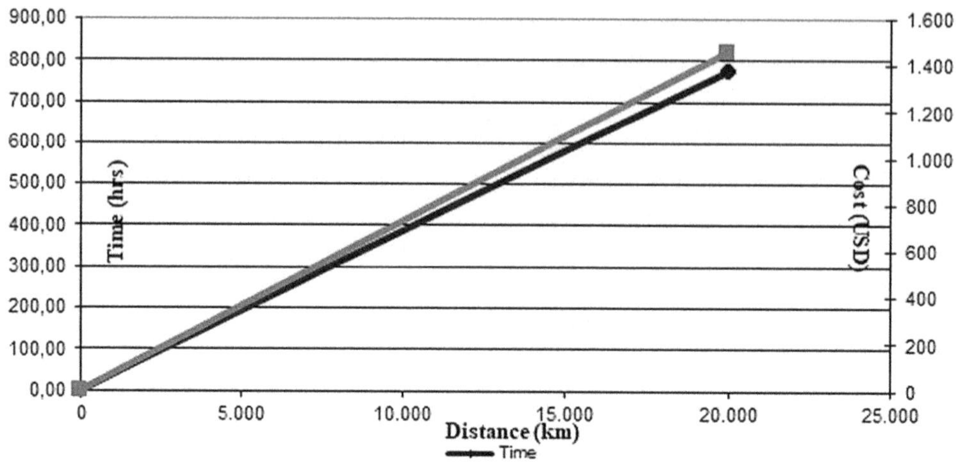

regard to One Belt and One Road policy planning guidelines, it will provide numerous economic benefits:

1. Sustainable development in infrastructure projects for developing countries such as Afghanistan and Pakistan;
2. Economic growth;
3. Increase in trade and decrease in transit times of goods;
4. International cooperation;
5. Peace building between nations.

The OBOR Iniatives is not limited to Eurasia but it is a global strategy and thus, the benefits are to increase relations in the five areas of policy, finance, trade, infrastructure, and people-to-people exchanges. Although OBOR Iniatives is in very large extent and still under development in numerous areas and countries, this study confirms that the project may provide the efficiency in the carriage of containerized cargoes and fastest transit times at the early stages of OBOR Iniatives. Hence, this analysis compares the unimodal and multimodal alternatives between China and Europe. Costs, transit time and distance related data were considered. Beresford Cost Model assists countries to maintain aforementioned elements for effective operational performance of OBOR Initiatives. Table 5 shows the comparison of the alternative routes analyzed in the study in terms of costs, time and distance.

Both route 1 and route 2 have around 18-20 days transit time. But route 3, which uses traditional sea transportation, has a longer transit time compared to other routes due to the time spent during sea voyage. Cost figures are also different in

Table 5. Evaluation of multimodal route alternatives between Shanghai (China) and Rotterdam (Europe)

Routes	Modes	Distance (Km)	Time (hrs)	Cost ($)
Route 1 (Shanghai to Rotterdam via Duisburg)	Railway	10.724	476	4.900
Route 2 (Shanghai to Rotterdam via Venice)	Seaway + Railway	17.544	494	5.448
Route 3 (Shanghai to Rotterdam via Yantian and Tanjung Pelepas)	Seaway	19.942	775	1.456

route 3 when compared to other routes due to the cost of maritime transportation is considerably low. While sea transportation in route 2 represents %80 of the total distance, it accounts for 49% of the total costs. However, it is still so much expensive for customer requirements in the supply chain of containerized cargoes. As mentioned in future research trends, "CPEC" may offer alternative route to decrease the total transportation cost and eventually would require time and cost analyses as new route. It may also contribute to reducing gas emmisions from cargo movements compared to existing routes, due to the decline in trade distance. Development of free trade zones and industrial zones along with "CPEC" may change manufacture production lines from China, Vietname and Taiwan. In summary, the development of freight railways and dry ports in China's inland regions would affect cargo flows, environmental issues, relocation of manufacturing production line in and around strategic trade or intermodal hubs.

Some findings, such as the principle of "sea maximizing and land minimizing" in transportation of big cargoes by sea fit comfortably with logistics theory for cost minimizing, but on the margins there can be room for alternative solutions for optimizing transit times. Traditional sea transportation with containerized cargo can be logical and cheaper when it is used in long distance as intermediate leg of the transportation. Although ocean and rail freight have limitations as to the geographical locations they can deliver the goods, OBOR Iniatives optimize transit times more flexible than traditional sea transportation. However, route 1 is quicker, taking roughly half the time of the sea journey. But it is hard to think of any goods for which it would be worth paying such a hefty premium to get them to their destination in 18 days rather than 35. High-value products – expensive pharmaceuticals, perishable foods, valuable electronic components which must arrive on schedule to comply with strict just-in-time inventory management and they can be considered to be carried by route 1. Additonally, when the railway transportation scale up to the extent of huge amount of cargoes, a single large container ship can carry 10,000

40 foot container boxes between China and Europe in five weeks. To shift as many boxes by rail would require 294 of the trains that left Rotterdam two weeks ago. And to get them all to their destination within five weeks, they would have to leave at intervals of no more than 80 minutes apart constantly for 18 days.

Considering the crucial importance of transportation with less time consuming for OBOR countries has started to compete with traditional seaway transportation but its cost is still so low. OBOR Iniatives needs the optimum utilization for cost advantage rather than other alternatives. It may be useful to reinvestigate the time-cost analysis for OBOR initative when other economic corridors work completely.

REFERENCES

Banomyong, R., & Beresford, A. K. (2001). Multimodal transport: The case of Laotian garment exporters. *International Journal of Physical Distribution & Logistics Management*, *31*(9), 663–685. doi:10.1108/09600030110408161

Beresford, A., Pettit, S., & Liu, Y. (2011). Multimodal supply chains: Iron ore from Australia to China. *Supply Chain Management*, *16*(1), 32–42. doi:10.1108/13598541111103485

Beresford, A. K. (1999). Modelling freight transport costs: A case study of the UK-Greece corridor. *International Journal of Logistics: Research and Applications*, *2*(3), 229–246. doi:10.1080/13675569908901583

Beresford, A. K. C., & Dubey, R. C. (1990). Handbook on the management and operations of dry ports. UNCTAD.

Brînză, A. (2016). *How a Greek Port Became a Chinese 'Dragon Head'*. Retrieved September 21, 2018, from https://thediplomat.com/2016/04/how-a-greek-port-became-a-chinese-dragon-head/

Bulis, A., & Skapars, R. (2014). Development of "New Silk Road" Northern Branch through Seaport of Riga in Latvia. *Procedia: Social and Behavioral Sciences*, *150*, 1222–1229. doi:10.1016/j.sbspro.2014.09.138

Chen, D., & Yang, Z. (2017). Investment in container ports along the Maritime Silk Road in the context of international industry transfer: The case of the port of Colombo. *Maritime Economics & Logistics*, 1–17.

Chu, Y., & Gao, Y. (2015). China's Belt and Road Initiative: Three questions to be answered. *International Economic Review*, *2*, 90–99.

Denktas Sakar, G. (2010). *Transport mode choice decisions and multimodal transport: A triangulated approach*. Izmir: Dokuz Eylul University Publications.

Eisenhardt, K. M. (1989). Building theories from case study research. *Academy of Management Review*, *14*(4), 532–550. doi:10.5465/amr.1989.4308385

He, M.-C., Zhang, J.-B., Zhang, Y.-F., & Tian, B. (2015). Strategy of "one Belt and one Road" confronted with barriers and countermeasures. *Journal of Xinjiang Normal University*, *36*(3), 36–45.

Herrero, A. G., & Xu, J. (2017). China's Belt and Road Initiative: Can Europe Expect Trade Gains? *China & World Economy*, *25*(6), 84–99. doi:10.1111/cwe.12222

Huang, H.-T. (2015). "The Belt and Road" Initiative: The nature of interaction and the building of trust. *Tianjin Social Sciences*, *6*, 87–92.

Islam, D. M. Z., Dinwoodie, J., & Roe, M. (2005). Towards supply chain integration through multimodal transport in developing economies: The case of Bangladesh. *Maritime Economics & Logistics*, *7*(4), 382–399. doi:10.1057/palgrave.mel.9100144

Jinchen, T. (2016). *One Belt and One Road': Connecting China and the world.* Global Infrastructure Initiative website. HKTDC Research, The Belt and Road Initiative. Retrieved September 21, 2018, from http://china-trade-research.hktdc.com/business-news/article/The-Belt-and-Road-Initiative/The-Belt-and-Road-Initiative/obor/en/1/1X000000/1X0A36B7.htm

Lee, P. T. W., Hu, Z. H., Lee, S. J., Choi, K. S., & Shin, S. H. (2018). Research trends and agenda on the Belt and Road (B&R) initiative with a focus on maritime transport. *Maritime Policy & Management*, *45*(3), 282–300. doi:10.1080/03088839.2017.1400189

Li, M. (2015). *China's "one belt, one road" initiative: New round of opening up.* Academic Press.

Li, X. Y. (2015). Relations to be prioritized in China's "Belt and Road Initiative". *International Economic Review*, *1*, 54–63.

Liu, W. D. (2015). Scientific understanding of the Belt and Road Initiative of China and related research themes. *Progress in Geography*, *34*(5), 538–544.

Liu, X., Zhang, K., Chen, B., Zhou, J., & Miao, L. (2018). Analysis of logistics service supply chain for the One Belt and One Road initiative of China. *Transportation Research Part E, Logistics and Transportation Review*.

Mcgregor, R. (2006). The trillion dollar question: China is grappling with how to deploy its foreign exchange riches. *Financial Times*, 25.

Peters, B. G. (1998). *Comparative politics: Theory and methods.* NYU Press. doi:10.1007/978-1-349-26926-6

Sheu, J. B., & Kundu, T. (2017). Forecasting time-varying logistics distribution flows in the One Belt-One Road strategic context. *Transportation Research Part E, Logistics and Transportation Review*.

Su, H. (2015). A study on the transfer of China's manufacturing under "the Belt and Road" Initiative. *International Trade*, *3*, 18–21.

Timmer, H., Bussolo, M., Gould, D. M., Letelier, R. A., Nguyen, T. C., Panterov, G. L., . . . Sanchez, C. (2016). The impact of China on Europe and Central Asia. Europe and Central Asia economic update. Washington, DC: World Bank Group.

Yang, D., Pan, K., & Wang, S. (2017). On service network improvement for shipping lines under the one belt one road initiative of China. *Transportation Research Part E, Logistics and Transportation Review*.

Yang, F.-H., & Yan, C.-F. (2015). A study on the implementation mechanism of Chinese direct investment under "the Belt and Road" Initiative. *Theoretical Investigation*, *5*, 80–83.

Yin, R. K. (2009). *Case study research: Design and methods (applied social research methods)*. London: Sage.

Zeng, Q., Wang, G. W., Qu, C., & Li, K. X. (2017). Impact of the Carat Canal on the evolution of hub ports under China's Belt and Road initiative. *Transportation Research Part E, Logistics and Transportation Review*.

Chapter 8
The Analysis on Railway Transportation Competitiveness and Influencing Factors of Typical Goods in Beijing-Tianjin-Hebei Region:
A Case of Coal Transportation

Shiqi Li
Beijing Jiaotong University, China

Maoxiang Lang
Beijing Jiaotong University, China

Xueqiao Yu
Beijing Jiaotong University, China

Yanling Wang
Beijing City University, China

Xiao Yu
China Academy of Railway Sciences Corporation Limited, China

ABSTRACT

This chapter takes the Beijing-Tianjin-Hebei region as the research scope, selects coal transportation as the research object, and finds out the current situation and supply capacity of railway transportation in the context of the transportation
DOI: 10.4018/978-1-5225-8440-7.ch008

industry's active promotion of transportation structure adjustment. The chapter chooses coal as an example, bases on the different influencing factors such as transportation distance and freight rate, combines with the current situation of railway transportation, quantitatively analyzes the superior distance and competitiveness of typical cargo railway transportation, and obtains the superior distance between railway transportation and road transportation the influence degree of various influencing factors on the sharing rate of railway transportation market. Finally, the chapter puts forward corresponding measures to improve the competitiveness of railway transportation market.

INTRODUCTION

At present, China's economic development mode is shifting from scale-type and extensive growth to quality-efficiency and intensive growth, from a high-speed growth phase to a high-quality development phase. The logistics is a comprehensive service industry that runs through the first, second and third industries industry, contacts the Production and Consumption, and involves a wide range of fields, great development potential and strong driving force. The high-quality development of the logistics industry is not only an important part of high-quality economic development, it is also the inherent requirement of the logistics industry to achieve higher level and higher stage development. Transportation is the basic link and important carrier of the logistics industry, and it has a basic and main role in promoting the development of the logistics industry. In recent years, the transportation industry has made efforts to promote the transformation and upgrading of transportation services, and has achieved positive results. However, the structure of the comprehensive transportation system is irrational, the comparative advantages of various modes of transportation have not been fully utilized, the level of comprehensive transportation organization is not high, and the infrastructure is not well connected. The problems are still outstanding. It is urgent to accelerate the adjustment of transportation structure, promote the high-quality development of transportation and promote the logistics industry to reduce costs and increase efficiency. Promoting the adjustment of transportation structure is based on The Beijing-Tianjin-Hebei region and its surrounding areas, The Yangtze River Delta region, and The Fenwei plain. In order to promote the transportation of bulk cargo, the "Road Transportation to Railway Transportation, Road Transportation to Waterway Transportation" is the main direction. Implementing six major operations of the railway transportation capacity upgrading, the water transportation system upgrading, the road freight transportation management, the multimodal transport speed increase, the information resource integration, and the urban green distribution nationwide.

The coordinated development of Beijing-Tianjin-Hebei is a major national strategic move aimed at exploring the optimal allocation model of economic and industrial resources within the economic sector of international-level urban agglomerations. The Beijing-Tianjin-Hebei region has also become the main battlefield for the adjustment of transportation structure. In the process of adjusting the transportation structure and improving transportation efficiency, the Beijing-Tianjin-Hebei region should focus on deepening the structural reform of the transportation supply side, and strive to promote the road transportation and simple tax reduction, and promote the "Road Transportation to Railway Transportation" for cargo transportation. The authors will promote the market-oriented reform of railway freight transportation, give better play to the backbone role of railways in bulk material transportation and long-distance transportation, and further increase the proportion of railway freight traffic in the total volume of freight in the Beijing-Tianjin-Hebei region.

The main transportation modes of coal includes railway, highway, waterway and multimodal transportation in China. The existing coal transportation system is mainly based on railway transportation and railway-river combined transportation, supplemented by road transportation, and adopts the following strategies: Transporting Coal from West to East, Transporting Coal from North to South, and Railway-sea Combined Transportation. Due to its low cost, large capacity, good safety and fast speed, the railway is very suitable for coal transportation. In China, the coal is the main cargo of railway transportation. Waterway transportation has become another important way of coal transportation because of its large volume and low cost. It provides an alternative capacity for railway transportation and relieves the pressure of railway transportation. Road transportation has the advantages of convenience and "door-to-door" transportation. In coal transportation, it mainly undertakes short-distance transportation of coal-producing areas and surrounding provinces, or coal gathering and transportation of railway stations and ports. Although large-scale coal transportation over long distances is not an advantage of road transportation, when the railway transportation capacity is insufficient, the objective coal transportation demand will also turn to road transportation. Long-distance cross-regional road coal transportation is mainly concentrated in Shaanxi and Inner Mongolia. Some of the coal transportation distance is short, there is no railway line, thus becoming a "blind area" for railway transportation, which needs to be picked up by the road transportation to fill the gap.

For the research of the competitiveness model based on generalized cost. He Yuqiang (2006) based on the Logit model to study the passenger flow sharing rate model of high-speed passenger line, choose economic, rapidity, convenience, comfort, safety as five metrics, and establish Its generalized cost function. Luo Jun (2012) applied the utility theory to the evaluation and selection between different modes of cargo transportation. Feng Xujie (2014) added carbon emission factors to the generalized cost function model. Wang Ying (2014) established a passenger flow sharing rate calculation model based on passenger flow type and sub-train level and proposed a correction method for passenger flow sharing rate based on passenger utility value. Zhang Wei (2015) selected cost, time and reliability to construct multiple Logit models for utility function property variables. Tang Jimeng (2018) based on the truck-only transport and Rail-road Intermodal Transport's generalized cost function, established the competitiveness modell of Rail-road Intermodal Transport based on stochastic utility theory. Zhang Zheng (2018) constructed a generalized cost function based on the whole life cycle of coal circulation, and established a mathematical model that characterizes the competitiveness of coal transportation routes.

Based on the above background, this paper takes the Beijing-Tianjin-Hebei region as the main research area, and shifts the road transportation volume to the railway transportation as the main research target in the main direction of transportation structure adjustment. Taking coal transportation as an example, the current situation of railway transportation in Beijing-Tianjin-Hebei region is analyzed. To study the railway transportation competitiveness and its influencing factors of typical goods in the Beijing-Tianjin-Hebei region. The rest of the paper is as follows. The second part is based on the generalized cost construction market share rate logit model to describe the competitiveness model of railway coal transportation and road coal transportation. The third part analyzes the competitiveness of railway coal transportation and calibrates the model parameters. The fourth part analyzes the structure of the competitiveness model and different influencing factors. Finally, some countermeasures and suggestions are proposed around the further development of railway coal transportation in the Beijing-Tianjin-Hebei region.

CONSTRUCTION OF RAILWAY COAL TRANSPORTATION COMPETITIVENESS MODEL BASED ON GENERALIZED COST

The economic, timeliness and environmental protection of different modes of transportation are the main reasons that affect their competitiveness. In terms of the choice of freight mode, the generalized cost is a perception of the "comprehensive cost" paid by the shipper to the transportation mode chosen by him. Assuming that the shipper is completely rational, the shipper will choose the transportation mode with the least general cost among all the alternative modes of transport.

The calculation of generalized expenses mainly includes two algorithms of addition and multiplication. If the effects of each factor are independent of each other, the addition factors can be used to combine the influencing factors. If the influence of a factor can be applied to other factors, the multiplication rule can be used to solve it. The generalized cost function of railway coal transportation and road coal transportation is composed of economic, timeliness and environmental protection. It analyzes the cost, time spent and carbon emissions generated in all aspects of the transportation process. Through time value, time is converted into time cost, and carbon emission is converted into one part of generalized cost through the social cost of carbon emission. Because the three components are independent of each other, each has a certain impact on the competitiveness of transportation mode. Therefore, this paper constructs a generalized cost function using additive operation to solve the problem, and constructs a generalized cost function for railway coal transportation and road coal transportation as follows:

$$GTC_m = C_m + VOT \cdot T_m + P_{carbon} \cdot E_m \quad m = 1,2 \tag{1}$$

In the formula, m=1 stands for rail transportation, m=2 stands for road transportation:

- GTC_m stands for generalized expenses;
- C_m stands for the total cost of transportation unit weight of coal;
- T_m stands for the time spent in the transportation process, in days;
- E_m stands for the carbon emissions generated by the transportation unit's volume of coal, in • $kgCO_2$;
- VOT stands for the time cost of unit weight of coal for 1 day;
- P_{carbon} stands for the unit cost of carbon emissions, in Yuan/$kgCO_2$.

For the construction of the competitiveness model of railway coal transportation and road coal transportation, the classical model of calculating the sharing rate is adopted—Discrete selection model. The theory of stochastic utility is the theoretical basis of the discrete selection model, which assumes that decision makers always choose the most effective solution when faced with multiple alternatives. The shipper has a perceptual utility on the railway coal transportation and road coal transportation, which is random utility:

$$U_m = V_m + \varepsilon_m \tag{2}$$

The random utility U_m represents the revenue obtained by the shipper in selecting the transportation mode m, Including the identification utility consisting of observable influencing factors V_m and unobservable influencing factors ε_m. The determined utility V_m for the transportation mode m can be expressed by the inverse of its generalized cost:

$$V_m = -GTC_m \tag{3}$$

Therefore, the shipper's perceived utility is:

$$U_m = -GTC_m + \varepsilon_m \tag{4}$$

According to the theory of random utility, the shipper chooses the transportation mode with the greatest perceived utility. Because the perceived utility is random, the shipper's choice of the transportation mode is actually a probability problem, namely:

$$P_m = \Pr(U_m \geq U_n, m \neq n) \tag{5}$$

The P_m indicates the probability that the shipper chooses the transportation mode m and has the following properties:

$$0 \leq P_m \leq 1, \sum P_m = 1 \tag{6}$$

Different discrete selection models can be obtained by assuming that the random item ε_m obeys different distribution hypotheses, such as Multinomial Logit Model(MNL), Nested Logit Model(NL), Generalized Extreme Value Model(GEV), Mixed Logit Model(MXL), Multinomial Probit Model(MNP). This paper assumes that the random items ε_m are independent of each other and obey the Gumbel distribution. Then the selection probability P_m of the transportation mode m can be calculated using the commonly used and fairly mature MNL model:

$$P_m = \frac{\exp(-\theta GTC_m)}{\sum \exp(-\theta GTC_m)} \tag{7}$$

θ stands for the parameters that needs to be determined, Its value is related to the variance of the ε_m, θ can be seen as a measure of the shipper's familiarity with the entire network.

In the model, the selection probability of the transportation mode m is determined by the absolute difference in utility between transportation modes. When the generalized cost value is too large, some unreasonable results will be generated. Therefore, this paper uses the relative utility to calculate the selection probability of the transportation mode. Improve the model to:

$$P_m = \frac{\exp(-\theta GTC_m / GTC_{\min})}{\sum \exp(-\theta GTC_m / GTC_{\min})} \tag{8}$$

In the formula, $GTC_{\min}$ indicates that the generalized cost is relatively small among the railway coal transportation and road coal transportation.

THE CASE ANALYSIS ON RAILWAY COAL TRANSPORTATION COMPETITIVENESS IN BEIJING-TIANJIN-HEBEI REGION

Coal belongs to the typical bulk cargo and is an important part of China's transportation market. At present, there are two main types of coal shipments in China. One is to transport by railway after short-distance transportation to a dedicated line (or railway station). Another is to directly access the dedicated line at the coal loading point and transports it to the main line by dedicated line. The way the coal is transported from the coal mine pit to the railway line is different. As the Beijing-Tianjin-Hebei region is China's main coal use zone, coal is transported from the "The Sanxi Area" regions through the "Transporting Coal from West to East" . It is also the main issuing place of "Transporting Coal from North to South". Therefore, considering that coal transportation is mostly issued by major coal-producing bases and transports to major ports or large power plants, steel plants and other end points, there are many coal- dedicated lines connecting to the land. The coal transportation studies is mainly based on the second type of shipping in this paper.

Determination of Parameter Values

Railway Transportation Costs

The transportation cost is the main component of the cost of railway coal transportation. The main line transportation price between the railway station and the station is mainly based on the base price of the first part and the base price of the second part, plus the railway construction fund and other expenses. The cost is relatively stable and is mainly related to the railway transportation distance. At present, the base price of the first part of the railway coal transportation is 16.3 yuan/t, the base price of the second part is 0.098 yuan/tkm.The railway construction fund rate is 0.033 yuan/tkm. The railway electrification surcharge decreased from 0.012 yuan/tkm to 0.007 yuan/tkm on June 1, 2017.

The Dedicated Line Usage Fees

The dedicated line that liked the "capillary" is the important supplement to the railway transportation. Due to restrictions on transportation volume and funds, some enterprises are unable to build dedicated lines themselves, and they need to use dedicated lines of other enterprises. Therefore, they need to pay dedicated line usage fees. Some enterprises have their own dedicated lines. Considering the use of dedicated lines to generate depreciation, maintenance, dust suppression, etc., it is also necessary to calculate the dedicated line usage fees. According to the actual research results, the dedicated line usage fees is 25.87 yuan/t.

Road Transportation Costs

Since the rectification of road transportation overload on September 21, 2016, the number of road transportation vehicles has been insufficient, and it is difficult to meet the demand for coal transportation, and transportation costs have risen rapidly. According to the trend of China's coal road freight rate, the cost of road coal transportation in 2018 is long-distance 0.3 yuan/tkm (400 km or more), medium-distance 0.49 yuan/tkm (100-400 km) and short-distance 0.71 yuan/tkm (0- 100 km). Since the coal transportation studied in this paper is mainly transported from the "Shanxi, Shaanxi and West of Inner Mongolia" to the Beijing-Tianjin-Hebei region, most of them are long-distance transportation, so the road freight rate is 0.3 yuan/tkm.

Other Relevant Parameters of Coal Transportation

- Dedicated line pick-up fare: 9 yuan/car km;
- Average line distance of dedicated lines: 4 km at each end;
- Railway loading and unloading operation fees: 11.2 yuan/t;
- The static load of the coal-traffic railway wagon: 70 tons/car;
- Road transportation loading and unloading fees: 6.9 yuan/t;
- Unit weight coal value: 640 yuan/t;
- Daily interest rate: 0.02%;
- The carbon emissions per unit of freight turnover of diesel locomotives: 9.07g/tkm.

The carbon emissions per unit of freight turnover of electric locomotive: 11.37g/tkm; (The carbon emission intensity of cargo trains drawn by electric locomotives is larger than that of diesel locomotives. The main reason is that the proportion of coal power in China's power production is quite large, resulting in a higher carbon emission coefficient of China's power life cycle. It is more than twice the European average.)

- The carbon emissions per unit of freight turnover of railway transportation: 11.24g/tkm;
- The carbon emissions per unit of freight turnover of road transportation: 48g/tkm;
- The carbon emission cost: 0.000166 yuan/g.

Parameter Determination

Taking the trunk transportation distance of 600km, the dedicated line distance of 8km, and the coal transportation capacity of 70 tons as the example, the example calculation can be used to obtain the general cost of 70t coal for railway and road transportation as follows:

$$GTC_1 = C_1 + VOT \times T_1 + P_{carbon} \times E_1 = 10384.4 + 9 \times 4 + 0.166 \times 472.1 = 10498.8 yuan$$

$$GTC_2 = C_2 + VOT \times T_2 + P_{carbon} \times E_2 = 13566 + 9 \times 1 + 0.166 \times 2016 = 13909.7 yuan$$

According to the survey, the number of coal transported by Shanxi Province to other provinces accounted for 73%, and the amount of coal transported by road transportation to other provinces accounted for 11% in 2017. The ratio of railway transportation to road transportation is 87%: 13%.

The above calculation result is brought into the Formula (8), thereby calculating the parameter θ of 5.85.

Substituting the parameter θ=5.85 into the Formula (8), the distribution rate of the railway transportation and road transportation market are both 50% when the trunk line distance is 322km, which means that road transportation has an advantage in the range of [0,322] km, and when the trunk line distance is more than 322km, the railway transportation advantage becomes more and more obvious with the increase of the transportation distance.

THE ANALYSIS ON COMPETITIVE MODEL STRUCTURE AND INFLUENCING FACTORS OF RAILWAY COAL TRANSPORTATION IN BEIJING-TIANJIN-HEBEI REGION

The Analysis on Competitive Model Structure

Due to the combination of different trunk transport distances and dedicated line distances, the general cost of road transportation and railway transportation will vary greatly. Therefore, based on the examples constructed by the actual survey and the parameters given in 3.1, this section analyzes the changes in the generalized costs of railway transportation and road transportation at the combination of different trunk transport distances and dedicated line pick-up distances.

The generalized cost components of railway coal transportation and road coal transportation are numbered. The generalized cost of railway transportation includes 5 parts, and the generalized cost of road transportation includes 4 parts, as shown in Table 1.

With a trunk transportation distance of 600km and a dedicated line distance of 8km as the benchmark, in the case of a combination of different trunk transportation distances (300km, 400km, 500km, 600km, 700km) and dedicated line distances (4km, 8km, 12km, 20km), Calculate the proportion of the various components of the generalized cost of railway coal transportation and road coal transportation. The proportion of the generalized cost of the road at the combination of different transportation distances is shown in Figure 1.

As can be seen from Figure 1, the generalized cost of road transportation is mainly composed of road transportation costs, and with the increase of transport distance, the proportion of this part has increased, the transport distance is 300km, 400km, 500km, 600km, 700km respectively. At that time, their proportions were

Table 1. The generalized cost of railway transportation and road transportation

Number	The Generalized Cost of Road Transportation	Number	The Generalized Cost of Railway Transportation
1	Road transportation loading and unloading fees	1	Railway transportation loading and unloading fees
2	Road transportation cost	2	Railway dedicated line operation fees
3	Road transportation time cost	3	Railway transportation costs
4	Road transportation carbon emission social cost	4	Railway transportation time cost
		5	Railway transportation carbon emission social cost

Figure 1. The proportion of the various components of the generalized cost of road coal transportation

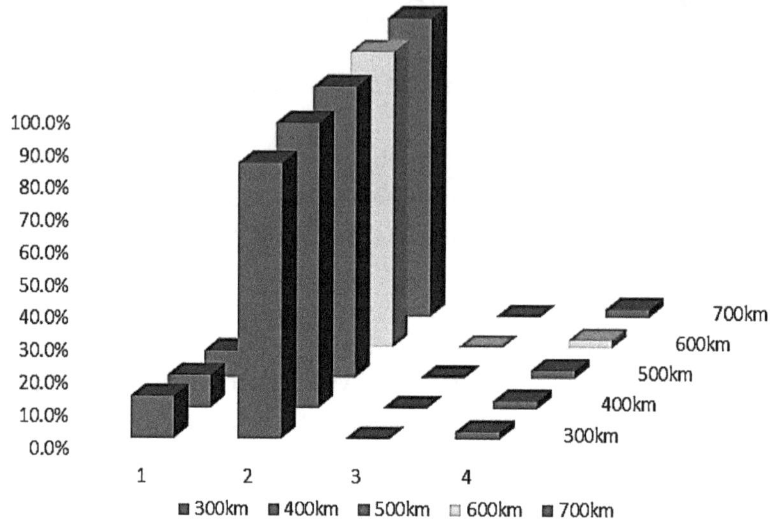

84.7%, 87.5%, 89.3%, 90.6%, and 91.5%, respectively. Since the Road transportation loading and unloading fees are independent of the transportation distance, the costs incurred are unchanged, and as the transportation distance increases, the proportion is gradually reduced. Since the transportation time is within one day, the proportion of this part is consistent with the road transportation loading and unloading fees. Although the social cost of road transportation carbon emissions has increased with the increase of transportation distance, its proportion in generalized expenses is relatively small, about 2.4%.

Therefore, road transportation costs account for the vast majority of generalized expenses, and increase with the increase of transportation distance, while the proportion of the total of the road transportation time cost, the road transportation carbon emission social cost and road transportation loading and unloading fees are small, indicating the road transportation is a costly, time-efficient means of transportation.

Similarly, when the trunk transportation distances are respectively 300km, 400km, 500km, 600km, 700km, and the dedicated line distances are 4km, 8km, 12km, 20km, the authors calculate the combination of different trunk transportation distances and dedicated line distances is calculated. The proportion of the generalized cost of railway coal transportation are shown in Figure 2.

It can be seen from Figure 2 that at the combination of different trunk transportation distances and dedicated line distances, the proportion of each component of the

Figure 2. The proportion of the various components of the generalized cost of railway coal transportation

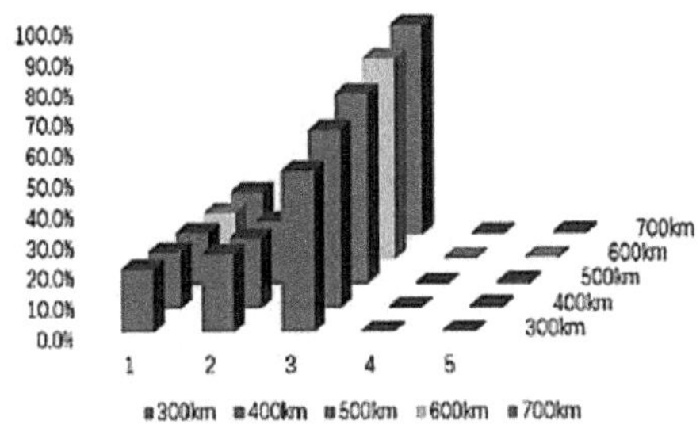

a the dedicated line distance is 4km

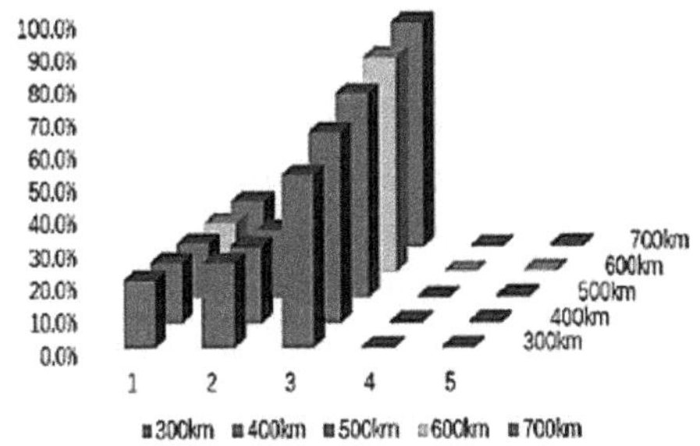

b the dedicated line distance is 8km

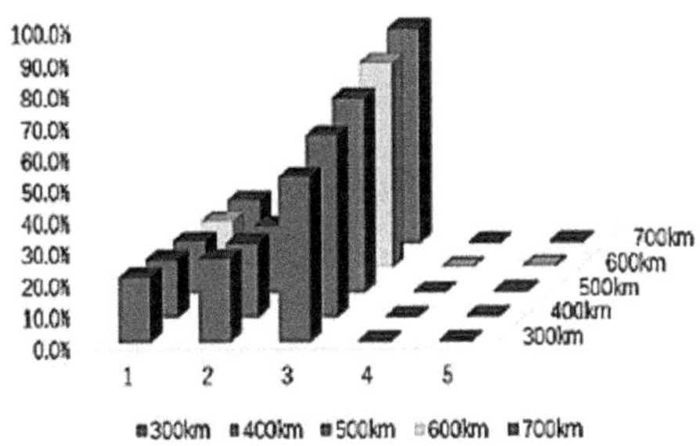

c the dedicated line distance is 12km

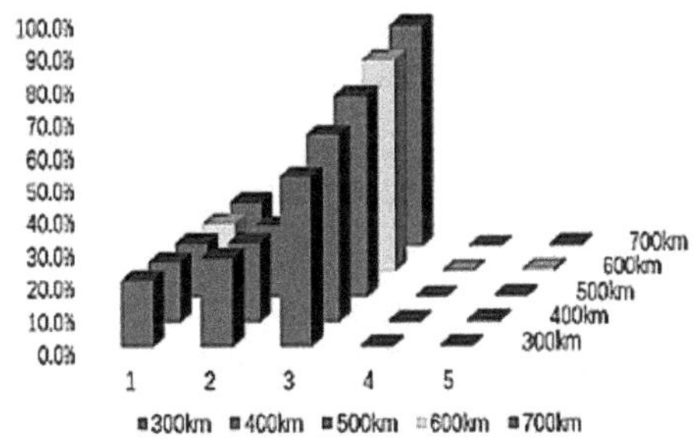

d the dedicated line distance is 20km

generalized cost of railway transportation has a certain difference. The higher proportion of the generalized cost of railway transportation is mainly the railway transportation cost and the dedicated line operation fees. The former increases with the increase of the transportation distance, and the latter decreases with the increase of the transportation distance, for example, at the dedicated line distance is 8km, when the trunk transportation distance are 300km, 400km, 500km, 600km, 700km respectively, the proportion of the dedicated line operation fees are 26.0%, 23.0%, 20.7%, 18.8%, 17.2%, and the proportion of railway transportation costs are 52.5%, 57.7%, 61.9%, 65.2%, 68.0%, and the other similar line distances have the similar trends.

In addition, as the distance of dedicated lines increases, the proportion of dedicated line operation fees increases gradually, while the proportion of railway transportation costs decreases. For example, when the trunk transportation distance is 600km, the distance of dedicated lines increases (4km, 8km, 12km and 20km), the proportion of dedicated line operation costs are 18.5%, 18.8%, 19.1% and 19.6%, respectively.

The proportion of railway transportation costs are 65.4%, 65.2%, 65.0% and 64.5%, and the other similar line distances have the similar trends.

At the combination of different trunk transportation distances and dedicated line distances, the proportion of the two main types of railway transportation are between 78.4% and 85.3%, compared with 84.7%--91.5% of the proportion of road transportation costs. The difference between the two is about 6%.

Although the railway transportation time cost is not very large, compared with the road transportation time cost, the railway transportation time cost is about three times that of road transportation time cost. In terms of carbon emission social costs, the railway transportation carbon emission social cost accounts for between 0.5% and 0.8%, while the road transportation carbon emission social cost is relatively large, accounting for between 2.2% and 2.4%.

Analysis of Influencing Factors of Railway Coal Transportation

Since the generalized cost is directly related to competitiveness, therefore, according to the analysis of the proportion of the generalized expenses of railway coal transportation and road coal transportation in Section 4.1, the sensitivity analysis is carried out by selecting the influencing factors with a large proportion, including road freight rate, railway freight rate, dedicated line operation fees and railway transportation loading and unloading fees.

According to the analysis of Section 4.1, at the combination of different trunk transportation distances and dedicated line distances, the proportion of each component of generalized expenses is different. As a result, the impact of various influencing factors on the competitiveness of railway coal transportation may be different. Therefore, when analyzing the sensitivity of each factor, the dedicated line distances are taken as 4km, 8km, 12km, and 20km, and the trunk transportation distance varies between [300, 1000]km, and the step length is 100km.

Road Freight Rate

The other parameters are fixed, and the road freight rate are in the interval [0.26, 0.34], and the step length is 0.02, unit: yuan/tkm. At the combination of different trunk transportation distances and dedicated line distances, the sharing rate calculation formula is used to analyze the impact of the road freight rate changes on railway coal transportation competitiveness. The results are shown in Figure 3.

As can be seen from Figure 3.

At the distance of each dedicated line, when the road freight rate takes different values, the share of the railway transportation market has maintained the same growth with the increase of the transportation distance. It has a similar phenomenon when

Figure 3. The impact of the road freight rate changes on railway coal transportation competitiveness

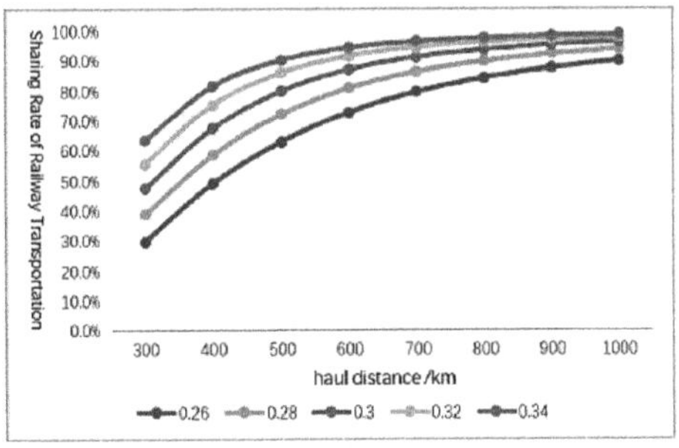

a The dedicated line distance is 4km

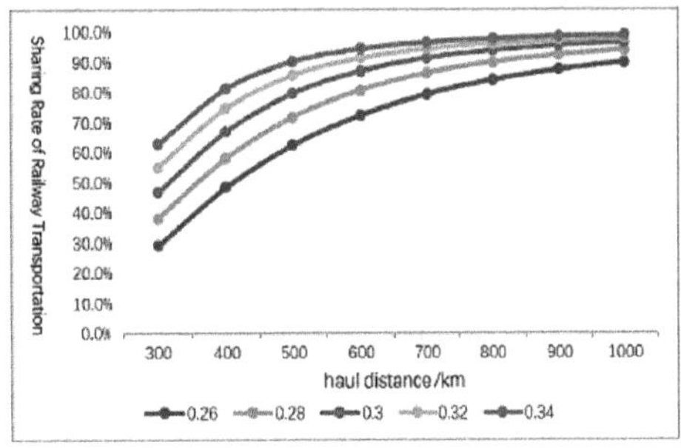

b The dedicated line distance is 8km

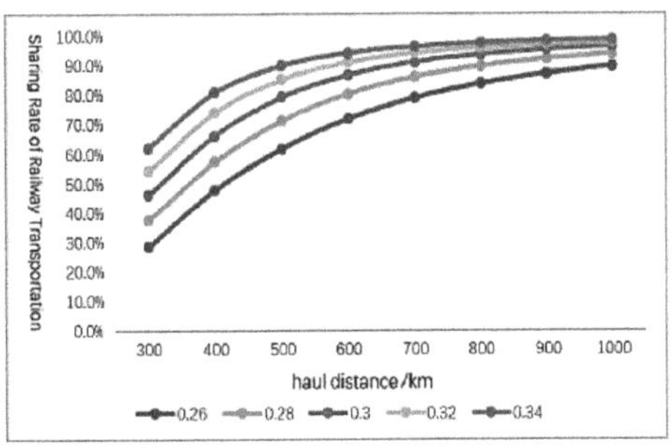

c The dedicated line distance is 12km

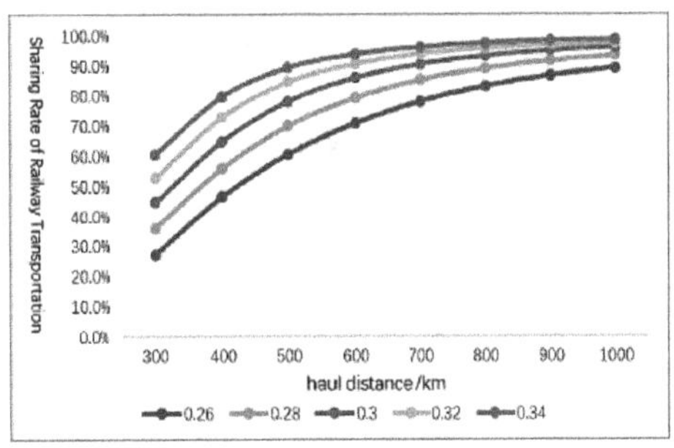

d The dedicated line distance is 20km

the sensitivity analysis of other influencing factors is carried out. Which shows that with the increase of the transportation distance, the advantage of low freight rate of railway transportation becomes more and more obvious. It can make up for the disadvantages of the high loading and unloading operations fees and the long railway transportation time. Thereby increasing the competitiveness of railway coal transportation.

At the distance of 600km, when the road freight rate increases from 0.26 yuan/tkm to 0.34 yuan/tkm, the sharing rate of the railway transportation market corresponding to the dedicated line distances of 4km, 8km, 12km and 20km are 21.7%, 22.1%, 22.4%, 23.0% respectively. It can be seen that the greater the distance of the dedicated line, the more obvious the effect of the increase in the road freight rate on the competitiveness of railway transportation.

When the current road freight rate is 0.3 yuan/tkm, it will have a greater impact on the railway transportation market share rate if it rises by 0.02 yuan/tkm and decreases by 0.02 yuan/tkm. If the road freight rate decreases by 0.02 yuan/tkm (0.28 yuan/tkm), when the transport distance is 600 km, the railway transportation market share rate is 80.7% (the dedicated line distance is 8km, as shown in Figure 3b). If the increase is 0.02 yuan/tkm, the same trunk transportation distance and dedicated line distance, the railway transportation market share rate reaches 91.4%. However, the road freight rate continues to rise, and the effect of improving the competitiveness of the railway transportation market has been weakened. If the road freight rate increases from 0.32 yuan/tkm to 0.34 yuan/tkm, the railway transportation market share rate only increases by 3%.

It can be seen that the small fluctuations in the road freight rate will have a greater impact on the sharing rate of the railway transportation market. Especially when the transportation distance is short, the effect is more obvious. Therefore, in the context of "Road Transportation to Railway Transportation", with the implementation of road rectification overload and the rise of oil and labor costs, not only can the road freight market return to a normal and orderly state, but also a greater role in promoting the development of railway coal transportation.

Railway Freight Rate

The railway freight rate mainly affects the railway transportation cost part of the railway generalized cost. This part mainly analyzes the influence of the base price of the second part of the railway freight rate and the electrification surcharge on the railway coal transportation competitiveness.

1. The base price of the second part of the railway freight rate.

The other parameters are fixed, and the base price of the second part of the railway freight rate are in the interval [0.049,0.123], and the step length is 0.0247, unit: yuan/tkm. At the combination of different trunk transportation distances and dedicated line distances, the sharing rate calculation formula is used to analyze the impact of the base price of the second part of the railway freight rate changes on railway coal transportation competitiveness. The results are shown in Figure 4.

As can be seen from Figure 4.

When the base price of the second part of the railway freight rate are between 0.049 yuan/tkm and 0.123 yuan/tkm, the corresponding railway transportation market share rate curve is surrounded by a reverse "horn" pattern. That is, as the distance increases, the decline in the base price of the second part of the railway freight rate has gradually weakened the effect of increasing the share of the railway transportation market. When the dedicated line distance is 8km (as shown in Figure 4.4b), if the base price of the second part of the railway freight rate drops from 0.123 yuan/tkm to 0.049 yuan/tkm, at the trunk line distance of 300km, 600km and 900km, corresponding the share of the railway transportation market increases by 31.6%, 21.0% and 10.5% respectively. The current base price of the second part of

Figure 4. The base price of the second part of the railway freight rate changes on railway coal transportation competitiveness

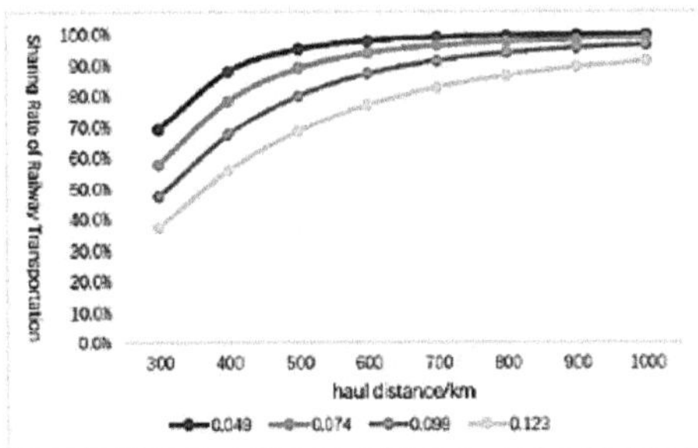

a The dedicated line distance is 4km

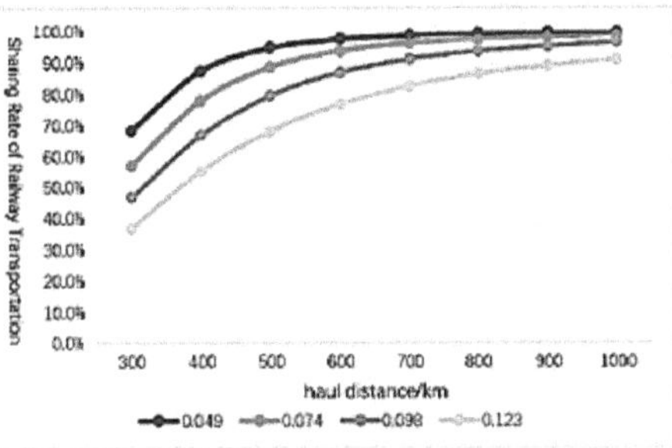

b The dedicated line distance is 8km

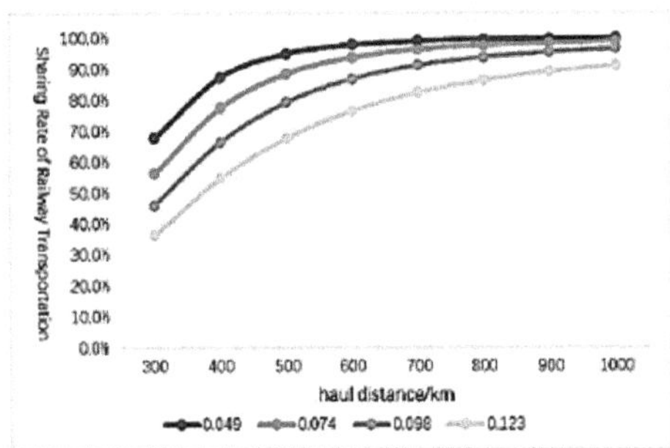

c The dedicated line distance is 12km

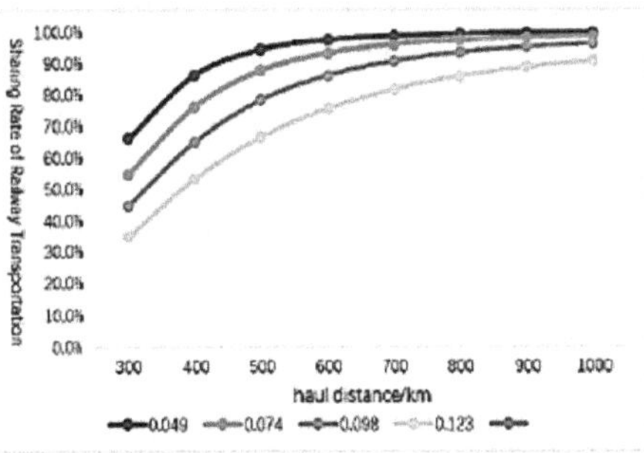

d The dedicated line distance is 20km

the railway freight rate is 0.098 yuan/tkm, and if it is reduced by 50% (0.049 yuan/tkm), when the dedicated line distance is 8km, at the 300km, 600km and 900km mainline transport distances, the corresponding railway transportation market share ratio increases by 21.6%, 10.8% and 4.2% respectively.

It can be seen from the above analysis that when the transportation distance is short, the change of railway freight rate has a great influence on the sharing rate of the railway transportation market. When the transportation distance is long, the impact of changes in railway freight rates on the sharing rate of the railway transportation market has been reduced. Therefore, railway transportation enterprises can change the current single freight rate strategy and formulate a new segmented freight rate strategy. For short-distance transportation, the freight rate should be appropriately reduced in order to expand its market share rate and increase transportation revenue. For long-distance transportation, it has already occupied an absolute advantage in market share, and no further price cuts can be made.

2. The electrification surcharge.

The other parameters are fixed, and the electrification surcharges are 0 yuan/t·km, 0.007 yuan/t·km and 0.012 yuan/t·km. At the condition that the dedicated line distance is 8km, the sharing rate calculation formula is used to analyze the impact of the electrification surcharge changes on railway coal transportation competitiveness. The result is shown in Figure 5.

According to the Notice of the National Development and Reform Commission on Abolishing the Repayment of Electricity Prices for Electrified Railway Power Supply Projects (Development and Reform Price [2017] No. 1005), China Railway Corporation research decision, since June 1, 2017, the railway electrification surcharge has been reduced. The electrification surcharge for the approval of the national railway electrification section of the national railway unified tariff will be lowered. The electrification surcharge for railway vehicle transportation is reduced by 0.005 yuan/ton. At the trunk transportation distances of 300km, 600km and 1000km, compared to before the downgrade, the share of the railway coal transportation market increased by 1.4%, 1.2% and 0.5% respectively. If the electrification surcharge is cancelled, the share of the railway coal transportation market will increase by 2.0%, 1.6% and 0.7% compared with the current level. It can be seen that the electrification surcharge has a relatively small impact on the market share rate in long-distance transportation, but in the short-distance transportation market, reducing the electrification surcharge is conducive to improving the market competitiveness of railway transportation.

Figure 5. The electrification surcharge changes on railway coal transportation competitiveness

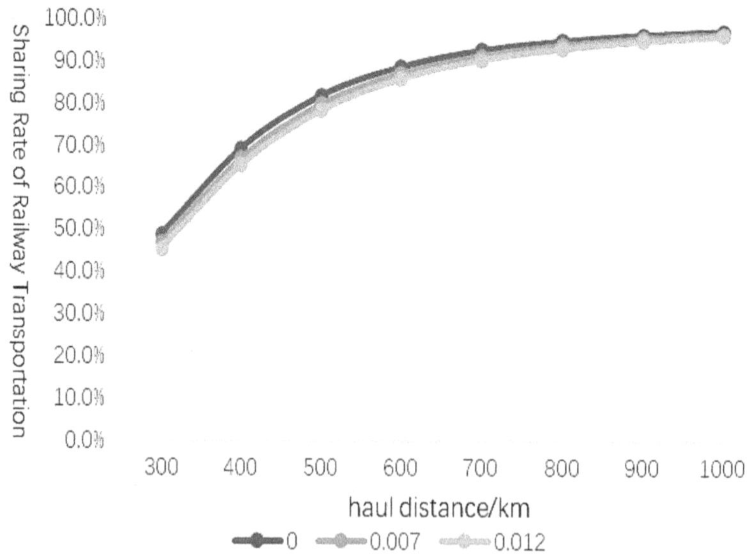

Figure 6. The dedicated line operation fees and railway transportation loading and unloading fees changes on railway coal transportation competitiveness

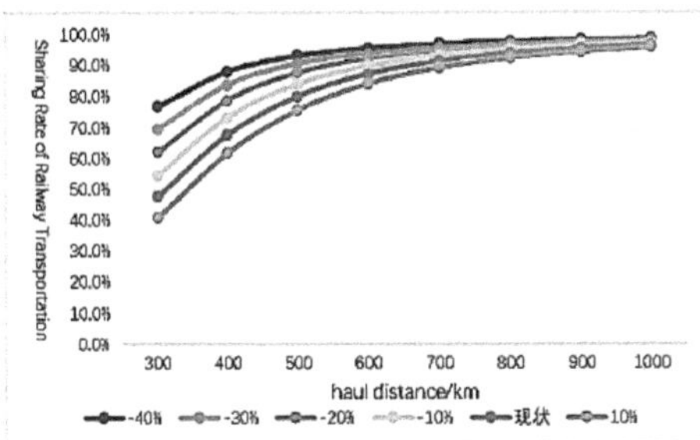

a The dedicated line distance is 4km

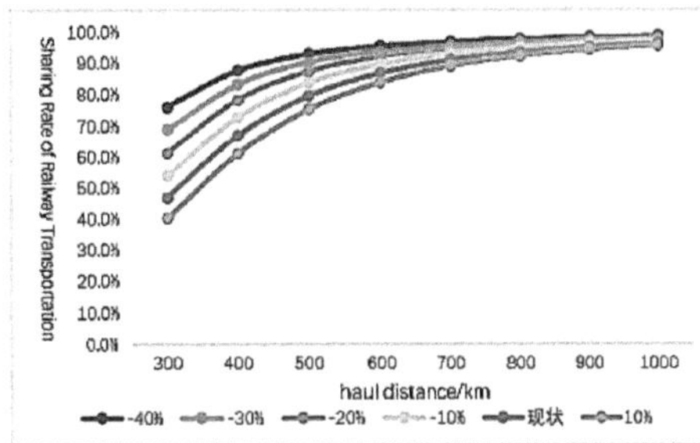

b The dedicated line distance is 8km

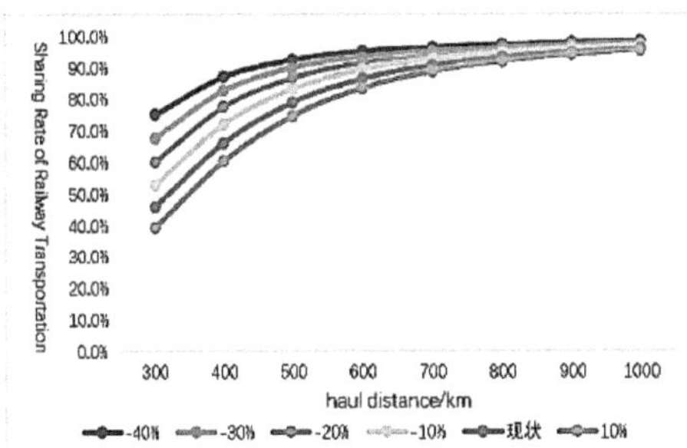

c The dedicated line distance is 12km

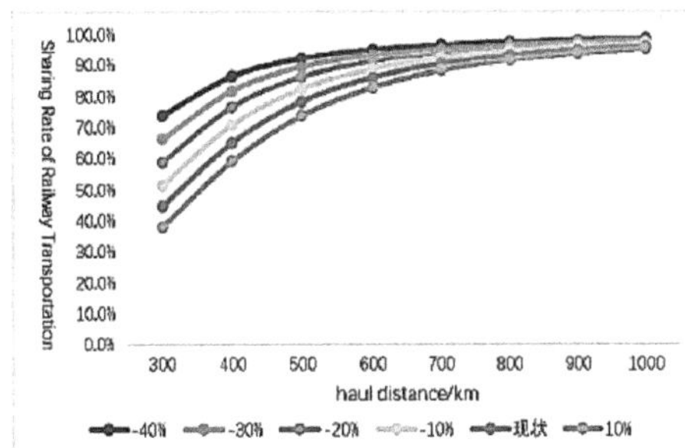

d The dedicated line distance is 20km

Dedicated Line Operation Fees and Railway Transportation Loading and Unloading Fees

In the baseline scenario, the dedicated line operation fees and railway transportation loading and unloading fees is 3468.9 yuan. The other parameters are fixed, the dedicated line operation fees and railway transportation loading and unloading fees are in the interval [2081.3,3815.8]yuan, and the step length is 10% of the dedicated line operation fees and railway transportation loading and unloading fees. At the combination of different trunk transportation distances and dedicated line distances, the sharing rate calculation formula is used to analyze the impact of the dedicated line operation fees and railway transportation loading and unloading fees changes on railway coal transportation competitiveness. The results are shown in Figure 6.

As can be seen from Figure 6.

Since the dedicated line operation fees and railway transportation loading and unloading fees do not change with the change of the dedicated line distance and the trunk transportation distance, it is a relatively fixed expenditure. Therefore, as the distance of the dedicated line increases and the distance of the trunk line increases, the total cost has increased, while the proportion of dedicated line operation fees and railway transportation loading and unloading fees has gradually decreased. Therefore, with the increase of dedicated line distance and trunk transportation distance, the railway transportation market share rate is gradually increasing.

At present, the proportion of special line operation fees and railway transportation loading and unloading fees in total expenses is second only to the main line transportation costs. Therefore, with the reduction of dedicated line operation fees and railway transportation loading and unloading fees, the market share of railway transportation will increase. With the increase of the dedicated line distance and the trunk transportation distance, there is a "end gathering" phenomenon in the railway transportation sharing rate curve corresponding to the operation cost of different special lines and the railway loading and unloading fee. When the dedicated line distance is 8km, if the dedicated line operation fees and railway transportation loading and unloading fees decrease from 3815.8 yuan (up 10%) to 2081.3 yuan (down 40%), when the trunk transportation distance are 400km, 600km, 800km and 1000km respectively. The corresponding railway transportation sharing rates increases by 26.7%, 11.7%, 5.5% and 2.9% respectively.

Therefore, at this stage, the relevant operational links of railway coal transportation are optimized, and the related operating costs are lowered, which has a positive effect on improving the competitiveness of railway coal transportation.

CONCLUSION

Taking coal transportation as an example, this paper analyzes the competitiveness of railway transportation market and its influencing factors of typical goods in Beijing-Tianjin-Hebei region. The main findings are as follows.

In the whole process of railway coal transportation, railway transportation costs and dedicated line operation fees are the main components of the generalized cost of railway transportation. The former increases with the increase of the transportation distance, while the latter decreases with the increase of the transportation distance. In addition, with the increase of the distance of dedicated lines, the proportion of dedicated line operation costs has gradually increased, while the proportion of railway trunk line transportation costs has decreased. Although the transportation time cost is not very large, compared with road transportation, the railway transportation time cost accounts for about three times the road transportation time cost. In terms of the social cost of carbon emissions, the railway transportation is about a quarter of the road transportation.

It is understood that when it is about 322 kilometers, the road transportation market share rate and the railway transportation market share rate are both 50% by calculating. The advantage of the railway transportation is gradually manifested above 322km. And with the increase of the distance, the advantage is more and more significant.

Through the analysis on the competitiveness of railway coal transportation, the factors such as road freight rate, railway freight rate, dedicated line operation fees and railway transportation loading and unloading fees have a great influence on the market share of railway transportation. The fluctuation of the road transportation rate level will have a greater impact on the railway transportation market share rate, especially when the transportation distance is short, the impact effect is more obvious. When the transportation distance is short, the change of railway freight rate has a greater impact on the sharing rate of the railway transportation market. When the transport distance is long, the impact of changes in railway freight rates on the share of the railway transportation market has decreased. At this stage, the relevant operation links of railway coal transportation are optimized, and the related operating costs are lowered, which has a positive effect on improving the competitiveness of railway coal transportation.

ACKNOWLEDGMENT

Author Contributions: Writing: S.L. and M.L.; Providing case and idea: X.Y., Y.W., and X.Y..

Funding: This research was supported by National Key R&D Program of China (2018YFB1201402) and National Key R&D Program of China (2016YFE0201700).

Conflicts of Interest: The authors declare no conflict of interest.

REFERENCES

Feng, X. (2014). *Modeling Life Cycle Energy Consumption and Greenhouse Gas Emissions for High-speed Railways*. Beijing, China: Beijing Jiaotong University.

He, Mao, Chen, & Yang. (2006). The Mode Share Model of the High-speed Passenger Railway Line and Its Application. *Journal of the China Railway Society, 2006*(3), 18-21.

Jun, L. (2012). *Research on Model of Freight Transportation Mode Choice Based on Behaviour Analysis*. Wuhan, China: Wuhan University of Technology.

Tang, J. (2018). *Competitiveness of Container Rail-road Intermodal Transport and Its Improving Strategies in China*. Beijing, China: Beijing Jiaotong University.

Wei, Z., Jian, W., & Zhu, L. (2015). Reliability Analysis of Railway Container Transport Time. *Journal of the China Railway Society*, *37*(11), 10–15.

Ying, W. A. N. G., Dan, H. A. O., Hai-ying, L. I., Xiao-jie, Y. A. N., & Huan-dong, W. A. N. G. (2014). Research on Share Rate of Passenger Flow in Railway Transportation Corridor Based on Matching between Supply and Demand. *Journal of the China Railway Society*, *36*(12), 1–5.

Zheng, Z. (2018). *Empirical Study of Coal Transportation on Multimodal Transport Network in China*. Beijing, China: Beijing Jiaotong University.

KEY TERMS AND DEFINITIONS

Beijing-Tianjin-Hebei Region: The "capital economic circle" of China, including Beijing, Tianjin, and Hebei Province.

Fenwei Plain: The Fenhe Plain, Weihe Plain, and their surroundings in the Yellow River Basin.

Road Transportation to Railway Transportation: Adjusting the transportation structure, converting some of the goods originally transported by road into railway transport.

Road Transportation to Waterway Transportation: Adjusting the transportation structure, converting some of the goods originally transported by road into waterway transport.

Sanxi Area: Including Shanxi Province, Shaanxi Province, and Western Inner Mongolia.

Transporting Coal From North to South: Transporting abundant coal resources in the North Region to the South Region where coal resources are scarce.

Transporting Coal From West to East: Transporting abundant coal resources in the Western Region to the Eastern Region where coal resources are scarce.

Yangtze River Delta Region: Including Shanghai, Jiangsu Province, and Zhejiang Province.

Chapter 9
The Development of Electrolytic Aluminum Industry and the Belt and Road Strategy:
A Collaborative Innovation Perspective

Ping Zhou
City University of Macau, China

Gexin Han
City University of Macau, China

Xinyao Li
Northeast Electric Power University, China

ABSTRACT

Innovation ability is the key to enterprise development. China's electrolytic aluminum enterprises have maintained a high growth rate for many years and have become one of the industries with the highest social contribution rate in the non-ferrous metal industry. However, a prominent problem in the development process of the industry is to put less emphasis on innovation and investment. Excessive production capacity due to blind investment has become a common disease of enterprises, which has seriously affected their performance. This chapter tries to explore cooperative motivation, innovation, and development of the electrolytic aluminum enterprise. The aim is for the enterprise to find source sex power basis, combined with the strategy of "area," all the way to the electrolytic aluminum enterprise value influence, understand all kinds of system to the importance of the synergy of electrolytic aluminum enterprises, in order to further promote collaborative innovation measures to provide adequate basis.

DOI: 10.4018/978-1-5225-8440-7.ch009

BACKGROUND

As one of the major non-ferrous metal mineral resources, aluminum is an indispensable and important element in modern industry, agriculture, national defense, and the development of science and technology. It has been widely used in many fields, such as architecture, transportation, electricity, and packaging, and is a basic raw material that cannot be replaced by modern high-tech development. As the basic raw material of industrial development, aluminum, which is one of the industries with the highest social contribution rate in China's non-ferrous metal industry, does not pollute the environment during use and is highly sought after for its high recycling and utilization. In China, aluminum has become the second largest metal material after steel, and the electrolytic aluminum industry has maintained rapid growth. Among all non-ferrous metal varieties, the growth rate has been the fastest for many years.

In the early 20th century, as a result of the guidance of China's industrial policy and the encouraging guidance of macro-control policy, China's aluminum industry has achieved very rapid development and made relatively important contributions to the economic development of the motherland. However, in recent years, the reckless activity of investors has led to a remarkable acceleration of the development of China's electrolytic aluminum projects, which eventually led to the extreme excess of China's electrolytic aluminum production capacity. The phenomenon of oversupply has become increasingly serious, and it is difficult to reverse in the short term. In addition, still a few enterprises have used to build first, cause already become fact hind to declare to examine and approve to wait for a method to build or expand electrolytic aluminum project. Since competition in the electrolytic aluminum industry is more intense, the market price has flagged for a long time. Consequently, the contradiction, such as a gradually enlarged loss area of the enterprise, is highlighted more and more. Since 2003, the Chinese government has stepped up its regulation of the electrolytic aluminum industry, hoping to slow down the biggest problem in the industry: excess capacity. However, the actual situation is not as the government expected. For more than 10 years, this state has not been effectively alleviated. Excess capacity leads to oversupply of electrolytic aluminum, low market price, weakened profitability of enterprises, and strong difficulty with surviving.

Proposed in 2013 by the Chinese President Xi Jinping, area along the "backbone" port of more than six galleries all nations" big pattern gradually forming. "Six corridors" refers to the corridor through six international economic cooperation areas, including the new Asia-Europe continental bridge, in Russia, China, central Asia, west Asia, China and Indochina China and India, Pakistan, Bangladesh, and Myanmar economic corridor. "Six roads" refers to the six major road networks, which facilitate the interconnection of railway, highway, waterway, airway, pipeline, and information superhighway. "Multinational" refers to the cultivation of a number of fulcrum countries. In accordance with the need to promote the construction of "One Belt, One Road" and the initiative of countries along the belt and road, a number of fulcrum countries will be cultivated in Central Asia, Southeast Asia, South Asia, West Asia, Europe, and Africa. "Multi-port" refers to the construction of several maritime fulcrum ports, the construction of a number of important ports centering on the 21st century maritime silk road, and the promotion of a number of important ports with prominent regional advantages and obvious supporting functions through various means. Infrastructure construction, such as railway transportation, oil pipelines, industrial plants, and power investment, will effectively drive the growth of consumption and export of at least six non-ferrous metal varieties in China, including copper, aluminum, lead, and zinc. "One Belt, One Road" is conducive to China's electrolytic aluminum industry to carry out international production capacity cooperation and transfer China's production capacity, as well as technology and capital. It is not only beneficial to countries along the belt and road, but also China can seize the opportunity to optimize the industrial structure and upgrade enterprises' operation and management mode. In recent years, the pace of "going out" has been accelerating, the scale is getting larger and higher, and remarkable results have been achieved. Taking an active part in the construction of "One Belt, One Road" will help Chinese electrolytic aluminum enterprises to seize the historic opportunity of the new round of international production capacity cooperation, deeply explore new modes and new paths of foreign economic cooperation, and comprehensively integrate the advantageous resources inside and outside the industry (Zahra, 1996).

DEVELOPMENT OF ELECTROLYTIC ALUMINUM ENTERPRISES FROM THE PERSPECTIVE OF COLLABORATIVE INNOVATION

Theoretical Research on Collaborative Innovation

All aspects of innovation complement each other, so none can be excluded. Undoubtedly, the establishment of enterprise innovation system and the use of system innovation is the inevitable choice to improve the success rate of enterprise innovation. Therefore, if an enterprise wants to survive and develop in the fierce market competition, it must rely on technological innovation, management innovation, and system innovation.

The economic development of electrolytic aluminum enterprises is a complex system engineering. It is difficult to realize the action of a certain innovation. Only the innovation in various aspects can coordinate cooperation with each other, so as to effectively promote the prosperity of regional economy. No matter which kind of innovative thinking theory, the internal operation process of the system is complex, and the process is a very complex organizational behavior. Therefore, in order to understand the technological innovation in electrolytic aluminum enterprise's innovation system accurately, it is necessary to introduce the category of self-organization theory (i. e., the theory of synergetics) to comprehensively and systematically explore (Adner & Kapoor, 2010).

In the 1970s, Harken established the theory of synergy. Synergetics theory to mutation theory, information theory, and cybernetics are some new achievements of modern science theory (Hitt & Ireland, 1985). At the same time, the adoption of the combination of the statistical and dynamic test method, drawing on the successful experience of the theory of dissipation structure, further reveals the various systems and phenomenon, from disorderly to orderly, shift in common law. According to the theory of synergetics, the generation and transformation of self-organization in the social system is determined by competition and collaboration. The key to the transformation of a system from disorder to order lies in whether the subsystems that make up the system can produce coherent effect and synergistic effect through nonlinear interaction under certain conditions, and generate order in structure and function through this effect. This kind of cooperative movement means the emergence of a new ordered state of the system, showing the self-organization phenomenon of the system on the macro level. In addition, the synergetic theory further points out that the transformation of a system from disorder to order lies in the synergetic phenomena and coherent effects of the nonlinear interactions between subsystems, which is an important leap based on the theory of dissipative structure (Stalk, Evans & Shulman, 1992).

In the process of technological innovation in electrolytic aluminum enterprises, the nonlinear interaction among the elements or subsystems in the innovation system is reflected in many aspects. Firstly, nonlinear and complicated relations occur among production factors, such as capital, technology, talent, information, and equipment. In addition, these relations often mutually cause and effect, which jointly promote the development of the electrolytic aluminum enterprises' innovation system. In particular, the nonlinear relationship between technical elements and non-technical elements (e.g., strategy, culture, and organization) is of particular concern. Secondly, nonlinear interrelations occur among the functional departments of the electrolytic aluminum enterprise innovation system. The internal functional departments of electrolytic aluminum enterprises, such as research and development, production, marketing, human resources, and financial departments, have interactive relations in the process of technological innovation, and jointly participate in the practice of innovation to promote the successful realization of innovation. Literature research indicates that the good coordination of internal functional departments is the key to the successful practice of enterprise technological innovation. Thirdly, a nonlinear interaction occurs between electrolytic aluminum enterprises and universities, research institutes, or enterprises. In most cases, technology innovation in electrolytic aluminum enterprises cannot be isolated (Gao, 2009). Not only is mutual cooperation necessary between the various functional departments within the enterprise collaborative, it is also paramount for electrolytic aluminum enterprises to actively seek external forces and resources. Further, the external form of the interaction relationship between the main body and promotes the improvement of ability and level of enterprise technology innovation.

The concept of fluctuation in synergetic theory deserves attention. Order parameter is one of the most important concepts. The order parameter is a kind of macroscopic parameter which is integrated by the complex nonlinear interaction among the subsystems during the operation of the system. The small fluctuations the system produces during operation can be amplified into huge fluctuations through the nonlinear interaction, which makes the system present significant characteristic changes. Therefore, fluctuation is regarded as an important inducement of system evolution. In the electrolytic aluminum enterprise innovation system, the fluctuation phenomenon exists, generally. For example, the introduction of new technology, the improvement of quality of scientific research personnel, and research and development funds investment relative to the previous level will form a fluctuation. Again, through the internal complex nonlinear interaction of the electrolytic aluminum enterprise innovation system, the fluctuation factors be amplified, eventually form to promote significant changes in the huge fluctuations of the electrolytic aluminum enterprise innovation system. Thus, electrolytic aluminum enterprises produce and enhance the resulting innovation performance. In conclusion, the purpose of constructing the theory of synergetics is to use a systematic perspective to examine the object of study and establish a series of theories and methods to deal with complex systems, so as to better understand the operation rules of the system.

Internal Collaborative Innovation Model of Electrolytic Aluminum Enterprises

At present, domestic and foreign innovation research on electrolytic aluminum enterprises mainly focuses on technological innovation, management innovation, and system innovation. On the basis of integrating previous research results, this chapter tentatively proposes the relationship model between collaborative innovation and traditional innovation performance (Figure 1).

Figure 1.

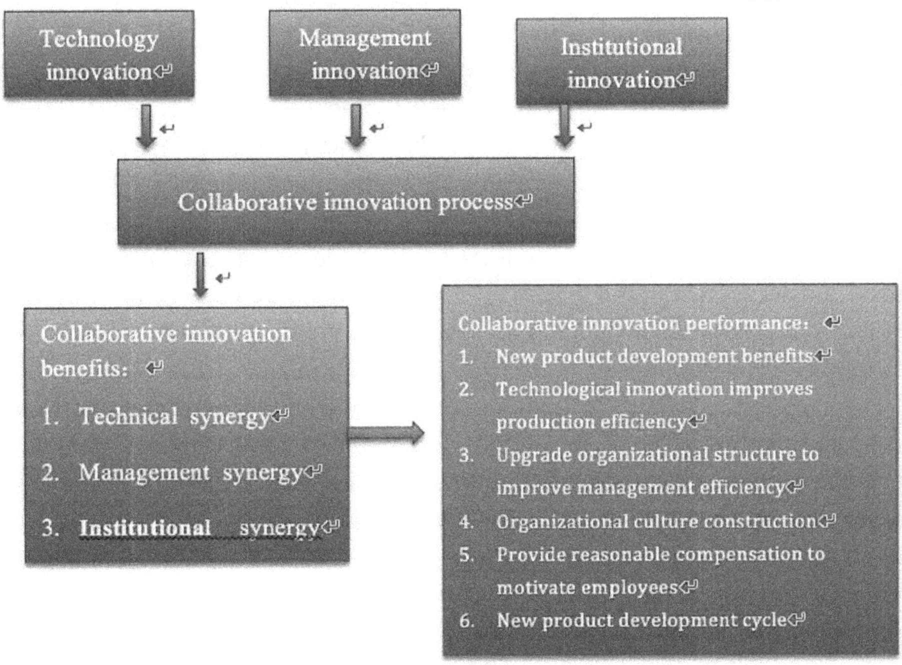

Analysis of Internal Collaborative Innovation of Electrolytic Aluminum Enterprises

For the micro individual of the enterprise, innovation refers to obtaining higher benefit by establishing a new system with stronger efficiency and higher efficiency. The reason for the continuous development of the enterprise is that it constantly introduces innovation in the operation system. At present, in electrolytic aluminum enterprises in excess capacity, or in market downturn in the severe situation, innovation has become the main melody of development. The Central Economic Work Conference proposed that the fundamental way out of overcapacity is innovation, including technological innovation, management innovation, and institutional innovation.

Technological Innovation

Innovation of electrolytic aluminum enterprises is the focus of technological innovation. Through operation and management, production conditions and factors are reorganized to establish a production system with higher efficiency and lower cost, so as to launch new products and production methods, and open up new markets.

This is a comprehensive process of a series of activities. Technological innovation is an important prerequisite for electrolytic aluminum enterprises to develop high technology and realize industrialization.

In the market competition, the technological innovation of electrolytic aluminum enterprises is related to their survival and development. In a narrow sense, it refers to the proposal and development of new products and new technologies. In a broad sense, technological innovation refers to the innovation process of an enterprise. The idea of new products or new technologies is put forward by the enterprise. After research and development, industrialization and commercial production are realized and successful in the market. The product is the symbol of the enterprise, and the popularity of the product in domestic and foreign markets is the main sign of the market competitiveness of electrolytic aluminum enterprises.

In the meantime, product technology innovation cannot leave the improvement of craft and method. The production process is the general flow and method of manufacturing products in electrolytic aluminum enterprise. Workers use production equipment to process raw materials, parts, or semi-finished products in specific production links. The innovation of the production process and operation method requires not only changing the process and specific method of product manufacturing on the basis of equipment innovation, but also continuously researching and improving the specific operation technology and adjusting the process sequence to make the production process more reasonable. Its means mainly includes two aspects: First, advanced science and technology are used to transform and renovate the original equipment, extend its technical life or improve its efficiency; the second aspect is to replace the old and backward machinery and equipment with more advanced and economical means of production, so that enterprise production is based on more advanced materials.

Management Innovation

In the era of knowledge-based economy, enterprise management should make new changes and combinations in terms of quality and quantity of various functions of enterprise production factors, so as to create a new and more effective resource integration system. According to professor Mingjie's point of view, organization is the form of effective allocation of resources, and the reform of organizational form can help resources achieve more effective allocation. Therefore, organizational innovation is part of management innovation. Large and medium-sized electrolytic aluminum enterprises should not only carry out industrial management innovation from the aspects of resource management, operation mode, sales means, investment, and financing, but also introduce organizational innovation from the aspect of institutional setup, and use organizational change to help resources achieve more effective allocation. Undoubtedly, organizational innovation also refers to the change and innovation in production mode and production rental (e.g., assembly line production technology and flexible manufacturing system). Also, it includes institutional innovations, such as joint stock companies and group company formation. Electrolytic aluminum enterprises shall, in different periods, with the changes in business activities, require the organizational structure to be constantly adjusted, aiming at more reasonable organizational management personnel and improving management efficiency. This kind of innovation has important influence on the deepening reform of Chinese electrolytic aluminum enterprises and the establishment of a modern enterprise system.

Institutional Innovation

The system is the principle that the organization runs a way to stipulate. The system innovation is the fundamental factor that the enterprise can develop continuously. The enterprise system mainly includes three elements: Property rights system, operation system, and management system.

The property right system stipulates the rights, interests, and responsibilities of the owners in relation to the most important factors of production for an enterprise.

The management system is the principle of the ownership related to the right of management and its conditions, scope, and restrictions. It shows the enterprise mode of operation, to determine: Who is the operator; who is to organize the production data of possession, use, and the exercise of discretion; who will determine the direction of enterprise production, production content, and mode of production; who is going to ensure the integrity of the enterprise production and its proliferation; who is responsible to the owner of the enterprise production and negative what responsibility. As the innovation direction of electrolytic aluminum enterprise management system, it should be the most effective way of using enterprise production data.

Management system is the general term of various specific rules for exercising the right of management and organizing the daily operation of enterprises, including provisions for the acquisition and use of various elements, such as materials, equipment, personnel, and funds. Among the many contents of the management system, the distribution system is one of the most important. Distribution systems involve how to properly measure the members' contribution to the organization and, on that basis, how to provide sufficient compensation to sustain such contributions (Lin & Xu, 2015). The laborer is the decisive factor of the efficiency of use of all the elements of the enterprise; therefore, providing reasonable remuneration to arouse the laborer's enthusiasm has very important meaning to the enterprise's management. The innovation of electrolytic aluminum enterprise distribution system lies in the continuous pursuit and realization of a higher level of compensation and contribution balance (Schuler, 1996).

The relationship between the three is complex. Generally speaking, certain property right systems decides corresponding management system. However, under the condition that the property right system remains unchanged, the specific operation mode of the enterprise can be adjusted continuously. Similarly, when the operating system remains unchanged, specific management rules and methods can be improved continuously. Once the improvement of the management system is developed to a certain extent, it will need corresponding adjustments. The constant adjustment of the management system will inevitably lead to the reform of the property rights system. Therefore, in turn, changes in the management system will be counterproductive to the operating system, and changes in the operating system will be counterproductive to the property rights system. The direction of enterprise system innovation is to constantly adjust and optimize the relationship between enterprise owners, operators, and laborers, so that the power and interests of all aspects are fully reflected, and the role of each member in the organization is fully played (Xu, Ao & She, 2012).

INFLUENCE OF THE "ONE BELT, ONE ROAD" STRATEGY ON THE DEVELOPMENT OF ELECTROLYTIC ALUMINUM ENTERPRISES

Chinese electrolytic aluminum enterprises are facing new breakthroughs in internal reform and opening up. The strategy of "One Belt, One Road" defines a new path for opening to the outside world, and lays a foundation for the development, transformation, and upgrading of electrolytic aluminum enterprises. With the promotion of the "One Belt, One Road" strategy, going out along "One Belt, One Road" will become the "new normal" of electrolytic aluminum enterprises' future development. "One Belt, One Road" provides Chinese electrolytic aluminum enterprises with new opportunities as well as challenges.

Opportunities Brought by the "One Belt, One Road" Strategy for the Development of Electrolytic Aluminum Enterprises

From the international experience, one of the most effective means to reduce overcapacity is international industrial transfer. This is also an important part of the process of economic globalization. "One Belt, One Road" is the concept and initiative of cooperative development. It is to take the initiative to develop the economic cooperative partnership with countries along the belt and road, by relying on the existing bilateral and multilateral system between China and relevant countries and the existing and effective regional cooperation platform. China said it would first set up a $40 billion silk road fund to provide investment and financing support for interconnected projects, such as infrastructure, resource development, and industrial and financial cooperation in countries along the Belt and Road initiative. It is also proposed to make breakthroughs in transportation infrastructure to realize the early harvest of Asian connectivity, and give priority to the development of railway and highway projects between China and neighboring countries. This is also the beginning of a new round of market competition. "One Belt, One Road" for the development of the aluminum industry provides new opportunities.

Data showed that, in recent years, excess capacity has been the development of China's "evil" electrolytic aluminum enterprises, but less developed countries are not saturated. Especially in the "neighbourhood" all the way along the route of the less developed countries, industry development is not perfect. Transfer of excess production capacity in China to go to these places, not only helps their development, but also solves the problems of excess production capacity in China. At the same time, these trade exchanges are conducive to deepening the economic and cultural exchanges between China and other countries. Due to the strategy of "area," all the way along the country the difference of industrial development is larger. China can transfer the low-end industries to the relative backward area to absorb excess production capacity and promote the adjustment of its industrial structure. Besides, some advantageous industries can be spread to Europe developed areas, and thus achieve the goal of technology upgrade and access to sales channels. The construction of infrastructure in countries along "One Belt, One Road" increases the demand of environmental protection and lightweight. As a light metal, aluminum plays an irreplaceable role in the development of modern society. In addition to rail transit use of aluminum profile, automobile use of aluminum is also in great demand. As the requirement of environmental protection and energy saving becomes more and more strict, the lightweight of automobiles has become the trend of automobile development in the world.

The "One Belt, One Road" Strategy Challenges the Development of Electrolytic Aluminum Enterprises

Chinese electrolytic aluminum enterprises will face various risks and challenges in the process of going out under the "One Belt, One Road" strategy. From the perspective of the tax system, many countries have set relatively low tax rates to attract foreign investment. Chinese enterprises still pay taxes in accordance with China's corporate income tax rate when they invest overseas, and they cannot enjoy the preferential tax rates abroad. In terms of politics, some countries along the Belt and Road have low political stability and irregular political rule, which is easy to bring political risks. From the perspective of economy, each country has different degree of exchange rate fluctuations, and investors have certain risks. In addition, the existing pollution problems in the aluminum industry need to be properly solved. The aluminum industry's output should also include low-energy materials and clean production, as well as innovative green and environmental technologies. The launch of the latest atmospheric emission standards will spur aluminum enterprises to move towards green, low-carbon, and efficient production.

China's aluminum processing industry still has the characteristics of being weak at both ends and over in the middle, that is, the product varieties, quality, and output of high-value-added and high-technology aluminum deep-processing materials are seriously insufficient. For aluminum enterprises seeking development abroad, they should be aware of the disadvantageous institutional and cultural environment for enterprise development, and consider the advantages and disadvantages comprehensively from the perspective of the whole. Countries along the Belt and Road differ in their resources endowment, stage of development, and environment for development. However, their economies are highly complementary to each other, and there is great room and potential for future cooperation. We will adhere to the principle of enterprises and market orientation, strengthen coordination, improve the service guarantee system, effectively combine China's industrial and financial advantages with the needs of the host countries, and vigorously promote international cooperation in production capacity and equipment manufacturing.

Key to the Integration of Electrolytic Aluminum Enterprises Into the "One Belt, One Road" Strategy

Electrolytic aluminum enterprises, as a key industry integrated into the "One Belt, One Road" strategy, should take the following factors into full consideration.

First, factor demand, they should find the right investment direction and find out what "One Belt, One Road" countries need. According to the data, China's primary aluminum demand is expected to be 34.7 million tons in 2017, up of about 6.78%. Global demand for raw aluminum was 62 million tons, up of about 4.8%. With the continuous development of intelligent automobile and new energy automobile, the demand of international high-end automobile aluminum is increasing day by day, which is expected to become an important growth point of aluminum demand in the future.

Second, they should establish extensive cooperation mechanisms. At bilateral and multilateral levels, China has signed relevant documents on production capacity cooperation with Kazakhstan, Malaysia, and more than 30 countries along the Belt and Road. China actively participates in and leads regional cooperation, promotes the issuance of the important document of Chinese-Asian joint statement on production capacity cooperation, and speeds up the formation of an open, inclusive, and win-win cooperation pattern. Today, on the outskirts of the northern city of Pavlodar, a Kazakh electrolytic aluminum plant which is financed by China nonferrous corporation and built by China color corporation, is the country's first.

Third, they should continue to improve the support system. We will give full play to the role of policy, development, and commercial finance, launch and set up financial platforms, such as the production capacity cooperation fund, encourage various financial institutions to support production capacity cooperation projects in various ways, and provide strong support to electrolytic aluminum enterprises in carrying out production capacity cooperation. In order to gradually improve the investment environment, China should constantly deepen the reform of "streamlining administration, delegating power, delegating control, and optimizing services," improve the facilitation and standardization of enterprises' outbound investment, urge enterprises to abide by the laws and regulations of the host country, and guide enterprises to actively fulfill their social and environmental responsibilities.

CONCLUSION

Collaborative innovation is an effective means to solve the practical problems Chinese electrolytic aluminum enterprises face, especially under the condition that the "One Belt, One Road" initiative is proposed and warmly responded by most countries in the world, which provides broader space for the development of collaborative innovation in China's electrolytic aluminum industry. Although China's electrolytic aluminum industry will encounter many difficulties on the way forward, with the development of collaborative innovation and the promotion of the "One Belt, One Road" initiative, the collaborative innovation of China's electrolytic aluminum industry is bound to usher in a brilliant future.

REFERENCES

Adner, R., & Kapoor, R. (2010). Value creation in innovation ecosystems: How the structure of technological interdependence affects firm performance in new technology generations. *Strategic Management Journal*, *31*(3), 306–333. doi:10.1002mj.821

Gao, F., Nie, Z., Wang, Z., Li, H., Gong, X., & Zuo, T. (2009). Greenhouse gas emissions and reduction potential of primary aluminum production in China. *Science in China Series E: Technological Sciences*, *52*(8), 2161–2166. doi:10.100711431-009-0165-6

Hitt, M. A., & Ireland, R. D. (1985). Corporate distinctive competence, strategy, industry and performance. *Strategic Management Journal*, *6*(3), 273–293. doi:10.1002mj.4250060307

Lin, B., & Xu, L. (2015). Energy conservation of electrolytic aluminum industry in China. *Renewable & Sustainable Energy Reviews*, *43*, 676–686. doi:10.1016/j.rser.2014.11.021

Schuler, D. A. (1996). Corporate political strategy and foreign competition: The case of the steel industry. *Academy of Management Journal*, *39*(3), 720–737.

Stalk, G., Evans, P., & Shulman, L. E. (1992). Competing on capabilities: The new rules of corporate strategy. *Harvard Business Review*, *70*(2), 57–69. PMID:10117369

Xu, G. D., Ao, H., & She, Y. G. (2012). Current status and development trend of aluminum industry in world and strategy suggestions in China under background of sustainable development. *Chin J Nonferrous Met*, *22*(7), 2040–2050.

Zahra, S. A. (1996). Technology strategy and new venture performance: A study of corporate-sponsored and independent biotechnology ventures. *Journal of Business Venturing*, *11*(4), 289–321. doi:10.1016/0883-9026(95)00128-X

Section 3

Regional Case Studies Under the Belt and Road Strategy

Chapter 10
Making Use of Geographic Advantage:
Building "One Belt One Road" Vital City

Ping Zhou
City University of Macau, China

Zhanwen Zhang
City University of Macau, China

Siwei Sun
Xi'an Jiaotong-Liverpool University, China

ABSTRACT

The "One Belt One Road" strategy has been fully implemented since 2016, and the unlimited potential of Macau needs to be developed. The excellent geographic location enables Macau to be a significant geographic node on the maritime silk route; the internalized business regulation and advantages in talent enables Macau to be a significant regulation node of system ensuring the operation of the policy "One Belt One Road"; the advantages in political aspect enables Macau to be a significant financial node of the process of "One Belt One Road" financing and management.

INTRODUCTION

For Macau, being enrolled in the program of One Belt One Road creates a significant opportunity to develop the economy and society. During the visits to central Asian and Southeast Asian countries from September to October 2013, President Xi Jinping,

DOI: 10.4018/978-1-5225-8440-7.ch010

the president of the People's Republic of China proposed two initiatives called the silk road economic belt and the 21st century maritime silk road and appealed countries to establish and cooperate together, which received high attention from the international community (Ferdinand, 2016). Actually, the "One Belt And One Road" strategy are formally named and proposed by Premier of the state council of the People's Republic of China, Li Keqiang. He suggested to pave the maritime silk road for countries of ASEAN and create the strategic fulcrum for development of hinterland on the Sino-ASEAN expo in 2013. Accelerating the development of One Belt And One Road can be regarded as a great project, not only promoting economic prosperity and deepen regional cooperation among countries along the belt and road, but also enhancing exchanges and mutual learning among different civilizations and promoting the peaceful development of all countries in the world (Lo, 2015; Swaine, 2015). In March 2015, the national development and reform commission, the ministry of foreign affairs and the ministry of commerce jointly put forward the announcement named "the vision and action of Promoting the construction of the Silk Road Economic Belt and the 21st Century Maritime Silk Road" (hereinafter referred to as the" vision and action ") and state council released to the public. Macao has been an important node city of China's "maritime silk road" since ancient times, and it is a natural bridge connecting China's inland and overseas countries. 1 In particular, compared with mainland cities, Macao has many advantages such as beneficial geographical location, culture2, and economic system and political system.

THE VISION OF PARTICIPATING IN "ONE BELT ONE ROAD"

As a national top-level design, "One Belt One Road" will help Macao gets rid of excessive dependence on gambling industry and better develops Macao's business service platform, featured financial industry, cultural industry, tourism, hotel, cuisine, etc. As early as 2001, Edmund Ho, chief executive of the Macao special administrative region, put forward the industrial policy of "enhancing the leading role of tourism and gambling industry and service industry, promoting the coordinated development of all kinds of industries" in his command paper. In particular, according to the data of Macao's statistics bureau, Macao's gambling industry experienced negative growth for the first time in 2014, which made the danger of excessive dependence on gambling suddenly appear and the call for promoting the diversified development of Macao's economy and industry is stronger than before. Therefore, Macao should take advantage of the "One Belt One Road" and follow the trend to inspire new industry leaders, adjust the direction of capital use and talent cultivation, so as to play a role as the bridgehead or node city in the new pattern of "One Belt and One

Road". Additionally, it also should seek for a new breakthrough and growth point for the diversification of Macao's economic structure and the integration of China's economy and global economy.

In 2014, the Macao submitted to the central government of China the text of "Suggestions on Macao's participation in the national 13th five-year plan", which clearly expressed Macao's willingness to participate in and integrate into the construction of "One Belt and One Road". It was also clearly stated in the 2015 policy address of the Macao SAR government that "Macao will commit to the construction of 'One Belt One Road' and strengthen economic and trade exchanges and cultural exchanges with ASEAN countries."1 " In March 2015, Macao was approved to be included in the "One Belt And One Road" strategy by the central government. Mr. Shian Chui, the present chief executive of Macao declared that the government of the Macao special administrative region would attach great importance to and cooperate with central government to make efforts to carry out a series of detailed actions to support the implementation of the vision and action in building the silk road economic belt and the 21st century maritime silk road.

UNIQUE ADVANTAGES OF MACAU

An Important Geographic Node City

Tracing back to history, hundreds of years ago, Macau was an important node of the significance and exportation trade of Maritime Silk way of China. Macau's unique geographical location and its close personal and economic resources along the "One belt one road" regions and nations have determined that Macau has an important geographic node function in the Maritime Silk Road's construction. Judging from the overall strategic layout of the planning of the central government, the starting point of the "One belt one road" is the prosperous Asia-Pacific economic circle, which is centered in the Central Asian Economic Circle, the South-West Asian Economic Circle, the African National Economic Circle, and the Eurasian National Economic Circle. Get into the European countries' economic circle with the most excellent economic growth. It can be considered that the middle realm of the "One belt one road" is an economic gloom, and there will be much room for improvement in its evolution phase and resources; the two ends of the "One belt one road" strategy being pushed by the multinational societal economy's two prime engines. It can supply tremendous economic growth momentum and create more evolution possibilities. As far as Macau is concerned, starting from the Asia-Pacific economic circle and contacting the European economic circle closely, its strategical place can play a bridge function and we need to concentrate on growth. "One country two systems" policy has given a unique mileage to Macau, which has enabled Macau to have a higher level of open and liberal economic system on a worldwide scale. Coupled with historical accumulation, Macau has turned into a model for the convergence of West and East. Macau's international business rules and the cultural condition of West and East integration are favorable at the same time. In the collection of passenger flow and talents, capital flow, information flow and other resources in Macau, the Macau economy will be upgraded to a novel degree.

System Node of "One Belt One Road"

In economic and trade exchanges with Western nations, Macau owns the benefits of the international business network, international talents, and capitalist economic system. This possesses a significant role for the Chinese central government to evade Western countries' ideology, the barriers to high-tech, to create an international business environment, and to cultivate international talents. It will make a system node of the One belt one road for Macau ". We have seen that although the "One belt one road" strategic concept has been widely endorsed by the international community as a whole, a number of countries yet have some uncertainties about the factual implementation of China's "One belt one road". For instance, within the EU, "China is managing to use the new Silk Road to carry capital exportation, resource development, and merchandise expansion out to Central Asian countries." There is also a Western public opinion that "One belt one road" Initiative may make for China increase its erosion of the European market and The international status of Europe poses a threat. "In August 2014, the" Asian and Asian Academic Research Associations' International Federation "was built in Ulaanbaatar by American countries and European. It is headquartered in Europe and has an Asian branch in Mongolia. And this will exclude the participation of China completely. A number of countries even compare China's "One belt one road" strategic concept with the "Marshall Plan" that the United States brought in in the past. It has had good cooperation with Western countries since the opening markets of Macau from 480 years ago. The "One belt one road" strategy through Macau to connect European countries and Asia-Pacific countries can dilute ideological conflicts and help the mainland of China better integrate with the international community. Macau has exerted the institutional advantages of "one country, two systems" and its good past relations with Western countries, helping eliminate the misunderstanding of the "One belt one road" the above-mentioned countries' strategy and promoting the implementation of the "One belt one road".

Internationalized Business Rules and Internationalized Talents

The operating costs of the implementation of the "One belt one road" strategy can be reduced by Macau's international system and business rules. Chinese companies may go abroad because they are not familiar with international business rules and bear large commercial risks in trade and overseas investment. A lot of multinational projects may be stranded in the middle, which will increase Chinese companies' transaction costs greatly in overseas distribution. Macau has rich experience in international trade, has always followed international business operations' rules, and has maintained close cooperation with American countries and European for a long time. It has attracted a lot of multinational companies to set branches up in Australia, which has a solid economic foundation and reserves a number of talented people. In the future, the implementation of the "One belt one road" in Eurasia's countries will require mainland enterprises and Macau to carry effective and deeper integration and grafting in the aspects of business rules and international systems out, and assist mainland enterprises to take risks in foreign investment and make up for them. The shortcomings in Chinese enterprises' process going global and improving mainland enterprises' comprehensive competitiveness in foreign investment. Macau can also provide the implementation of the "One belt one road" initiative with international talent. Macau has professional and high-level talents who are familiar with international rules and have competitive advantages in finance, law, consulting and accounting. Compared with the mainland, Macau's professionals have a high level of advanced international concepts and foreign language generally. Elites and professionals participate in the "One belt one road" foreign negotiations, which can help to resolve international trade frictions (such as anti-dumping). Disputes, at the same time, can represent China in international organizations, etc., which will provide a strong talent guarantee for the implementation of the "One belt one road". It can be said that the promotion of the "One belt one road" Initiative requires an elite's cultivation with a national consciousness, global vision, pioneering capabilities and innovative thinking. The young elites rooted in Macau and have the mainland's in-depth understanding and have global thinking will become the mass base for Macau's upgrading and industrial transformation. This group of Macau will also open its gain experience and horizons during the implementation of the "One belt one road" initiative.

Featured Financial Node

In the "One belt one road" strategy, the financial instruments are relying on the Asian Infrastructure Investment Bank, the BRICS Bank, the $40 billion Silk Road Fund and the proposed SCO Bank. These four institutions are known as the "Four Big Funds" of the "One belt one road". The efficient operation of these financial institutions also requires the cooperation and support of Macau. Compared with the developed European and American financial markets, the financial markets of Asian countries are not developed to a high degree, and the degree of financial integration is lower. Due to differences in legal, administrative and regulatory mechanisms, the flow of resources between economies has been greatly limiting.

The business of the "Four Major Funds Pool" of the "One belt one road" initiative will also face competition and boycotts from ADB and the World Bank. The "four major fund pools" will have a long history from negotiation, signing, preparation to high-efficiency operation. The accumulated successful experience in the financial sector in Macau, the financial services professionals, and the evolution of financial products in the early stage can provide strong support for the efficient operation of the "Four Capital Pools". The Chinese government will also use the "One belt one road" opportunity to carry out various economic and trade settlements, construction financing and RMB investment with the assistance of Macau, thus accelerating the internationalization of the RMB. Macau's active integration into the "One belt one road" construction is also conducive to promoting the internationalization of the RMB. For example, there are currently 29 banks operating in Macau, including mainland China, Taiwan, Singapore, the United States, the United Kingdom, and Portugal. Macau has also actively expanded cross-border financial services and further strengthened its financial links with the Mainland. Macau's renminbi deposits accounted for 10% of total Macau's total deposits, and cross-border renminbi trade settlements grew more rapidly. Cross-border renminbi trade settlements completed in the first half of 2015, a year-on-year growth rate of 52%.

FEASIBILITY MEASURES AND IMPLEMENTATION RECOMMENDATIONS

The "One belt one road" strategy has been rolled out gradually in 2015, and a series of usable projects will be introduced one after another. It can be said that the "One belt one road" is a major strategical arrangement for China to adjust to the new modifications in the global economic development pattern, international and domestic overall situation of coordinate China, and focus on fostering new benefits in long-term international economic competition. This will be China's promotion of a new round of extraneous reforms. A major platform for openness. In the grand strategy and great tendency of China, Macau should, therefore, make use of the tendency, comprehensively, actively and join in the formulation deeply and implementation of the "One belt one road" plan, and suppose geographical nodes, finance, and institutional nodes. The node's important aspects.

Actively Integrate Into the National Strategy to Achieve a Seamless Connection Between the System and the System

In "Action and Vision", the cooperation mechanism was explained by the central government. "Reinforcing policy communication is an important commitment for the construction of the" One belt one road ". Reinforcing inter-governmental co-operation, establishing exchange mechanisms and multi-level inter-governmental macro-policy communication actively, and increasing interests. Integration, boost political mutual trust and achieve an advanced consensus on cooperation. Nations along the route can fully exchange and coordinate countermeasures and economic growth strategies, formulate measures and projects jointly for promoting regional cooperation, negotiate and resolve problems in cooperation, and apply large-scale projects and pragmatic cooperation together. Supply policy protection. To this end, in the top-level system's design, its own functions should be better defined by Macau in the "13th Five-Year Plan" of the central government, so as to share the development achievements of comprehensive deepening reform of China. On the other hand, In terms of specific implementation, we can refer to international standards, formulate cooperation plans with Guangdong in the form of pre-entry national treatment plus negative list, and step the development and cooperation up in Nansha, Qianhai, and Hengqin to create a high-standard Guangdong-Hong Kong-Macau free trade zone. At the same time, Action and Vision proposed "to strengthen bilateral cooperation, carry multi-level and multi-channel communication and consultation out, and promote bilateral relations' all-round development. Promote the signing of cooperation plan or a cooperation memorandum and build a number of bilateral cooperation demonstrations. Establishing and improving the bilateral joint working mechanism, with the study and implement the action roadmap and implementation plan is all service for the construction of the "One belt one road". It is predicted that giving full play to the bilateral committees, mixed committees, association committees, steering committees, management committees, and other bilateral mechanisms to coordinate and promote cooperation implementation. Supporting local people to explore the cultural and historical heritage on the "One belt one road" is one of the aims. At the meantime, organizing trade and cultural exchange activities for investment is beneficial for the Silk Road International Cultural Expo, the Silk Road International Film Festival, and the Book Fair, for instance, the activities like supporting to found the "One belt one road" International Summit Forum. From this, we can see that there are a large number of jobs Macau can carry through. By embedding the national grand strategy completely and exerting its own advantages fully, Macau merely has the opportunity to begin to be an indispensable economic node in the promotion of the "One belt one road"; and only by implementing the mechanism in a down-to-earth manner can the economic node's function be effectively utilized. To turn theoretical thoughts into reality.

Using our Advantages to Establish Close Cooperation Mechanisms With Mainland Financial Institutions

In "Vision and Action", in terms of financial resources, it is clearly stated that the financial financing is an important support for the implementation of the "One belt one road" strategy. "Deepening financial cooperation, promoting the construction of Asian monetary stability system, investment and financing system and credit system. Expanding the scope and scale of bilateral currency swaps and settlements along the line. Promoting the opening and development of the Asian bond market. Promoting the Asian Infrastructure Investment Bank, The BRICS Development Bank is preparing for construction, and all parties concerned will hold consultations on establishing a financing organization for the Shanghai Cooperation Organization. Accelerate the establishment and operation of the Silk Road Fund, and carry out multilateral financial cooperation through syndicated loans and bank credits, etc. Support the governments along the line and the higher credit rating. Enterprises and financial institutions issue RMB bonds in China. Eligible Chinese financial institutions and enterprises can issue RMB bonds and foreign currency bonds abroad, and encourage the use of funds raised in countries along the route." "One belt one road" construction requires a lot of money, the future in 10 years, China's total investment in the "Belt and Road" will reach 1.6 trillion US dollars. To this end, Macau's financial advantages should be fully utilized to assume the corresponding functions of financial nodes. In addition to the general requirements of the top-level design and implementation mechanism, it is also necessary to strengthen the close cooperation mechanism between Macau and mainland financial institutions, so that Macau funds can enter and leave the Mainland relatively loosely. Macau's financial institutions and financial talents can touch the "One belt one road" in practice. "The investment project." In this regard, Macau should actively promote the depth and breadth of financial market development, optimize the cooperation mechanism with mainland financial institutions, so that Macau funds and talents can participate in the country's "One belt one road" investment and financing activities, and integrate into the AIIB. In the preparatory activities of financial institutions such as the Silk Road Fund, this will strengthen the role of the national foreign investment strategic contact.

Fully Explore the Inherent Advantages of Business Nodes With Portuguese-Speaking Countries

Based on the historical connection between Portugal and Macau, Macau should give full play to economic and trade links' position with Portuguese-speaking nations. As early as 2003, Macau established the Permanent Secretariat of the China-Portuguese-Speaking Countries Economic and Trade Cooperation Forum. The forum's main objective was to push the economic and trade development between the Portuguese-speaking nations and China. In November 2010, Premier Wen Jiabao of China's State Council arrived in Macau and attended the third ministerial meeting of the "Chinese-Portuguese National Development Forum" and delivered an important speech, proposing a series of measures to promote Macau as a platform for China-Portugal economic and trade cooperation. With the "Chinese-Portuguese National Development Forum" as the medium, Macau plays an increasingly significant role in promoting economic and trade cooperation with Portuguese-speaking countries. Now, China's economic and trade exchanges with Portuguese-speaking countries are progressively close, and there is likewise a huge need for relevant financial services. Macau can play a platform role in providing the multilateral economic and trade development of Portuguese-speaking countries and China with financial services. There are differences in economic evolution between Portuguese-speaking nations and China. The trade complementarity effect that is brought about by this difference is apparent. Reinforcing economic and trade exchanges can create more opportunities for economic development. Tangible benefits will be also gained by Macau by playing a platform role. For instance, for the Chinese mainland, the Portuguese Capital Bank and a long time have a substantial market share in the banking industry. Various cooperation agreements have been signed by Chinese banks with the Portuguese-speaking national financial institutions through financial institutions that were based in Macau. The financial industry has been promoted by these measures in Macau for further development. Macau can also serve as a business node for Portuguese-speaking countries. Macau can play a role as a node that connects Portuguese-speaking countries' renminbi market: one is to realize the circulation of RMB funds that are required for trade's settlement in two markets, and the other is to realize financial products' interoperability between the two markets. Through this connection, not only can the circulation efficiency and use of the renminbi in the

Portuguese-speaking countries be enhanced, but the renminbi's internationalization can be further promoted. It ought to be pointed out that Portugal has turned into a hot spot for Chinese investment. Following a report by the American News Agency on March 2, 2015, as stated by the latest statistics, Portugal has been the fourth biggest Chinese investment destination country in Europe in the past decade, and its ranking is higher than that of European countries like Germany. Statistics reveal that in 2014, China's investment in Europe totaled 18 billion US dollars, doubled in 2013. Among them, the investment amount to the United Kingdom was 5.1 billion US dollars, Italy's 3.5 billion US dollars, and the Netherlands 2.3 billion US dollars. During the period, Portugal absorbed a sum of US$2 billion in investment funds from China, ranking fourth, and Germany, which graded fifth, absorbed US$1.6 billion. It can be seen that the integration of Macau into the "One belt one road" will also help to increase international investment in Portugal.

Strengthen Cooperation With Hengqin Free Trade Zone, Guangzhou, and Other Regions to Break Through the Restriction of the Narrow Region

"Action and Vision" puts the advantages of Macau, Taiwan, and Hong Kong forward clearly. Leverage the role of Guangzhou Nansha, Zhuhai Hengqin, Shenzhen Qianhai and other open co-operation zones, can deepen cooperation with Macau, Taiwan and Hong Kong, also build Guangdong, Hong Kong and Macau Dawan District, with Strengthening Shanghai, Tianjin, Guangzhou, Shenzhen, Zhuhai, Zhanjiang, Shantou, Xiamen, Haikou Construction of coastal cities such as Sanya, we reinforce the Guangzhou International Hub Airport's function. To expand the blooming and deepen reforms, governments innovate the mechanism and open economic system, increase technological and scientific innovation, and form a new advantage of leading the competition and international cooperation and participating in (Liu, et al., 2018). All the way the vanguard and principal force are in the construction of the 21st Century Maritime Silk Road. We will especially give full play to overseas Chinese's unique mileages and the particular administrative areas of Macau and Hong Kong, and participate in activities and contribute to the construction of the "One belt one road". Macau is limited by geographical area.

The development opportunities should be expanded by more actively in Hengqin New District. For instance, Macau's Hengqin New District in Zhuhai already has a Chinese medicine park and a university campus with 1.09 square kilometers. This cooperation with the mainland and Hengqin can be further deepened. Zhuhai Hengqin New District is an active exploration of cooperation's new model between Guangdong, Hong Kong, and Macau. Macau can invest in the construction of exhibition venues and other public infrastructures direct and integrate into the construction and development of Hengqin New District in Zhuhai. To undertake more work for the resource sharing, common development, and interconnection of infrastructure in Macau and Zhuhai. The "One belt one road" encourages the development of various free trade zones (Du, 2016; Du & Zhang, 2018). In 2015, Hengqin New District had been included in the Guangdong Free Trade Zone's scope and is the most important. The Guangdong Free Trade Zone was renamed from the Hong Kong, Macau Free Trade Zone and original "Guangdong". The advantage of strengthening Guangdong's local advantages and relying on Guangdong is emphasized. This is obviously the new realm of the "Hong Kong, Macau Free Trade Zone and Guangdong and the Central Government". At present, the Macau economy is more advanced than Guangdong, but from the perspective of international vision and long-term development, and Guangdong's local advantages exceed Hong Kong and Macau will be the general trend. The free trade agreement signed between China's domestic free trade zone and countries along the "One belt one road" will be internal and external, and will play an important role in promoting the economic integration of the Eurasian continent, thus having an important impact on the current global economic landscape. Therefore, as an important node city in the "One belt one road" pattern, Macau should actively expand and deepen cooperation with Hengqin New District, Guangdong, and the mainland provinces and cities. This will not only benefit the diversified development of the Macau economy but will also expand the broader geographical space for Macau's economic development.

REFERENCES

Du, J., & Zhang, Y. (2018). Does one belt one road initiative promote Chinese overseas direct investment? *China Economic Review*, *47*, 189–205. doi:10.1016/j.chieco.2017.05.010

Du, M. M. (2016). China's "One Belt, One Road" initiative: Context, focus, institutions, and implications. *The Chinese Journal of Global Governance*, *2*(1), 30–43. doi:10.1163/23525207-12340014

Ferdinand, P. (2016). Westward ho—the China dream and 'one belt, one road': Chinese foreign policy under Xi Jinping. *International Affairs*, *92*(4), 941–957. doi:10.1111/1468-2346.12660

Liu, W., Shi, H. B., Zhang, Z., Tsai, S. B., Zhai, Y., Chen, Q., & Wang, J. (2018). The Development Evaluation of Economic Zones in China. *International Journal of Environmental Research and Public Health*, *15*(1), 56. doi:10.3390/ijerph15010056 PMID:29301304

Lo, C. (2015). China's Silk Road Strategy. *Inter Economics*, *29*(4), 54.

Swaine, M. D. (2015). Chinese views and commentary on the 'One Belt, One Road'initiative. *China Leadership Monitor*, *47*(2), 3.

Chapter 11
Belt and Road Initiative:
The Case of Malaysia

Teo Poh Chuin
Tunku Abdul Rahman University College, Malaysia

ABSTRACT

With the aim of the Belt and Road Initiative in search of synergies with participating countries, infrastructure development projects are expected to arise incrementally and will be adapted accordingly to fulfil local regulatory requirements and needs. Malaysia embraces opportunities brought by the Belt and Road Initiative by penetrating deeper into overseas market with the availability of rail lines that will drive connectivity and foster economic growth. The potential of the Belt and Road Initiative lies not just within the infrastructure sector, but also offers plenty of opportunities for human capital development, which made available through technology transfer and knowledge sharing arising from the cooperation between China and Malaysia. While it is believed that Malaysia will experience a strong growth, this motion definitely requires a high level of mutual cooperation, understanding, and trust in managing regulatory, political, and financial risks, as well as challenges involved.

INTRODUCTION

President Xi Jinping's Belt & Road Initiative's (一带一路), a key element of China's 21st century diplomacy, clarity of vision, powerful means and combining movement, has created a strong impact on global businesses and international relations (Benjamin & Viktor, 2017). The overland 'Belt' involves the founding of a trade corridor and economic expansion from the west of China through Central Asia, and finally to

DOI: 10.4018/978-1-5225-8440-7.ch011

Europe; whilst, the maritime 'Road', China's development of hubs and ports across the Indo-Pacific is a main aspect of this initiative (The Economist, 2017).

Even though the underlying concept, scope and framework of the Belt & Road Initiative seem vague in nature, it has since gathered notable influences by positioning itself as an enormous and comprehensive infrastructure development programme based on the utilisation of China's massive economic leverage abroad and exports of its strong capabilities to other regions in the infrastructure development area (Lehmannet *et* al., 2016). Formally, the Belt & Road Initiative covers five key areas of cooperation comprising hammering infrastructure and facilities networks, improve financial cooperation, coordinating development policies, strengthening trade relations and investment and intensifying cultural and social exchanges (Benjamin & Viktor, 2017).

Even though it is believed that the Chinese companies will be the big winners from the Belt & Road Initiative, but non-Chinese companies are also increasingly seeing themselves benefiting from this initiative. President Xi hopes to find a more profitable venture for China's vast foreign-exchange reserves, which are presently interested in low-interest-bearing American government securities (David, 2017). Besides, he also hopes to establish a new market for Chinese companies, such as the high-speed rail firms, as well as to export some of China's vast excess capacity in steel, cement and other metals. Apart of giving an overview on the Belt and Road Initiative, this study also discusses the opportunities and challenges in the context of Malaysia.

BACKGROUND OF THE BELT AND ROAD INITIATIVE

Conceptualization

Prior of the introduction of the overarching term 'One Belt, One Road' or also known as the 'Belt & Road' (or 'B&R') – an initiative that could reshape the world order potentially, Xi Jinping, the China's president announced two major initiatives which are the land-based 'Silk Route Economic Belt (SREB)' and the ocean going 'Maritime Silk Road' in 2013 (Leer & Yau 2016; Lehmann *et* al., 2016). Figure 1 illustrates the Silk Route Economic Belt and the Maritime Silk Road under the Belt & Road Initiative.

The primary objective of the Belt & Road Initiative is to build a trade and infrastructure network connecting Asia with Europe and Africa along the ancient Silk Road trade routes. The 'Belt' refers to an infrastructure network of mainly transport, communication and energy projects stemming from Xi'an in China via Central Asia to Moscow, Rotterdam and Venice; whereas, the 'Road' refers to the

Figure 1. Silk road and maritime silk road of the belt and road initiative
Source: China Institute of International Studies (2016)

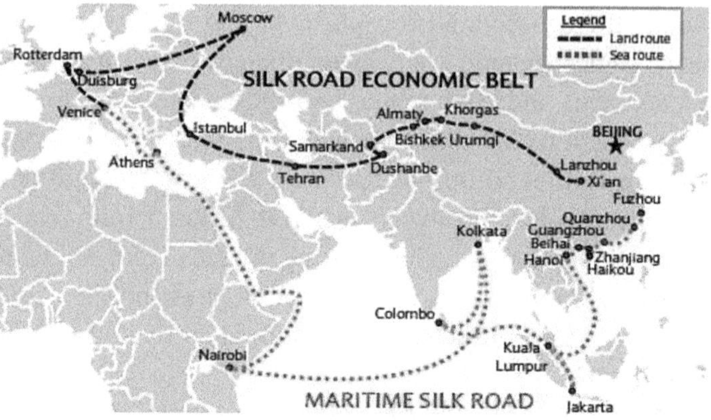

infrastructure network in terms of maritime which comprises of planned ports and other coastal infrastructure from South China and Southeast Asia to East Africa and the northern Mediterranean Sea (Lehmannet *et* al., 2016). As a joint effort between the National Development and Reform Commission (NDRC), Ministry of Foreign Affairs and the Ministry of Commerce, the Belt & Road plan was eventually established (Leer & Yau, 2016).

Scope

China has slowly opened its economy and initiated several internal and external developmental strategies since its participation into the World Trade Organisation (WTO) in 2001, and the Belt & Road Initiative is one of the most vital drives toward its developmental effort (Lehmann *et* al., 2016). The concept of Belt & Road Initiative is to build a trade and infrastructure network connecting Asia with Europe and Africa along the ancient Silk Road trade routes, with the purpose of not only improving the trade flows, driving long-term economic growth and developments in the region, which in turn is expected to bring advantages to the economies of countries along the routes, as well as also offering solutions to the global economic difficulties (Belt & Road Portal, 2017). In aligning with China's search for new economic thrust due to recent slower economic growth, the Belt & Road Initiative is implemented to structurally solve the problem of weaknesses in both state enterprises and real estate market bubbles attributed to economic globalization and where growth is now provided with greater platform to expand due to the Belt & Road Initiative focusing on infrastructure development (el Namaki 2017).

In line with the historical framework of harmonious co-existence and mutual cultural enrichment, the China government introduces the "Five Principles of Peaceful Coexistence" as fundamental values of the Belt & Road Initiative (Barcelona Centre of International Affairs, 2016). These five principles are:

1. Mutual respect for each other's sovereignty and territorial integrity;
2. Mutual non-aggression;
3. Non-Interference in each other's internal affairs;
4. Equality and mutual benefit; and
5. Peaceful co-existence.

China sees connectivity and co-development as the common interests and keys to peace and prosperity (Chinese National Development and Reform Commission, 2015). Through the introduction of the Belt & Road Initiative, China strives to promote Five Connectivities, which are:

- Policy coordination
- Facilities connectivity
- Unimpeded trade
- Financial integration; and
- People-to-people bonds

Although the Belt & Road Initiative is usually referred to as a national vision and foreign strategy which seems like a conceptual propaganda, in actual fact, it also involved a series of concrete investments and projects (Leer & Yau 2016). Thus, a huge series of on-going, planned and future infrastructure projects, which are accompanied by various bilateral and regional trade agreements are made available under the initiative of Belt & Road. The focus of these projects is on the development of a vast array of resources consists of roads, railways, ports, airports, oil and gas pipelines and refineries, power plants, Free Trade Zone as well as information technology, telecommunication and financial infrastructure (Leer & Yau, 2016). Amongst all the projects, infrastructure comprising railways, ports and roads, together with telecommunications networks receive the most attention (The Economist, 2017).

Many advantages can be brought by the Belt & Road Initiative and one of them is the reduction in trade expenses resulted from infrastructure improvement, which also helps to foster the economy growth and strengthen stability amongst the region as the inland and coastal China are integrated by setting up land corridors along the major Eurasian countries, through China-Mongolia-Russia, China-Central and West Asia, China-Indochina Peninsula, China-Pakistan, and Bangladesh-China-India-Myanmar

(Lehmann *et* al., 2016). For instance, companies like BMW and Hewlett-Packard (HP) are using the Trans-Eurasia Chongqing-Xinjiang-Europe international railway route, which begins from Chongqing and arises in Duisburg, Germany for a total of 16 days of travel along 11,179 km route. Moreover, the Belt & Road Initiative also acts as a common platform for economic security in conjunction with the United Nation's Sustainable Development Goals by connecting global north to global south (United Nations, 2017).

Thus, a massive financing commitment and platform are needed to support the initiative. Indeed, US$1 trillion of outbound financing is expected to be initiated by the Belt & Road Initiative from Chinese government in the coming 10 years, either in the form of preferential debt funding or equity funding (Leer & Yau, 2016). The funding to the appropriate initiatives and projects will be allocated through specific channels created by the China's government such as New Silk Road Fund (NSRF), Asian Infrastructure Investment Bank (AIIB), foreign exchange reserves and some of its largest state-owned banks. For instance, AIIB is complemented by the Belt & Road Initiative as an effort in financial development with the purpose of improving regional collaboration and economic empowerment along with social changes (Hu *et* al., 2017).

The trade and exports with China's neighbours are expected to be stimulated by advocating the connectivity along the two main routes and the investment across the continents, in which the new market will be opened through the Belt & Road Initiative, and the issues of China domestic overcapacity can be resolved particularly in terms of construction, engineering and manufacturing capacity (el Namaki, 2017). With the purpose of seeking market driven collaboration among these countries, this initiative is also intended to be beneficial to the internationalisation of Chinese currency Renminbi and the harmonisation of diplomatic relations amongst many of its neighbouring countries (Leer & Yau, 2016; Lehmann *et* at., 2016). Hence, it is important for the Chinese leaders to ensure that peace in its fragile neighbourhood can be maintained and safeguarded through economic prosperity. The Belt & Road Initiative is initiated to align with China's strategic and geopolitical interest in building a cordon sanitary of regional stability around the country itself.

Involvement of Other Countries

Covering 30% of global Gross Domestic Production and 35% of global trade, the Belt & Road Initiative encompass more than 60% of the world's population through the 71 participating countries are connected in its current shape, and even that China still welcome other countries that are out of the Belt & Road region to join the forces, as detailed in the 2017 report of the Malaysia's Ministry of International Trade and

Industry. Hence, the current and future participating countries in the Belt & Road Initiative are estimated to be more diverse and inclusive.

The routes under theBelt & Road Initiative are more alike to a range of network instead of a fixed route (Mustafic, 2017). The Belt & Road Initiative consists of two physical routes, a land route and a maritime route that connect China with Europe, Southeast Asia and Africa region by having numerous side-branches along the way. The land route is stemming from inner China to Southern Europe through Netherlands; whilst, the sea route is running from Shanghai's port through India and Africa to the end-point of the land-based route in Venice (Leer & Yau, 2016).

The outbound focus of China in three directions is reflected by the Belt & Road Initiative, which includes West (West China, Central Asia, the Middle East and Europe), East (Southeast Asia), and South (South Asia and Africa) (Leer & Yau, 2016). As a result, underdeveloped countries will learn from developed countries through economic globalization and economic integration, China's outward foreign direct investment can be promoted overall through reducing the institutional differences (Gao, 2017). Due to the closer distance to Western China, demand for higher regional stability and natural resources abundance, Eurasia will be given priority in conjunction of the initiative, as well as Southeast Asia which will also be prioritized due to its importance in trading relationship with China (Leer & Yau, 2016).

THE CASE OF MALAYSIA

The Relationship Between China and Malaysia

Malaysia is the first Southeast Asia country establish diplomatic relations with China (Selat 1987), since the historical visit of its former Prime Minister Abdul Razak to Beijing in 1974. Malaysia has been attentive to China's development after its opening-up process and economy reform. In 2013, the relationship of Malaysia-China upgraded to "Comprehensive Strategic Partnership." As expected, Malaysia is emerging the largest trading partner of China in Southeast Asia where the bilateral annual trades amounting to US$ 100 billion.

Since the implementation of the Belt & Road Initiative, Malaysia and China have been reaping the early benefits of economic investment and have pledged to build a stronger all-round strategic partnership in areas including trade, finance, military defence, port development, as well as supply chain and logistics. The Malaysia government has shown its strong dedication and priority in this Initiative by the establishing Belt & Road Initiative National Secretariat (BRINS) Malaysia in 2017 in the Ministry of International Trade and Industry, with the objectives to coordinate, monitor and facilitate the Belt & Road projects in Malaysia. According to the Economic Report 2017/18 released in conjunction with Budget 2018, Malaysia's annual trade with countries that which run along the Belt & Road exceeded RM850 billion in 2016. With the Belt & Road Initiative, it is expected to increase further in the coming decades.

In fact, Malaysia has been continuously gaining from China's economic expansion (HSBC 2017). Since 2009, China has remained as Malaysia's largest trading partner for the ninth consecutive year, and Malaysia's trade with China has registered a growth of 20.6% to RM290.65 billion, where exports to China were valued at RM126.15 billion with an increase of 28%, while imports rose by 15.5% to RM164.5 billion (Malaysian External Trade Development Corporation, 2018). Amongst others, higher exports were recorded for electrical and electronic products, petroleum products, rubber products, liquefied natural gas, chemicals and chemical products, optical and scientific equipments, manufacture of metal as well as natural rubber; whereas higher imports were registered for electrical and electronic products.

Opportunities for Malaysia

Malaysia's early embrace of China's Belt & Road Initiative has led to a flood of Chinese investments in the country, boosting the Southeast Asian nation's economy (Xin, 2017). China has invested more than US$50 billion in the Belt & Road countries since the initiative was proposed, and has achieved a great number of early harvest results (Belt & Road Portal, 2017). According to a recent report by the Wharton School of the University of Pennsylvania, they named Malaysia as the best country to invest in (Adilla, 2017). Therefore, Malaysia also decided to take the opportunity by signing agreements with China amounting to RM144 billion, which is a sign of the great confidence of Chinese investors have in Malaysia (The Star, 2017).

In November 2016, Malaysia and China inked 14 Memorandum of Understandings worth approximately RM 144 billion. These projects between Malaysia and China include urban developments and creating industrial parks, generation of power, upgrading and building new ports, train construction, logistics, investments in manufacturing plants and even building new rail lines (The Star, 2017). One of the major deals confirmed was the East Coast Rail Line (ECRL) infrastructure project amounting to RM 55 billion (South China Morning Post 2016). Supporting this project is one of the examples of Malaysia welcoming The Belt & Road Initiative. China's state-owned enterprise China Communications Construction Co Ltd (CCCC) will be funding this project together with a soft loan from the Export-Import Bank of China (The Star, 2017). Figure 2 illustrates the coverage of ECRL project.

Figure 2. Coverage of ECRL Project
Source: The Straits Times (2017)

Apart of that, Malaysia also signed a contract for the purchase of an initial four littoral mission ships (LMSs) from China for the Royal Malaysian Navy (RMN) (Jennings, 2017) which is estimated to provide jobs in both Malaysia and China. As two of the ships are being built in each country, it would involve a transfer of technical knowledge to Malaysia as well as safeguarding the safety and security of Malaysians (The Star, 2017).

Apart from that, Jack Ma, the Executive Chairman of Alibaba and Malaysia's former Prime Minister Datuk Seri Najib Razak worked together by launching the world's first "Digital Free Trade Zone (DFTZ)" in Kuala Lumpur early 2017 (The Star, 2017). This will undoubtedly be a catalyst for e-commerce and Small and Medium-sized Enterprises (SMEs). Najib Razak was positive that the small and medium entrepreneurs in the country will have the opportunity to access international markets more easily and increase their business returns (Bernama, 2017). Besides, Malaysia will also be the premier hub for global and local internet-based companies targeting Southeast Asia (The Star, 2017). In addition to shortening shipping times for key commodities like palm oil and fruits, such network would also allow the direct transfer of goods between China and Indian Ocean ports in Malaysia, Thailand and Myanmar (Business Monitor International, 2017).

The largest Business-to-Business agreement signed is the project of developing Robotic Future City in Johor by Johor Corporation and its Chinese partner Saisun Robot Investment. This project worth approximately RM 15 billion and involves the development of 404 ha (hectare) of land to set up the futuristic hub to develop the robotic industry as well as encouraging and promoting the growth of different supply chains in Malaysia (The Star, 2017).

Another major deal announced is the Methanol and Derivatives Complex, a project in Sarawak between Yayasan Hartanah Bumiputera Sarawak (YHBS), Consortium Huanqiu Contracting and Engineering (HQC) and MacFeam. This project is worth approximately RM 8.7 billion and will be located at Tanjung Kidurong and comprise of three plants to be built in two phases. With this project, Sarawak is expected to be transformed into a petrochemical hub in the region. It is estimated to be completed in 2021 (New Sarawak Tribune, 2017).

A Memorandum of Understanding to develop the Melaka Gateway project was also signed between KAJ Development (KAJD) and its Chinese partners Powerchina International Group, Shenzhen Yantian Port Group and Rizhao Port Group. Under this project, a total of four artificial islands of reclaimed land will be built, which include 1) Tourism, Entertainment and Property Development Island; 2) Free Trade Economic Zone Island; 3) Melaka Gateway Port Island; and 4) Maritime Industrial Park. Figure 3 illustrate the idea of Melaka Gateway.

Meanwhile, AirAsia, China Everbright Group and Henan Government Working Group signed a joint-venture Memorandum of Understanding to establish a low-cost carrier (LCC) terminal in Zhengzhou, capital of Henan province in central China. The three entities will also set up an aviation academy with the objective of developing and training talents such as pilots, cabin crew and engineers, as well as maintenance, repair and overhaul facilities to service aircraft (Reuters, 2017).

Besides, AgroFresh International has secured an approximately RM 6.6 billion deal with China's Dashang Group to export Cavendish bananas and tropical fruits to China (AgroFresh). Also, an engineering, procurement, construction and commissioning contract was signed between Titijaya Land Bhd and CREC Development to develop The Shore, a mixed-use commercial hub, in Kota Kinabalu, Sabah. This project worth approximately RM 576 million, and expected to be completed in four years (The Star, 2017).

Bursa Malaysia and Shanghai Stock Exchange also signed an agreement to explore potential ways to improve market accessibility and products in both markets. In

Figure 3. Graphic of Melaka Gateway
Source: EdgeProp (2016)

addition, a sister port relationship has also been reached between Northport in Port Klang and Weifang Sime Darby Port in Shandong province of China (Hanif, 2017).

Apart of that, with the aim to further strengthen Malaysia's leadership in Halal industry and develop Halal compliance infrastructure in Weifang Sime Darby port and industrial park in accordance to Malaysia Halal standards, Halal Industry Development Corporation (HDC) has signed a Memorandum of Understanding with Weifang Sime Darby Port Co., Ltd. China (WSD) (Ministry of International Trade and Industry, 2017). The collaboration includes facilitation of Malaysian Halal products into the Belt & Road connectivity for wider markets reach in Northern and Western region of China as well as neighboring countries. This joint effort benefits Malaysian exporters in the form of expanding their halal businesses worldwide.

In addition, Malaysia can also leverage on the Made in China (MIC) 2025 Initiative. In 2015, China has adopted the MIC policy to encourage technological innovation and enhance competitiveness in the country's manufacturing sector where the primary aim of this strategy is to upgrade China into a manufacturing powerhouse, from a quantity-based manufacturer of quality-driven manufacturing powerhouse to compete with top-notch players from the United States and Europe, Malaysia External Trade Development Corporation urges Malaysian exporters to leverage on this opportunity to export more products to China especially in the manufacturing sectors given China's strong motivations to leverage its Belt & Road investments in Malaysia for strategic purposes, consistent with the plan's revitalized focus (Sophie 2017). Based on the analysis of Malaysia External Trade Development Corporation, one of the key bottlenecks facing the Chinese manufacturing industry is in the manufacturing of high-end microchips as MIC 2025 encourages substantial automation within the manufacturing activities, which drives high consumption of microchips component, where Malaysian exporters should reap the opportunities in this sector and boost their exports of components and related materials.

As a result, the Belt & Road Initiative together with the MIC 2025 strategies will bring an effect where Malaysia has a higher potential to attract Chinese Multinational companies to grow their business in Greater Kuala Lumpur (GKL), which is an optimal location in Asia enabling them to leverage GKL as a gateway into the ASEAN region on the back of 633 million populations, with growing household income and increasing high standard of living (Sophie, 2017). Besides, with the rapidly rising labor cost in China and complex consumer demand in Asia region faced by the Chinese manufacturers, multinational organizations should now consider setting up their regional business, innovation and talent hubs in GKL as the principal hub and business hub models for not only facilitate quicker decision making and optimization of resources but also to offer a cost competitive advantage with optimal and global levels of operational excellence (John 2017). With the attraction of Chinese multinational organizations, the domestic transportation will be enhanced with the projects such as the Melaka Gateway and ECRL, tourism industry to boost the economic and industrial development whereby promoting job creation in domestic market where such projects are crucial to works toward attaining the status of a developed country (Xin, 2017).

Since the implementation of the Belt & Road Initiative, both countries have reaped the early benefits of economic investment and have pledged to build a stronger all-round strategic partnership in areas including trade, finance, port development and logistics. The opportunities for Malaysia to develop the infrastructure and boost economic growth would not be available if not for the Belt & Road Initiative pushed forward by China (The Star, 2017). By then Malaysia's trade figures can jump by up to three to four folds once Malaysia's able to export and import goods to the country's major trade partners including China, Europe and Middle East overland via the rail systems and enhance domestic transportation, industrial and tourism development, thereby promoting job creation (Han, 2017). This would be "win-win cooperation" between Malaysia and China.

Problems and Challenges for Malaysia

With the Belt & Road Initiative, each country faces a unique combination of problems and challenges that are caused by the complexity and extensivity of laws, rules and regulations shaping the business environment in each country. Amongst the risks faced by are macroeconomic risks such as unsustainable economic structures and exchange-rate volatility as well as the microeconomic risks including the social and political tensions, weak banking sectors, governance failures that are ranged from corruption to inefficient implementation of reforms (Liu, 2016).

Many of the Western critics have viewed this initiative as China's desire of expanding its influence to poor nations hungry for economic and infrastructure development (Ignatius, 2017). Some of the politicians in Malaysia also questioned its former Prime Minister Datuk Seri Najib Razak on the signing of certain agreements and Memorandums of Understanding, which can be interpreted as selling the sovereignty of Malaysia by agreeing to such projects (The Star, 2017). However, he claimed that the Belt and Road Initiative serves the purposes of building world-class infrastructure, bringing more trade and opportunities, improving living standards and prosperity.

Even though Malaysia companies could collaborate with the Chinese companies, nevertheless they will also be facing a greater challenge. This is in view that the competition is keen as many of the companies from the Belt & Road countries will also be seeking partnerships with the Chinese companies in order to benefit from the opportunities and over the past decade, many of these Chinese companies have actually built up strong levels of technical expertise due to their improved economy and technology and therefore no longer need to partner with international companies to carry out the business contracts (Business Monitor International, 2017).

It is also difficult to analyse the true state of the initiative as there are misleading official statistics being made and published. All of these misleading statements make it hard to assess whether most of the current Chinese investments are in fact going to these Belt & Road countries or not as compared to the previous years (Parameswaran, 2017). China, on the other hand, is ensuring the security of these maritime passageways including the Strait of Malacca and the country also seeks to extend the reach of the Chinese navy in the regional waters (Pitlo, 2016). If China attempts to use the initiative to tighten its influence over Malaysia, it could be a challenge to Malaysia by undermining Malaysia's effort to maintain a high degree of independence in its foreign policy while pursuing close economic ties. And if Malaysia is aligned too closely with China, this would complicate its relations with the United States (Han, 2017).

If Malaysia is too dependent on China for economic growth, this might give China undue leverage in its relations with Malaysia, permitting China to exert greater pressure on Malaysia to simply go along with China's strategic interests in the South China Sea region (Han, 2017). It raises questions about where the relationship is ultimately headed especially when a bilateral relationship shifts so dramatically, where China suddenly acquires a monopoly of major infrastructure projects into Malaysia and when a foreign power makes such rapid political and economic inroads in Malaysia (Ignatius 2017). This is because Malaysia has benefited tremendously from the gains in term of trades from the China-driven commodities boom that drive domestic demand, but as China moves away from a commodity-intensive investment-led growth model, the whole benefits can be wiped off (Sumathy 2017).

If China attempts to use the Belt & Road Initiative to tighten its influence over Malaysia, it could undermine Malaysia's effort to maintain a high degree of independence in its foreign policy while pursuing close economic ties and if Malaysia is aligned too closely with China, this would complicate its relations with the United State, while Malaysia seeks to capitalize on the lucrative Belt & Road Initiative, then it should be mindful to ensure that it does not serve as a foothold facilitating China's ambitions to become a regional hegemon that dominates geopolitics in Southeast Asia (David, 2017).

The project management and control of the Belt & Road Initiative are basically in the hand of the Chinese party, which means that all the decision making as well as resourcing and procurement will be done by China (Malaysiakini, 2017). This is obvious when it is linked with one of the projects in Malaysia, which is the ECRL project. In this project, China will use their nationals and materials for the construction and development rather than give Malaysia the opportunity to provide all the materials. This was unlike other past national development projects, where Malaysia's resources will be given priority when dealing with the needs of building resources and materials (Free Malaysia Today, 2017). Hence, the Malaysia government should impose standards such as local content requirements, in which enforced that a certain percentage of materials must be purchased from local suppliers or produced by domestic manufacturers, as well as set minimum requirements in terms of involvement of local workforce in these mega projects.

The Belt & Road Initiative brings a lot of business opportunities to most of the countries including Malaysia. It advocates to improve international business opportunities between China and Malaysia. The Belt & Road Initiative provides a platform for Malaysian SMEs to explore the business opportunities abroad, not only providing networking platform but also advice on the matters on financial services, legal services and others. However, at the same time it may also decreases the business opportunities of SMEs as they opined that they are not able to compete with other business that are bigger in size compared with them, hence they might not be able to seize the opportunity provided by the Belt & Road Initiative, and it is difficult for them to gain a foothold in the marketplace. SMEs might choose to exit the market due to the weak competitiveness and not able to afford the required cost to operate a business.

Also, Malaysia and China are different, culturally, and this does bring impacts to the business dealings. Greet Hofstede's five cultural dimensions are being adopted to analyze the cultural difference between Malaysia and China. Hofstede's cultural dimensions theory is a framework for cross-cultural by identifying the effects of a society's culture on the values of its members and how these values relate to behavior of the society in general (Hofstede, 2001). The five cultural dimensions of Hofstede's framework includes power distance, individualism, masculinity, uncertainty avoidance and time orientation. Please refer to Figure 4 for the cultural distance between China and Malaysia.

Based on Figure 4, China and Malaysia are different in terms of masculinity and long-term orientation. The Masculinity side of this dimension represents a preference in society for achievement, heroism, assertiveness and material rewards for success; whilst femininity refers to a preference for modesty, caring and cooperation for the weak and also emphasize on quality of life (Hofstede, 2001). According to Hofstede (2010), with the score of 66, China is a Masculine society which emphasizes on success is driven; whereas the preference for Malaysia on this dimension cannot be determined, given a score of 50. Many Chinese would rather sacrifice family and leisure priorities than to work have proven their needs to ensure success (Hofstede, 2010). This is being influenced by its need for social-ego of work status. And hence, material reward is appreciated and saving face is extremely important to the Chinese.

Figure 4. Culture index of China and Malaysia according to Hofstede's Five Cultural Dimensions
Source: Hofstede Insight (2018)

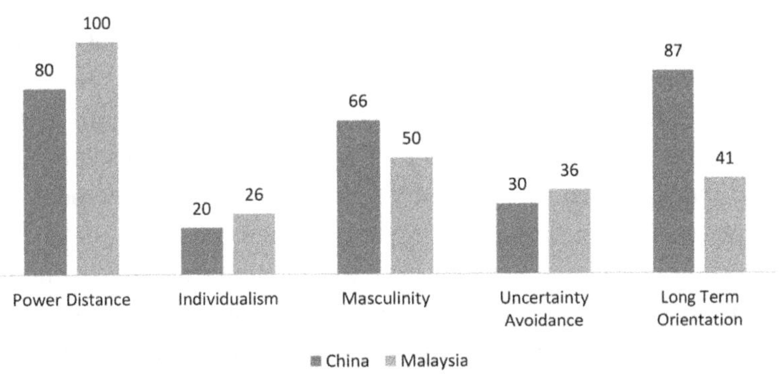

Every society has to maintain some links with its own past while dealing with the challenges of the present and the future, and this is explained by Hofstede (2001) in time orientation, which is classified as long-term orientation and short-term orientation. China scores 87 in long-term orientation which means that it is a very pragmatic culture. In this society, people show abilities to easily adapt traditions to change in conditions as well as a strong tendency to save and invest. Additionally, it is crucial to have thriftiness and perseverance in order to achieve results (Hofstede, 2010). In order to gain and achieve success in life, Chinese people are willing to persevere and work hard for a long period of time. Chinese people are not so much about instant gratification.

In contrast, a low score of 41 in long term orientation refers to Malaysia having a normative culture. People in such societies have a relatively small propensity to save for the future and that spending money is a more common practice than saving. Malaysians also wish to make decisions faster in order to achieve more immediate results and have a great respect for traditions (Hofstede, 2010).

It is important to understand the importance of mutually beneficial long-term relationships (guanxi) in China. According to Wei *et* al. (2012), networks could improve both job performance and personal career growth in China. Thus, having relationships in place is very critical. As Hofstede and Hofstede (2005) observed, guanxi lasts a lifetime in China so it would be unwise to waste it on a short-term objective. To develop relationship and trust before commencing any discussion on business, managers have to invest a considerable amount of time. Thus, it is essential to understand that business people in China prefer to establish a strong relationship before closing a deal by discussing business matters with the Chinese counterparts (Veras, 2016) as loyalty cannot be built from day one. Therefore, patience is vital in dealing with the Chinese parties.

In addition, Malaysian managers or companies operating or intend to operate in China should also emphasize on these emotional and relationship investments and make their subordinates feel that this company is not just a place where they come to work but provide them with more than just a workplace such as career prospect and sense of belonging (Goodall *et* al. 2007). As mentioned earlier that Chinese people like to invest in things in a long-term basis, thus it is crucial to ensure durability and permanence of the products or services offered as these are going to be more appealing than any short term benefits or pleasure derived (Hofstede 2007).

However, under a long term perspective, China's massive investment will reduce the sovereignty of Malaysia, by strangling its own socio-economic development and lead to a sinicization of Malay Nusantara culture, or known as 中国化Zhōngguóhuà, according to Embong *et* al. (2017), a group of professor from the Institute of Malaysian and International Studies. He also highlighted the concern on the possibly of over-reliant of Malaysia to China, in which Malaysia's once powerful geopolitical position of "connecting oceans" will be reduced to just a link to China's production chain.

Apart of that, Malaysia current Prime Minister Tun Dr Mahathir Mohamad, a 93-year-old leader, who returned for a second stint as premier following a shock election win in May 2018, has railed against a series of deals struck with Chinese state-owned companies by the administration of the toppled leader, Datuk Seri Najib Tun Razak (The Star, 2018). Dr Mahathir had pledged to raise the issue of what he views as unfair terms and conditions related to some of the deals, and his government has suspended the China-backed projects worth more than US$22 billion that were signed under his scandal-plagued predecessor. During his nine-year rule, Najib was accused of cutting quick deals with Beijing in return for assurance in paying off debts linked to a massive financial scandal that ultimately brought down his long-ruling Barisan National coalition, in which fuelling suspicions about Najib's real motives, critics said there was often a lack of transparency on the terms, such as interest rates on loans, which were unfavourable to Malaysia (The Star, 2018). All of these bring additional uncertainties on the political ties between China and Malaysia, which potentially affect the inter-country business-related activities.

CONCLUSION

Under the Belt & Road Initiative, the government of China will spur massive spending on global infrastructure and create abundant of opportunities that assure the active involvement from both China and foreign firms. Although the initiative of Belt & Road is being doubted over its overarching and ambitious undertakings in helping China to attain geopolitical goals by economically connect China's neighbourhood countries, there are many factual and concrete objectives implied that should not be neglected from the perspective of strategy, but instead to embrace it as a transcontinental infrastructure programme (Wijeratne et al. 2017).

By utilisation of China's ability in financing projects and leveraging on funding, industrial goods such as power generation equipment, high-speed railway and telecommunications infrastructure are going to be employed comprehensively amongst the countries involved in the Belt & Road Initiative. However, it remains questionable that the overcapacity problem in China, the lack of political trust and instability as well as the security threats with some of the Belt & Road countries can be resolved, as one of the goal and benefits brought by the Belt & Road Initiative is attributed to the willingness of its neighbours to absorb the excess manufacturing capacity (Cai, 2017).

With the Belt & Road Initiative, there will be a rapid and simultaneous industrialization and urbanization of the Malaysia economies along the Belt & Road. Apart from that, by having more transport routes and cargo transport modes, it will lead to lower transport fares, regionally and globally, and these will be reflected into the improved operational costs and economic efficiency (Pancea, 2017). Hence, companies should carefully recognize the difference of various Belt & Road projects and prepare contingency plans to cope with any short-term disruptions over lengthy project lifespans while building strong relationships with local authorities to enhance the chances of success (Wijeratne *et* al. 2017).

In short, the strategy has a huge potential for integrating Malaysia with the rest of the world. To achieve this goal, a fine balance must be reached between Malaysia and China's interests to develop not only connectivity between the two countries but also the connectivity between ASEAN member states and the countries included in the Belt & Road Initiative (Chia 2016). This initiative could draw states together and promote integration by narrowing space and time. Better connectivity will enhance Malaysia's development potential as well as facilitate the diffusion of not only technology but also of ideas and norms (Pandit & Basu 2014), and Malaysia could benefit greatly from this transformation.

REFERENCES

Adilla, J. (2017). Malaysia tops US-based '2017 best countries to invest in' survey. *New Straits Times*. Available from https://www.nst.com.my/news/2017/03/219850/msia-tops-us-based-2017-best-countries-invest-survey

Barcelona Centre of International Affairs. (2016). *One Belt, One Road: The Chinese Dream and its Impact on Europe*. Retrieved from https://www.cidob.org/en/publications/publication_series/notes_internacionals/n1_148_one_belt_one_road_el_sueno_chino_y_su_impacto_sobre_europa/one_belt_one_road_the_chinese_dream_and_its_impact_on_europe

Belt and Road Portal. (2017). *Xi Jinping and B&R Initiative*. Available from https://eng.yidaiyilu.gov.cn/info/iList.jsp?tm_id=139&cat_id=10089&info_id=9598&fbclid=IwAR0uzl34B042msFA9xWUzzwOSLgO_D5HbTjmbC7k0fDa3btqLM_pxHxuAA4

Benjamin, H., & Viktor, F. (2017). The Belt and Road Initiative: China's Vision for Globalisation, Beijing-Style. *The Conversation*. Available from http://theconversation.com/the-belt-and-road-initiative-chinas-vision-for-globalisation-beijing-style-77705

Bernama. (2017). Malaysia Expected to Benefit from One Belt One Road Initiative. *BERNAMA*. Available from http://www.bernama.com/malaysia/article/malaysia-expected-to-benefit-from-one-belt-one-road-initiative-says-najib

Business Monitor International. (2017). *Trillion-dollar trade route: Winners along the Belt and Road*. London: Business Monitor International.

Cai, P. (2017). Understanding China's Belt and Road Initiative. *Lowy Institute*. Available from https://www.lowyinstitute.org/publications/understanding-belt-and-road-initiative

Chia, S. Y. (2016). ASEAN Economic Integration and Physical Connectivity. *Asian Economic Papers*, *15*(2), 198–215. doi:10.1162/ASEP_a_00438

China Institute of International Studies. (2016). *The Belt and Road Initiative and Its Impact on Asia-Europe Connectivity*. Available from http://www.ciis.org.cn/english/2016-07/21/content_8911184.htm

Chinese National Development and Reform Commission. (2015). Vision and Actions on Jointly Building Silk Road Economic Belt and 21st Century Maritime Silk Road. *Chinese Ministry of Foreign Affairs and Chinese Ministry of Commerce*. Available from http://en.ndrc.gov.cn/newsrelease/201503/t20150330_669367.html

David, H. (2017). Malaysia Welcome OBOR but Keeps China at Arm's-Length. *World Politics Review*. Available from http://www.worldpoliticsreview.com/trend-lines/22091/malaysia-welcomes-one-belt-one-road-but-keeps-china-at-arm-s-length

EdgeProp. (2016). *Melaka Gateway Developer Ropes in China State Firm*. Available from https://www.edgeprop.my/content/870701/melaka-gateway-developer-ropes-china-state-firm

el Namaki, M. S. S. (2017). Is China's Belt and Road Initiative (BRI): A case of cross country dynamic synergy? *Scholedge International Journal of Management & Development*, *4*(5), 40–45.

Embong, E. A. R., Evers, H.-D., & Ramli, R. (2017). *One Belt One Road (OBOR) and Malaysia: A Long-Term Geopolitical Perspective*. Institute of Malaysia and International Studies Working Paper Series, Universiti Kebangsaan Malaysia.

Free Malaysia Today. (2017). *PPBM: Don't Compromise Security with 'One Belt, One Road'*. Available from http://www.freemalaysiatoday.com/category/nation/2017/05/14/ppbm-dont-compromise-security-with-one-belt-one-road

Gao, Y. (2017). Influences of institutional differences on Chinese enterprises' Investment on countries in "The Belt and Road" Strategy - Based on regulatory effects of ethnic Chinese in host countries. *Modern Economy*, *8*(4), 551–556. doi:10.4236/me.2017.84042

Goodall, K., Li, N., & Warner, M. (2007). Expatriate Managers in China: The Influence of Chinese Culture on Cross-Cultural Management. *Journal of General Management*, *12*(4).

Han, D. (2017). Malaysia welcomes 'One Belt, One Road' But Keeps China at Arm's Length. *World Politics*. Available from http://www.worldpolitics.com/trend-lines/22091/malaysia-welcomes-one-belt-one-road-but-keeps-china-at-arm-s-length

Hanif, L. (2017). China, Malaysia exchange 9 MOUs, agreements. *News of Asia*. Available from http://newsofasia.net/china-malaysia-exchange-9-mous-agreements

Hofstede, G. (2001). *Culture's Consequences: Comparing Values, Behaviors, Institutions, and Organizations across Nations* (2nd ed.). Thousand Oaks, CA: Sage Publications.

Hofstede, G. (2007). Asian Management in the 21st Century. *Asia Pacific Journal of Management*, *24*(4), 411–420. doi:10.100710490-007-9049-0

Hofstede, G. (2010). *What about China?* Available from https://geert-hofstede.com/china.html

Hofstede, G. (2010). *What about Malaysia?* Available from https://geert-hofstede.com/malaysia.html

Hofstede, G., & Hofstede, G. (2005). *Culture and Organizations: Software of the Mind*. New York: McGraw-Hill.

Hofstede, G., Hofstede, G. J., & Minkov, M. (2010). *Cultures and Organizations: Software of the Mind* (3rd ed.). New York: McGraw-Hill USA.

Hofstede Insights. (2018). *Compare Countries*. Available from https://www.hofstede-insights.com/product/compare-countries/

Ignatius, D. (2017). The new silk road: Is there a plan for Malaysia? *Free Malaysia Today*. Available from http://www.freemalaysiatoday.com/category/opinion/2017/05/29/the-new-silk-road-is-there-a-plan-for-malaysia

Jennings, R. (2017). Malaysia buying Chinese ships to protect its waters from China. *VOA*. Available from https://www.voanews.com/a/malaysia-buying-chinese-ships-to-protect-waters-from-china-others/3780026.html

John, T. (2017). Malaysia One of the Greatest Beneficiaries of OBOR. *New Straits Times*. Available from https://www.nst.com.my/opinion/columnists/2017/05/239626/malaysia-one-greatest-beneficiaries-obor

Leer, Y. V. D., & Yau, J. (2016). China's New Silk Route - The Long and Winding Road. *PwC*. Available from http://www.pwc.com/gx/en/issues/high-growth-markets/publications/china-new-silk-route.html

Lehmann, J. P., Buche, I., & Perrinjaquet, M. (2016). One Belt – One Road: China's re-Engineering of the Global Business Environment. *IMD*. Retrieved from https://www.imd.org/research/insightsimd/one-belt-one-road-chinas-re-engineering-of-the-global-business-environment

Liu, M. K. (2016). *The challenges and opportunities of China's new Silk Road*. Available from https://www.weeconomic.org/2016/01/the-challenges-and-opportunities-of-china-s-new-silk-road

Malaysia External Trade Development Corporation. (2018). *Tapping Business Opportunities along the Silk Route*. Available from http://www.matrade.gov.my/en/about-matrade/media/press-releases/4296-tapping-business-opportunities-along-the-silk-route

Malaysiakini. (2017). *Malaysia Inks Second Phase Deals on ECRL and Malacca-Pengerang Pipeline*. Available from https://www.malaysiakini.com/news/382127

Ministry of International Trade and Industry Malaysia. (2017). *Halal Industry Development Corporation Signs MoU with Weifang Sime Darby Port Co., Ltd China to Develop 1B1R Halal Infrastructure*. Available from http://www.miti.gov.my/index.php/pages/view/4239

Ministry of International Trade and Industry Malaysia. (2017). *MITI Report 2017*. Author.

Mustafic, A. (2017). China's One Belt, One Road and energy security initiatives: A plan to conquer the world? *Sarajevo Journal of Social Sciences - Inquiry*, *2*(2), 153-190.

New Sarawak Tribune. (2017). *CM Witnesses Exchange of MOU of Methanol Plant*. Available from https://www.newsarawaktribune.com.my/news/cm-witnesses-exchange-of-mou-for-methanol-plan

Pandit, S. D., & Basu, R. (2014). Connectivity, Development and Regional Integration: The Case of Indo-Myanmar Kaladan Project. *IUP Journal of International Relations*, *8*(3), 25–39.

Parameswaran, P. (2017). The real trouble with China's Belt and Road. *The Diplomat*. Available from http://thediplomat.com/2017/05/the-real-trouble-with-chinas-belt-and-road

Pencea, S. (2017). A Look Into the Complexities of the One Belt, One Road Strategy. *Global Economic Observer*, *5*(1), 142–158.

Pitlo, L. B. (2016). China-Southeast Asia connectivity: Opportunities and challenges for the Maritime Silk Road. *China US Focus*. Available from http://www.chinausfocus.com/foreign-policy/china-southeast-asia-connectivity-opportunities-and-challenges-for-the-maritime-silk-road

Reuters. (2014a). *Alibaba's Yuebao Dents Chinese Banks' Profitability*. Available from http://www.reuters.com/article/china-banks-idUSL2N0MG0BV20140320

Reuters. (2014b). *China Banks Strike Back against Threat from Internet Finance*. Available from http://uk.reuters.com/article/uk-china-banks-online-idUKBREA1M12I20140223

Reuters. (2017a). *AirAsia to Launch New Chinese Low Cost Carrier*. Available from http://www.reuters.com/article/us-airasia-china-idUSKCN18A0TL

Reuters. (2017b). *China loosens some license requirements for foreign banks.* Available from http://www.reuters.com/article/us-china-banking-regulations-idUSKBN16O0BS?il=0

Selat, A. M. (1987). *Malaysia's China policy: the bilateral relationship (Master's thesis).* Australian National University.

Sophie, Q. (2017). *One Belt One Road in Malaysia.* Retrieved from https://www.aspistrategist.org.au/one-belt-one-road-malaysia-chinas-strategic-enabler

Sumathy, P. (2017). China's One Belt One Road Initiatives: Strengthening Economic Linkage for Mutual Benefits. *New Straits Times.* Available from https://www.nst.com.my/opinion/columnists/2017/05/235414/chinas-one-belt-one-road-initiative-strengthening-economic

The Economist. (2017). *What is China's Belt and Road Initiative?* Available from https://www.economist.com/blogs/economist-explains/2017/05/economist-explains-11

The Star. (2016). *MayBank's ShenZhen Branch Opens.* Author.

The Star. (2017a). *OBOR lights the way to China.* Retrieved from http://www.thestar.com.my/business/business-news/2017/04/10/obor-lights-the-way-to-china

The Star. (2017b). *Prospering with Belt and Road.* Available from http://www.thestar.com.my/news/nation/2017/05/21/prospering-with-belt-and-road-malaysia-is-one-of-64-countries-to-reap-the-benefits-of-chinas-initiat

The Star. (2017c). *Robotic City among RM31bil worth of Deals Signed.* Available from http://www.thestar.com.my/news/nation/2017/05/15/robotic-city-among-rm31bil-worth-of-deals-signed

The Star. (2017d). *RM 55bil East Coast Rail Kicks Off.* Available from http://www.thestar.com.my/business/business-news/2017/03/29/east-coast-rail-kicks-off

The Star. (2017e). *Titijaya to tie up with CREC in RM575mil Sabah property project.* Available from http://www.thestar.com.my/business/business-news/2017/05/15/titijaya-to-tie-up-with-crec-in-rm575mil-sabah-property-project

The Star. (2017f). *Why Malaysia Supports China's Belt and Road.* Available from http://www.thestar.com.my/news/nation/2017/05/12/why-malaysia-supports-china-belt-and-road

The Star. (2018). *Dr Mahathir Calls for China's Help with Fiscal Problems*. Available from https://www.thestar.com.my/news/nation/2018/08/20/dr-mahathir-calls-for-china-help-with-fiscal-problems/#lmwA3d8Kyzfc5APk.99

The Straight Times. (2017). *East Coast Rail Link: Malaysia Touts Rail Trade Route as Rival to Singapore.* Available from https://www.straitstimes.com/asia/se-asia/east-coast-rail-link-malaysia-touts-rail-trade-route-as-rival-to-singapore

United Nations. (2017). *Sustainable development goals*. Available from http://www.un.org/sustainabledevelopment/sustainable-development-goals

Veras, E. Z. (2016). Cultural Differences between Countries: The Brazilian and the Chinese Ways of Doing Business. *Journal on Innovation and Sustainability*, *2*(2), 77–83.

Wei, L. Q., Chiang, F. T., & Wu, L. Z. (2012). Developing and utilizing network resources: Roles of political skill. *Journal of Management Studies*, *49*(2), 381–402. doi:10.1111/j.1467-6486.2010.00987.x

Wijeratne, D., Yau, J., Wong, G., Rathbone, M., Neu, B. L., & Lau, S. (2017). Repaving the ancient Silk Routes. *PwC.* Available from https://www.pwc.com/gx/en/issues/high-growth-markets/publications/repaving-the-ancient-silk-routes.html

Xin, J. (2017). Malaysia fast and firm to grasp Belt and Road opportunities. *CGTN.* Retrieved from https://news.cgtn.com/news/3d41444e34557a4d/share_p.html

KEY TERMS AND DEFINITIONS

Ancient Silk Road Trade Routes: An ancient network of trade routes that connected the East and the West.

Belt and Road Initiative: The Belt and Road Initiative, also known as One Belt One Road, the Belt and Road, or formally the Silk Road Economic Belt and the 21st-Century Maritime Silk Road, which can be abbreviated as B&R, is a huge infrastructure development and investment program introduced by the Chinese government that covers Europe, Asia and Africa regions.

Cultural Distance: A difference in human values that are rooted in national culture, which affect individuals' attitude and behavior.

Economic Globalization: The widespread of international movement of groups, capital, services, technology, and information that increase the interdependence of world economies.

Infrastructure: The fundamental physical facilities and organizational system that needed for the operations of a society.

Investment: Distribution of money in items or projects in the expectation of benefits in the future.

Small and Medium-Sized Enterprises (SMEs): Sales turnover and number of full-time employees are the criteria that been used in determining SMEs in Malaysia, in which for manufacturing sectors, SMEs are defined as firms with sales turnover not exceeding RM50 million or number of full-time employees not exceeding; whereas for service and other sectors, SMEs are defined as firms with sales turnover not exceeding RM20 million of number of full-time employees not exceeding 75.

Chapter 12
Opportunities of Tourism Development of Mongolia Under the Belt and Road Initiative

Huilian Han
Jilin University, China

Hui Li
Jilin University, China

ABSTRACT

The Belt and Road Initiative has had great impact on the countries on the road. The China-Mongolia-Russia corridor, as one of the six economic corridors, has seen rapid progress. In the progress, Mongolia not only plays important role as a bridge, but it actively participates in the initiative. As a leading industry, tourism has played an active role in Sino-Mongolian cultural exchanges and trade cooperation and has become a pillar industry in Mongolia. This chapter analyzes the limiting factors of Mongolian tourism and points out the new opportunities for tourism brought by the Belt and Road strategy. Though the analysis of the tourism industry in Mongolia and of the opportunities brought by the Belt and Road Initiative, the chapter has important practical significance for the investors of China and Mongolia to correctly understand the Mongolian tourism industry's development status and prospects. Thus, they will strengthen the tourism industry cooperation in the future.

DOI: 10.4018/978-1-5225-8440-7.ch012

INTRODUCTION

At present, the impact of the international financial crisis has not gone far in Mongolia. The large reduction in demand for mineral products and low prices have continuously affected the Mongolia's economic growth. What is more, the international debt crisis in 2016 is worse for the Mongolian National Economy. Under this background, the Mongolian government puts forward the green development idea. It is plans to vigorously develop agriculture, tourism and manufacturing industries in 2016-2030 to promote Mongolia's economic development. China has brought great development opportunities to the countries along the road since it proposed the strategy. As a leading industry, tourism plays an important role in the process of promoting the cultural exchange and trade among the countries along the route. Mongolia's Prairie Road program and China Silk Road docking brings new opportunities to Mongolia's tourism development.

STATUS OF TOURISM DEVELOPMENT IN MONGOLIA

Mongolian Tourism Development Stage

Mongolia is located in the central part of Asia, and adjacent to China and Russia. Mongolia has 15665 million square kilometers, and is divided into 21 provinces and one municipality, 342 Soum and 1681 bagg. The total population of Mongolia reached 3.1209 million at the end of 2016. After the transition of Mongolia's economy, Mongolian exported mineral resources to promote economic development, but the development of tourism was lagging behind. Mongolia is rich in tourism resources, but mineral development contributes more to the national GDP than other industries. In 2016, the mining output value was 4808.5 billion Mongolian tugrug, accounted for 20% of GDP, while the tourism revenue was 247.1 billion Mongolian tugrug, accounted for only 1% of GDP. Therefore, Mongolia still attaches great importance to mineral development and ignores the development of tourism. Besides, the backward infrastructure is also an important factor hindering the development of tourism in Mongolia.

According to the economic system, the development of Mongolian tourism can be divided into two stages: tourism of the planned economy and the market economy period. On the basis of the development stage of tourism is divided into initial stage, development stage and stable development stage. Tourism in Mongolia is now in the early stages of the development of tourism. In the planned economy period, the Ministry of Commerce of Mongolia set up the "Tourist Customer Service Bureau" to begin receive foreign tourists. In 1990 the Mongolian tourism market formed and developed. With the Mongolian economy entering the transition period, the tourism industry turned to the market, began to operate independently, and got good development. The Mongolian Tourist Association was established in 1992, and 125 enterprises have joined the association since then. The Mongolian government headed by Prime Minister Ponzag Zaseri in 1995 promulgated the first file which concerned about the development of tourism, "Mongolia Tourism Development Plan 1995-2005" on No.167 Decision, then established the tourism agency under the basis of the Ministry of Commerce and Industry. In 1996, the tourism industry was under the jurisdiction of the former Ministry of Infrastructure Development; In 1998, the government confirmed No.192 Decision to determine the Mongolian Resolution on Formulating and Developing Tourism Policies. In the same year, the government adopted the No. 214 resolution in response to the development of tourism, and established the Mongolian Tourist Information Center. In 1999, Mongolia joined the World Tourism Organization. In 2004, 1 "Tourism Information Center" was abolished, then was established Ministry of Road Transport and Tourism. After the reorganization of government agencies in 2008, Tourism Management Agencies were assigned to the Ministry of Nature, Environment and Tourism. In May, 2000, the state of Mongolia issued the first travel law, the Tourism Law of the Mongolia. Mongolia's Great Hural made the 2016-2030 Economic Development Vision Plan, which centered on the nomadic culture, actively participate in the "Silk Road Economic Belt" and develop the "Tea Road". This showed Mongolia's determination to accelerate the development of tourism in the market economy system.

Although Mongolia's tourism industry has entered the market economy period, Mongolia has proposed relevant policy, resolutions and laws, and established relevant supporting departments. However, the development of tourism has not received enough attention under the background of mining-based economy. Tourism development in Mongolia is still in its early stages.

Resources of Tourism in Mongolia

Resources of the tourism are the object and the foundation of developing tourism industry. The advantage of developing tourism in Mongolia lies in its abundant tourism resources. The tourism resources of Mongolia are divided into three categories:

Mongolian Natural Landscape

Mongolia belongs to the continental climate, with a wide variety of wild animals and plants. Mongolia, with vast land and sparse population, has rich natural scenery with little human intervention and high ornamental value. In addition, Mongolian nature reserve is also a good place for tourists to travel and sightseeing. Mongolia has not only the tourist attractions like the Altay Mountains, the Hangai Mountains, and the Kent Mountain Range, but also has the Leisure tourism Holy Land as Kusugu Lake, which is known as the "Oriental Blue Pearl". Mongolian are very respectful of nature, and have a strong sense of protection of nature. At present, Mongolia has established more than 40 nature reserves. These are important parts of Mongolian natural landscape. In a word, Mongolian tourism natural landscape resources are rich and environmentally friendly.

Mongolian History and Folk Culture

Jiangbo(2013)deems the culture is the soul of tourism, and tourism is the carrier of culture. Culture is the eternal theme of tourism, the mystical sense of cultural differences is pursued by tourists, and the culture of the original ecology is more attractive to tourists. For thousands of years, there have been many ethnic groups living in this vast grassland. They created a splendid history on this land, then silently withdraw from the stage of history, and leave a rich and colorful historical and cultural relics as well as human economic living fossil— "nomadic economy" culture. The Mongolian nationality has formed a unique national culture in this long history which becomes a historical and cultural resource of the development of modern tourism.

Nomadic Culture

Nomadic lifestyle, which is the most suitable way of life on the land, can make full use of grassland resources. According to Xie Zhiwei(2008),"Nomadic culture is all tangible or intangible cultural heritage created by the nomadic people and it is the living fossil of human economic production". More than half of populations of Mongolia have been engaged in nomadic herding directly or indirectly. In 2016, the livestock inventories were 61.549 million, and 341 livestock per capita. Nomadic herding is the traditional economy of Mongolia and one of the most important pillar industries. Mongolian mainly adopt the traditional nomadic production mode, and has maintained a profound nomadic culture foundation in the long-term production and life. The Mongolian have been procreating for generations, living in harmony with the nature and creating a unique nomadic culture. It is different from other regions and ethnic groups, and has distinctive features both in terms of its historical connotation and its extension. Nomadic culture produces products with simple, aesthetic, original ecological, and attracts tourists from all over the world.

Although Mongolia has beautiful natural landscape, history and folk cultural heritage, but the tourism development of Mongolia is still faced with poor infrastructure, lack of distinctive brand and lagging problems caused by the seasonal characteristics of tourism industry.

LIMITING FACTORS OF TOURISM DEVELOPMENT

The Lack of Unique Brands in Tourist Attractions

Zhao liming et al. (2002) regard as that tourism scenic spot brand refers to the comprehensive reflection of the terms such as the name and terminology, mark symbol, actual function, service facility, market development, corporate reputation and corporate image of the tourist attraction. Mongolia has a unique natural landscape, historical and cultural resources, which are not only the basis of tourism development, but also are the important factor of establishing unique brand. Mongolian scenic spots lack a unique brand. There are several factors restricting the Mongolian tourism brand. Firstly, Mongolia's tourism industry starts late, tour operators fail to understand the core value of tourism brands, and their brand awareness is very weak. At present, the tourism industry of Mongolia lacks a system. Travel agencies and tourism service companies are small in scale, with less mutual coordination. Secondly, the tourism projects of Mongolia is mainly based on natural landscapes. According to a Study on the Consumption Structure of Incoming Tourists in Mongolia, which conducted by the Mongolian National Bank and the Mongolian Tourism Center displayed, 36% of Mongolian inbound tourists are for visiting natural scenery, 30% of them want to experience folk culture, 13% of tourists are interested in Mongolian history, and 9% of people for adventure tourism. According to the above data, 76% of the inbound tourists want to visit or experience Mongolia's natural and humanistic. The exploration of national history and culture and its connotation are not enough. The connotation of the history and culture are not explored enough. Thirdly, the structure of tourism products in Mongolia is single and lacks local characteristics. Although the tourist products of scenic spot mainly have ethnic characteristics, they lack products embodying national cultural connotations. Many products are imported directly or copied abroad, lacking their own national cultural characteristics. In addition, some products with national characteristics are rough, which cannot meet the needs of tourists and affect the national brand image of tourists. Finally, Mongolia's tourism propaganda is not enough. Due to the insufficient funds, the brand innovation capability of Mongolian tourism enterprises is limited, and brand promotion is insufficient.

According to the data (shows in Table 1) issued by the National Statistics Office of Mongolia, the inbound of tourists in Mongolia for official, business and employment in 2017 accounted for 10%, 34%, and 11.3%, respectively. And 35.2% of the total visitors were purely for sightseeing, which increased by 3.3%. Compared with 2013, the number of passengers for official and employment in 2017 declined, but it still accounted for a large proportion of inbound tourists in Mongolia. As a whole, the

Table 1. The inbound tourist of Mongolia by purpose of visit 2013- 2016 (per 100 people)

Purpose of Visit	2013	2014	2015	2016	2017
Official	26.7	26	20.2	16.8	10
Business	30.7	25.4	32	30.9	34
Tourism	22.4	24.4	25.9	31.9	35.2
Employment	18.2	21.4	16	12.2	11.3
Transit	0.5	0.8	0.2	0.6	0.7
Other	1.5	2	5.7	7.6	8.8

Source: National Statistics Office of Mongolia

Table 2. Number of inbound tourists of Mongolia by countries 2013 -2016 (person)

	2013	2014	2015	2016	2017	Annual Growth*
Total	417815	392844	386204	404163	469309	16.2
China	178326	157561	145029	131312	142481	8.2
Russia	74468	73055	70668	84065	106885	27.2
Korea	45178	45476	47213	57587	74921	30.1
Japan	18178	18469	19277	19985	22519	12.7
America	14701	13987	14420	15859	16667	5.1
Germany	9499	9551	8992	9709	10582	9
France	7407	7733	7989	9026	10038	11.2
United Kingdom	6391	5758	6148	6161	5996	-2.67
Australia	6765	5118	4804	5631	7287	29.4

Source: National Statistics Office of Mongolia

number of inbound tourists in Mongolia has a rising trend, and they mainly come from northeast Asian countries.

Among them, (shows in Table 2)142 thousand tourists comes from China, accounted for 30.3%, and 10.7 thousand of them are from Russia, accounted for 22.7%. There are also a lot of tourists from developed East Asian countries; such as Japan and Korea, and less tourists from Europe and America. We can see from the analysis of the origin and the purpose of inbound passengers, It is shown that the tourism publicity of Mongolia is not strong enough, and therefore it is not attract the tourist from developed countries as Europe and the United States. It has limited the development of Mongolian tourism.

Underdeveloped Infrastructure in Mongolia

The development of tourism is closely related to the infrastructure. The region with good infrastructure has better opportunity to tourism development. To some extent, the level of tourism development reflects the level of infrastructure. Because perfect infrastructure will enhance the tourism development, otherwise it will impede the development of tourism. Mongolian tourism development is restricted by regional conditions and economic development, which makes Mongolia difficult to build infrastructure, especially the infrastructure of tourism industry.

A very important infrastructure for the tourism industry development is transportation. Transportation is as important to tourism like a person's meridian. However, the transportation facilities in Mongolia are relatively backward: is total existing railway 1815 kilometers, which are broad-gage railway and most of them are constructed by the Soviet Union. Fan Lijun (2012) stated, at present, in the capital cities of 21 provinces, only 5 cities in the central and eastern regions have railways. The rest of the cities are connected by road or air routes.

The infrastructure construction in Mongolia is relatively weak, and the facilities are not smooth, which restricts the development of Mongolia's tourism industry to a certain extent. In recent years, Mongolian government have put forward a set of projects on infrastructure construction, and have invested a lot of money, but compared with the other fields of investment, the fund investment in Mongolia infrastructure construction is still limited. According to Fig 1 and 2, statistics released by National Statistics Office of Mongolia, Mongolian Civil Aviation Development is limited. The passengers and freights are mainly carried out by roads and railways, therefore it cannot meet the service demands of passengers in the peak tourist season.

The service infrastructure of Mongolian tourist attractions is backward, thus as the accommodation, catering, entertainment and medical facilities of Mongolian scenic spots cannot meet tourists' different levels of needs. Statistical data displayed

Figure 1. Carried passengers by transportation sector
Source: National Statistics Office of Mongolia

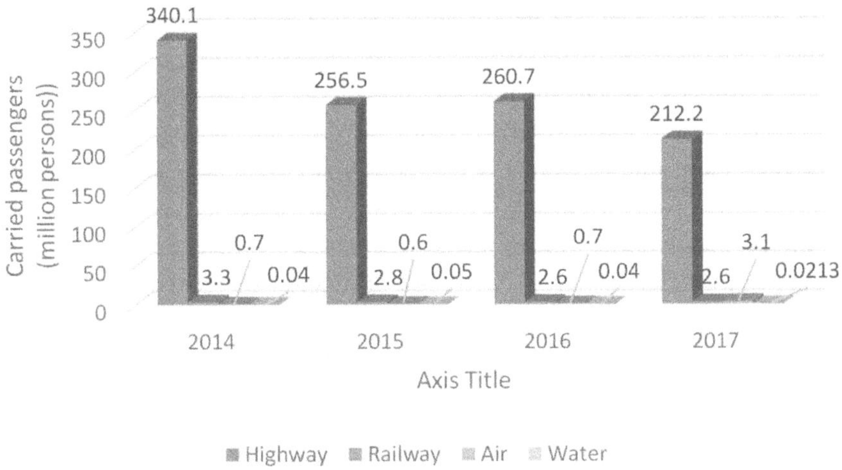

Figure 2. Carried freight by transportation type
Source: National Statistics Office of Mongolia

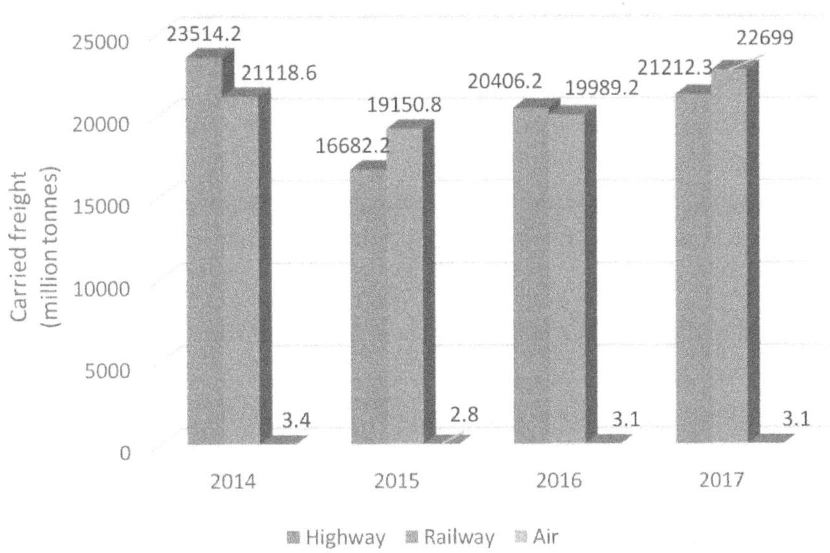

that Mongolia has 3632 restaurants, of which 2167 are in business, 470 are not open, 773 are suspended, 131 are closed which accounted for 59.6% of total. But beyond that, the safety measures and emergency ability of the scenic area are insufficient. However, the safety is very important for a tourist, but Mongolian scenic area, lacks the professional service personnel and rescuers to ensure the tourists safety.

Strong Seasonality of Mongolian Tourism

Mongolia is a landlocked country, its climate typical belongs to the continental climate, and has four distinct seasons. The annual minimum temperature in most areas is lower than -40°C, and the highest temperature is over 40°C. The seasonality is mainly reflected in the time distribution of inbound tourists and the tourism revenues. The winter in Mongolia is relatively long, generally from November to April of the following year. Spring is from May to June every year, Summer is from July to August, and Autumn from September to October. Because of low temperature and imperfect tourist facilities in Mongolia, in winter, the cost of tourist industry operators in Mongolia will increase and the tourism revenue will reduce.

Table 3 and Table 4 shows the arrival time of tourists is mainly in June, July and August. The tourist season mainly focuses on June, July and August. Even if it is extends from mid-May to mid-October, it only last for five months. Thus, the enthusiasm of local tourism enterprises is not high. Mongolian tourism industry is difficult to develop under the condition of cold weather and high cost.

OPPORTUNITIES BROUGHT BY THE BELT AND ROAD STRATEGY TO MONGOLIAN TOURISM INDUSTRY

The Belt and Road development strategy proposed by China aims to create a maritime economic corridor to connect Europe, Asia and Africa, so as to promote the coordination of countries along the routes, for the purpose of achieving mutual benefit. This development strategy will build the new economic structure, promote

Table 3. Number of inbound tourists of Mongolia by quarter 2010-2017 (person)

	Quarter I	Quarter II	Quarter III	Quarter IV	Total
2010	30310	187703	355627	456090	1029730
2011	75520	203481	372659	460360	1112020
2012	72496	198794	378839	475892	1126021
2013	58110	168855	332951	417815	977731
2014	57647	154533	315901	392844	920925
2015	53804	147145	317210	386204	904363
2016	49562	146923	325042	404163	925690
2017	63577	180775	383141	469306	1096799

*Source: National Statistics Office of Mongolia: [EB/OL].*http://www.nso.mn.*[2018-06-10].*

Table 4. Tourism revenue of Mongolia by quarter 2010-2017 (million tugrug)

	Quarter I	Quarter II	Quarter III	Quarter IV	Total
2010	1,058.80	3,821.10	7,252.00	6,688.20	18820.1
2011	1,443.60	2,968.50	16,044.80	3,388.00	23844.9
2012	1,411.70	13,784.40	12,831.10	9,854.30	37881.5
2013	4,465.80	12,218.40	28,340.00	8,674.60	53698.8
2014	9,913.50	16,288.80	34,894.30	4,173.40	65270
2015	37,526.70	51,589.50	73,819.20	31,761.00	194696.4
2016	40,947.70	69,641.80	78,373.50	58,129.60	247092.6

*Source: National Statistics Office of Mongolia: [EB/OL].*http://www.nso.mn.*[2018-06-10].*

economic cooperation among the countries, and accelerated economic development. The boundary line is 4710 kilometers between China and Mongolia, which is a geographical advantage for Sino-Mongolia coorporation. Mongolia is a developing country and its economic growth is relatively dependent on China's economic. The Belt and Road initiative development strategy plays a very significant role in the development of Mongolia's tourism and economic development.

Promoting Tourism Industry and International Cooperation of Mongolia

During the transitional period, the tourism industry in Mongolia developed rapidly. However, the scale of tourism industry was small, and the tourism route was not fully explored and developed, and unique tourism brand has not been established. Compared with Mongolia, China's tourism industry has comparatively perfect tourism infrastructure and service, and made remarkable achievements. In addition, The Belt and Road Initiative creates more cooperation opportunities for the tourism industry all the countries along the road, especially, it provide good chance to Mongolian tourism, to develop more tourist routes and speed up the unique image of Mongolian tourism brand in the international community.

Tourism plays an important role in the new round of opening-up and international cooperation represented by the Belt and Road Initiative of China. In recent years, with the concerted efforts of the travel agencies of China, Mongolia and Russia, these three countries have deepened their travel exchanges and cooperation, which has become an important highlight of the construction of the China-Mongolia-Russia Economic Corridor. The Belt and Road Initiative involves 65 countries, not only involving Asian countries, but also involving 16 countries in Central and

Eastern Europe. Mongolia has taken an active part in the Silk Road Economic Belt proposed by China with Mongolia's Prairie Road Program, which is docked with China's Silk Road and Russia's Eurasian Economic Union Plan. It playing the role of a bridge connecting the Eurasian Development Strategy in The Belt and Road.

Facilitating the Construction of Tourism Infrastructure of Mongolia

The backward transport infrastructure is one of the factors that affect the development of tourism in Mongolia. The traffic condition is imperfect, and it not enough to meet the traffic demands of inbound tourists, thus narrowing travel space range. However, the Belt and Road initiative promotes infrastructure construction in Mongolia.

Mongolia has only one railway, Beijing-Ulaanbaatar-Moscow, which has been aged because of years of disrepair. But beyond that, the difference in track gauge between China and Mongolia has increased transportation costs and extended transportation time, which has restricted the development of tourism in Mongolia. The China, Mongolia and Russia economic corridor signed in UFA, Russia, July 9, 2015. The three countries emphasize to build and develop international land transport corridors, ensuring the accessibility of passengers, goods and vehicles through the implementation of infrastructure co- construction projects. Under the initiative of the Belt and Road, enterprises from countries along the Belt and Road invest Mongolia's transport and production projects. For example: the Mongolian Bagnall Power Plant Project, which is contracted by Chinese enterprises, was officially opened in Ulaanbaatar on December 23, 2015. After the project put into operation, it will not only change the outlook of Mongolia's urban development, but also push forward the tourism development of Mongolia. The economic corridor of China, Mongolia and Russia takes the action to promote the interconnection of the infrastructure. After the opening up of "Channels and Collaterals" in the tourism industry, its development is bound to be rapid. In order to develop the tourism, Mongolia will improve the quality of tourist service, to perfect the accommodation environment and to add supporting facilities of the tourist attractions.

According to the statistics in the first half year of 2017, Mongolia's total population is 3.11 million. The Mongolian population is relatively small. The population of people aged 15 and above is 1.23 million. There are only 38000 people in the accommodation and catering industry. The development of tourism industry will boost the training mechanism of professional talents in the service industry. The investment in the infrastructure construction of countries along the Belt and Road will further improve the national infrastructure and promote the accessibility of tourism.

Increasing Mongolian FDI Inflows

The increasing of foreign direct investment (FDI) and inbound tourism revenue are main sources of the Mongolian foreign exchange income, which create the job opportunities, and promote the economic development of Mongolia. The Belt and Road initiatives advances Mongolian FDI. There is close relationship between FDI and inbound tourism in Mongolia. FDI pushes forward the development of tourism industry on the basis of the income generated by Mongolian inbound tourism industry. Business tourism is an important part of tourism income in Mongolia. FDI can cover the shortage of fund in the development of tourism industry. The inbound tourism attracts more direct investment from foreign counties to Mongolia. The essential relationship between FDI and inbound tourism is mutual funds and tourist flow. Therefore, in terms of flow pattern and economic purpose, Mongolia's FDI and inbound tourism are closely related with each other, and has a concomitant relationship.

Inbound tourism brings population flow, accelerates local infrastructure construction and economic development, and forming regional advantages. It can enhance the absorption of FDI, which has formed the development situation of inbound tourism to boost the FDI of Mongolia. The growth of FDI can also directly promote the exchange of business between Mongolia and source countries of the tourist. A certain scale of inbound business tourism can be formed. Bao Fuhua(2016) stated, at the same time, inbound business tourism indirectly promote the personnel exchanges between the two countries and reputation of the tourism service of Mongolia, to facilitate inbound tourism is for the purpose of visiting relatives and sightseeing. Therefore, the increase of FDI brings the trend of inbound tourism development.

Creating Revenues for Tourism

China puts forward the Belt and Road initiative, calling on countries to concern themselves promoting policy coordination, facilities connectivity, unimpeded trade, financial integration and people-to-people bonds. All of this is the top-level design policies of promoting tourism industry of countries along the route. Jiang Yiyi(2017) argued, under the Belt and Road initiative, the tourism industry deepen the cooperation, which shifts from the market cooperation to the resource flow and brand, service cooperation. In 2014, Chinese president Xi Jinping's visit to Mongolia promoted a China-Mongolia comprehensive strategic partnership. In the same year, the heads of China, Russia and Mongolia held their first meeting in Dushanbe, proposing practical cooperation in tourism and other fields. They approved the "Mid-term road map for the development of tripartite cooperation of the China-Russia-Mongolia" at the second summit in Ufa, in 2015, and clearly stated that the three parties would expand the cooperation in the tourism field and jointly built an international tourist route of the "Tea Road". At the third meeting in Tashkent, China, Russia and Mongolia agreed with the planning of economic corridor construction, and signed "The Outline of the Construction of China, Mongolia and Russia Economic Corridor". President Xi Jinping pointed out that China, Russia, and Mongolia rely on the advantages of each other as a neighboring country to carry out close cooperation and actively implement the "Mid-term road map for the development of tripartite cooperation of the China-Russia-Mongolia". Three countries have made positive progress and achievements in the fields of economic, trade, humanities, transit transport, tourism and sports. In July 22, 2016, the first China-Russia-Mongolia Tourism Ministers' Meeting was successfully held in Hohhot, Inner Mongolia for implementing the consensus approved at the third meetings. In July, 2016, Premier Li Keqiang successfully visited Mongolia and attended the Asia Europe Summit held in Mongolia, which provided new opportunities for both sides to strengthen further practical cooperation in various fields, including environmental protection, tourism and other fields.

The scale of tourism exchange among China, Russia, and Mongolia has exceeded 5.431 million (person) in 2016. Among them, Sino-Russian bilateral exchanges reached 3.264 million (person), two-way exchanges of Sino-Mongolia was 1.473 million (person), and Russian-Mongolian exchanges was about 0.606 million (person). The rapid growth of the number of tourists is a huge market support for the practical cooperation of China- Russia-Mongolia. The cross border tourism exchanges and cooperation of Sino- Mongolia have been increasing rapidly. At present, 15 Sino-Mongolian border tourism routes have been explored.

Jiang yiyi(2017) found that during the Thirteenth Five-Year Plan period, China will contribute 150 million tourists and 200 billion dollars in consumption to countries along the Belt and Road. The inbound tourists in Mongolia reached 404 thousand, and generated US $321 million income in 2016. In the past, mineral resources accounted for a large proportion of GDP in Mongolia. But mineral mining and export do not bring obvious increasing benefit to the ordinary people of Mongolia. On the contrary, tourism has driven the service industry in Mongolia, which has a huge impact on the income of ordinary people. The accommodation and catering industry in Mongolia is a part of the tourism industry. In 2016, the output of accommodation and catering industry reached 241812.7 million Mongolian tugrug, with annual growth rate of 12%. Obviously, "The Belt and Road" strategy has enabled Mongolia's tourism industry to generate income revenue and increase Mongolia's tourism output.

CONCLUSION

In the environment of economic crisis caused the world economic depression, and economy of the Mongolia which is based on the mining industry, enters a bottleneck period. Thus it Mongolia needs to expand the new development field. China, as Mongolia's largest trading partner of Mongolia, proposed the development strategy of The Belt and Road, which brought the new development opportunity and challenge to the countries on the road, especially to Mongolian economy which is under slow development. Although Mongolia's tourism industry has grown rapidly, it has not been fully appreciated by the government, Mongolia still focus economic development on mining.

The rich natural resources, beautiful ecological environment and long history of folk culture, etc. are the resource basis for the development of tourism in Mongolia. Under the background of the Belt and Road and construction of the China-Mongolia-Russia Economic Corridor, the resource of tourism give full scope to function, and the inadequacies of the tourism industry have been improved. The Belt and Road will not only promote Mongolia's tourism growth, but also promote the service industry and foreign investment, and the development of Mongolia's third industries. In this way, Mongolia's further economic development will be promoted. In the condition of the Belt and Road initiative, the development of tourism has great prospects Mongolia.

On the other hand, "the Belt and Road" development strategy is not only an opportunity for Mongolia to develop the tourism industry, but also a very good opportunity for development of Chinese tourism industry. The advantages of geographical and cultural identity are the strong foundations for Sino-Mongolian cooperation in various fields. The geographical location has unique advantages in the development of tourism cooperation between the two countries. Moreover, the Inner Mongolian and Mongolian have a high degree of similarity in the field of language and culture, which decreases the cultural identity barriers for the development of tourism and promotes the social and cultural exchange of the two countries, it pushes forward the Sino-Mongolian economic cooperation.

ACKNOWLEDGMENT

This research received no specific grant from any funding agency in the public, commercial, or not-for-profit sectors.

REFERENCES

Газрын.Засгийн (1998). оны 192-р тогтоолоор "Аялал жуулчлалын бодлого зохицуулах Үндэсний Зөвлөл"-ийг байгуулж, дүрмийг нь баталжээ.

Мөнх-ЭрдэнэБ. (n.d.). *Монгол улсад аялж буй гадаадын жуулчдын зардлын түвэр судалгаа*. Retrieved from www.mongolbank.mn

Bao. (2016). The Spatial Temporal Coupling Relationship between FDI and Inbound Tourism in China. *International Economics and Trade Research, 11*, 41-55.

Fan. (2012). Sino-Russian Games in Mongolia's New Railway Construction. *Russian Central Asian & East European Market, 6*, 45-52.

Jiang. (2017, Mary 15). Tourism cooperation and resonation with "The Belt and Road" initiative. *Chinese Tourism News*.

Jiangbo. (2013). Research on historical and cultural name of Phoenix, cultural tourism product planning. *Tourism Overview, 9*, 170-180.

Mongolian Tourism Association. (n.d.). Retrieved from http://www.travelmongolia.org/index.php?do=cat&category=1

Xie. (2008). Study on the development and sustainable development of tourism resources of nomadic culture. *Heilongjiang History, 24*, 89-90.

Zhao, Huang, & Zhang. (2002). *Management of tourist attractions*. Nanjing: Nankai University Press.

Glossary

Ancient Silk Road Trade Routes: An ancient network of trade routes that connected the East and the West.

Beijing-Tianjin-Hebei Region: The "capital economic circle" of China, including Beijing, Tianjin, and Hebei Province.

Belt and Road Initiative: The Belt and Road Initiative, also known as One Belt One Road, the Belt and Road, or formally the Silk Road Economic Belt and the 21 st -Century Maritime Silk Road, which can be abbreviated as B&R, is a huge infrastructure development and investment program introduced by the Chinese government that covers Europe, Asia and Africa regions.

Cultural Distance: A difference in human values that are rooted in national culture, which affect individuals' attitude and behavior.

Economic Globalization: The widespread of international movement of groups, capital, services, technology, and information that increase the interdependence of world economies.

Fenwei Plain: The Fenhe Plain, Weihe Plain, and their surroundings in the Yellow River Basin.

Infrastructure: The fundamental physical facilities and organizational system that needed for the operations of a society.

Investment: Distribution of money in items or projects in the expectation of benefits in the future.

Road Transportation to Railway Transportation: Adjusting the transportation structure, converting some of the goods originally transported by road into railway transport.

Road Transportation to Waterway Transportation: Adjusting the transportation structure, converting some of the goods originally transported by road into waterway transport.

Sanxi Area: Including Shanxi Province, Shaanxi Province, and Western Inner Mongolia.

Small and Medium-Sized Enterprises (SMEs): Sales turnover and number of full-time employees are the criteria that been used in determining SMEs in Malaysia, in which for manufacturing sectors, SMEs are defined as firms with sales turnover not exceeding RM50 million or number of full-time employees not exceeding; whereas for service and other sectors, SMEs are defined as firms with sales turnover not exceeding RM20 million of number of full-time employees not exceeding 75.

Transporting Coal From North to South: Transporting abundant coal resources in the North Region to the South Region where coal resources are scarce.

Transporting Coal From West to East: Transporting abundant coal resources in the Western Region to the Eastern Region where coal resources are scarce.

Yangtze River Delta Region: Including Shanghai, Jiangsu Province, and Zhejiang Province.

Compilation of References

Adilla, J. (2017). Malaysia tops US-based '2017 best countries to invest in' survey. *New Straits Times*. Available from https://www.nst.com.my/news/2017/03/219850/msia-tops-us-based-2017-best-countries-invest-survey

Adner, R., & Kapoor, R. (2010). Value creation in innovation ecosystems: How the structure of technological interdependence affects firm performance in new technology generations. *Strategic Management Journal, 31*(3), 306–333. doi:10.1002mj.821

Allen, F., Qian, J., & Gu, X. (2017). An overview of China's financial system. *Annual Review of Financial Economics, 9*(1), 191–231. doi:10.1146/annurev-financial-112116-025652

Amighini, A. (2018). China's new economic powerhouse. In A. Amighini & P. Magri (Eds.), *China Champion of (Which) Globalisation* (pp. 13–37). Milano, İtaly: ISPI.

Aoyama, R. (2016). One belt, one road: China's new global strategy. *Journal of Contemporary East Asia Studies, 5*(2), 3–22. doi:10.1080/24761028.2016.11869094

Arrighi, G. (2008). *Adam Smith Pekin'de: 21. yüzyılın soy kütüğü*. İstanbul: Yordam Kitap.

Balding, C. (2018). Is China a market economy? In A. Amighini & P. Magri (Eds.), *China Champion of (Which) Globalisation* (pp. 61–79). Milano, İtaly: ISPI.

Banomyong, R., & Beresford, A. K. (2001). Multimodal transport: The case of Laotian garment exporters. *International Journal of Physical Distribution & Logistics Management, 31*(9), 663–685. doi:10.1108/09600030110408161

Bao. (2016). The Spatial Temporal Coupling Relationship between FDI and Inbound Tourism in China. *International Economics and Trade Research, 11*, 41-55.

Barcelona Centre of International Affairs. (2016). *One Belt, One Road: The Chinese Dream and its Impact on Europe*. Retrieved from https://www.cidob.org/en/publications/publication_series/notes_internacionals/n1_148_one_belt_one_road_el_sueno_chino_y_su_impacto_sobre_europa/one_belt_one_road_the_chinese_dream_and_its_impact_on_europe

Belt and Road Portal. (2017). *Xi Jinping and B&R Initiative*. Available from https://eng.yidaiyilu.gov.cn/info/iList.jsp?tm_id=139&cat_id=10089&info_id=9598&fbclid=IwAR0uzl34B042msFA9xWUzzwOSLgO_D5HbTjmbC7k0fDa3btqLM_pxHxuAA4

Benjamin, H., & Viktor, F. (2017). The Belt and Road Initiative: China's Vision for Globalisation, Beijing-Style. *The Conversation*. Available from http://theconversation.com/the-belt-and-road-initiative-chinas-vision-for-globalisation-beijing-style-77705

Beresford, A. K. C., & Dubey, R. C. (1990). Handbook on the management and operations of dry ports. UNCTAD.

Beresford, A. K. (1999). Modelling freight transport costs: A case study of the UK-Greece corridor. *International Journal of Logistics: Research and Applications*, *2*(3), 229–246. doi:10.1080/13675569908901583

Beresford, A., Pettit, S., & Liu, Y. (2011). Multimodal supply chains: Iron ore from Australia to China. *Supply Chain Management*, *16*(1), 32–42. doi:10.1108/13598541111103485

Bernama. (2017). Malaysia Expected to Benefit from One Belt One Road Initiative. *BERNAMA*. Available from http://www.bernama.com/malaysia/article/malaysia-expected-to-benefit-from-one-belt-one-road-initiative-says-najib

Björkman, I., & Forsgren, M. (2000). Nordic international business research: A review of its development. *International Studies of Management & Organization*, *30*(1), 6–25. doi:10.1080/00208825.2000.11656780

Bottelier, P., & Dadush, U. (2011). *The future of Renminbi as an international currency*. Retrieved from https://carnegieendowment.org/2011/06/02/future-of-renminbi-as-international-currency-pub-44338

Bremmer, I. (2010). *The end of the free market: Who wins the war between states and corporations?* New York: Portfolio.

Brînză, A. (2016). *How a Greek Port Became a Chinese 'Dragon Head'*. Retrieved September 21, 2018, from https://thediplomat.com/2016/04/how-a-greek-port-became-a-chinese-dragon-head/

Bulis, A., & Skapars, R. (2014). Development of "New Silk Road" Northern Branch through Seaport of Riga in Latvia. *Procedia: Social and Behavioral Sciences*, *150*, 1222–1229. doi:10.1016/j.sbspro.2014.09.138

Business Monitor International. (2017). *Trillion-dollar trade route: Winners along the Belt and Road*. London: Business Monitor International.

Buzan, B., & Lawson, G. (2014). Capitalism and the emergent world order. *International Affairs*, *90*(1), 71–91. doi:10.1111/1468-2346.12096

Cai, P. (2017). Understanding China's Belt and Road Initiative. *Lowy Institute*. Available from https://www.lowyinstitute.org/publications/understanding-belt-and-road-initiative

Callaghan, M., & Hubbard, P. (2016). The Asian infrastructure investment bank: Multilateralism on the Silk Road. *China Economic Journal*, *9*(2), 116–139. doi:10.1080/17538963.2016.1162970

Carroll, A. B. (1979). Corporate social responsibility: Evolution of a definitional construct. *Business & Society*, *38*(3), 268–295. doi:10.1177/000765039903800303

Carroll, A. B. (1991). The pyramid of corporate social responsibility: Toward the moral management of organizational stakeholders. *Business Horizons*, *34*(4), 42. doi:10.1016/0007-6813(91)90005-G

Cavusgil, S. T., & Knight, G. (2015). The born global firm: An entrepreneurial and capabilities perspective on early and rapid internationalization. *Journal of International Business Studies*, *46*(1), 3–16. doi:10.1057/jibs.2014.62

Chang, H., & Grabel, I. (2005). *Kalkınma yeniden: Alternatif iktisat politikaları elkitabı*. Ankara: İmge Kitabevi.

Chen, C. (2011) The Development of China's FDI laws and policies after WTO accession. In J. Golley & L. Song (Eds.), Rising China: Global challenges and opportunities (pp. 85-97). ANU Press. doi:10.22459/RC.06.2011.06

Chen. (2007). Globalization, Regional Integration and Localization of Intellectual Property Law: Problems, Doctrines and Methods. Journal of Guangxi Normal University: Philosophy and Social Sciences, 43(6), 134.

Chen, D., & Yang, Z. (2017). Investment in container ports along the Maritime Silk Road in the context of international industry transfer: The case of the port of Colombo. *Maritime Economics & Logistics*, 1–17.

Chia, S. Y. (2016). ASEAN Economic Integration and Physical Connectivity. *Asian Economic Papers*, *15*(2), 198–215. doi:10.1162/ASEP_a_00438

China Institute of International Studies. (2016). *The Belt and Road Initiative and Its Impact on Asia-Europe Connectivity*. Available from http://www.ciis.org.cn/english/2016-07/21/content_8911184.htm

Chinese National Development and Reform Commission. (2015). Vision and Actions on Jointly Building Silk Road Economic Belt and 21st Century Maritime Silk Road. *Chinese Ministry of Foreign Affairs and Chinese Ministry of Commerce*. Available from http://en.ndrc.gov.cn/newsrelease/201503/t20150330_669367.html

Chu, Y., & Gao, Y. (2015). China's Belt and Road Initiative: Three questions to be answered. *International Economic Review*, *2*, 90–99.

Corden, W. (2009). China's exchange rate policy, its current account surplus and the global imbalances. *Economic Journal (London)*, *119*(541), 430–441. doi:10.1111/j.1468-0297.2009.02319.x

David, H. (2017). Malaysia Welcome OBOR but Keeps China at Arm's-Length. *World Politics Review*. Available from http://www.worldpoliticsreview.com/trend-lines/22091/malaysia-welcomes-one-belt-one-road-but-keeps-china-at-arm-s-length

Deng, P. (2004). Outward investment by Chinese MNCs: Motivations and implications. *Business Horizons*, *47*(3), 8–16. doi:10.1016/S0007-6813(04)00023-0

Denktas Sakar, G. (2010). *Transport mode choice decisions and multimodal transport: A triangulated approach*. Izmir: Dokuz Eylul University Publications.

Dollar, D. (2015). China's rise as a regional and global power: The AIIB and the 'One Belt, One Road'. *Horizons,* (4), 162-172. Retrieved from https://www.brookings.edu/wp-content/uploads/2016/06/China-rise-as-regional-and-global-power.pdf

Donnan, S., & Dyer, G. (2015). US warns of loss of influence over China bank. *Financial Times*. Retrieved from https://www.ft.com/content/71e33aea-ccaf-11e4-b94f-00144feab7de

Duanmu, J. L. (2012). Firm heterogeneity and location choice of Chinese multinational enterprises (MNEs). *Journal of World Business*, *47*(1), 64–72. doi:10.1016/j.jwb.2010.10.021

Du, J., & Zhang, Y. (2018). Does one belt one road initiative promote Chinese overseas direct investment? *China Economic Review*, *47*, 189–205. doi:10.1016/j.chieco.2017.05.010

Du, M. M. (2016). China's "One Belt, One Road" Initiative: Context, focus, institutions, and implications. *The Chinese Journal of Global Governance*, *2*(1), 30–43. doi:10.1163/23525207-12340014

Dunning, J. H. (2009). Location and the multinational enterprise: John Dunning's thoughts on receiving the Journal of International Business Studies 2008 Decade Award. *Journal of International Business Studies*, *40*(1), 20–34. doi:10.1057/jibs.2008.75

EdgeProp. (2016). *Melaka Gateway Developer Ropes in China State Firm*. Available from https://www.edgeprop.my/content/870701/melaka-gateway-developer-ropes-china-state-firm

Edmonds, C., Croix, S. L., & Li, Y. (2006). *The China's rise as an international trading power*. Economics Study Area Working Papers 88, East-West Center.

Eichengreen, B. (2018). *Globalization with Chinese characteristics*. Retrieved from https://www.project-syndicate.org/commentary/globalization-chinese-characteristics-by-barry-eichengreen-2018-08

Eisenhardt, K. M. (1989). Building theories from case study research. *Academy of Management Review*, *14*(4), 532–550. doi:10.5465/amr.1989.4308385

el Namaki, M. S. S. (2017). Is China's Belt and Road Initiative (BRI): A case of cross country dynamic synergy? *Scholedge International Journal of Management & Development*, *4*(5), 40–45.

Embong, E. A. R., Evers, H.-D., & Ramli, R. (2017). *One Belt One Road (OBOR) and Malaysia: A Long-Term Geopolitical Perspective*. Institute of Malaysia and International Studies Working Paper Series, Universiti Kebangsaan Malaysia.

Fan. (2012). Sino-Russian Games in Mongolia's New Railway Construction. *Russian Central Asian & East European Market, 6*, 45-52.

Fei & Yan. (2007). Regional Practice of the Patent's International Protection and Patent's Unification in Europe. *Journal of Dalian Maritime University: Social Science Edition*, (6), 15-18.

Feng, X. (2014). *Modeling Life Cycle Energy Consumption and Greenhouse Gas Emissions for High-speed Railways*. Beijing, China: Beijing Jiaotong University.

Ferdinand, P. (2016). Westward ho—the China dream and 'one belt, one road': Chinese foreign policy under Xi Jinping. *International Affairs*, *92*(4), 941–957. doi:10.1111/1468-2346.12660

Free Malaysia Today. (2017). *PPBM: Don't Compromise Security with 'One Belt, One Road'.* Available from http://www.freemalaysiatoday.com/category/nation/2017/05/14/ppbm-dont-compromise-security-with-one-belt-one-road

Gao, F., Nie, Z., Wang, Z., Li, H., Gong, X., & Zuo, T. (2009). Greenhouse gas emissions and reduction potential of primary aluminum production in China. *Science in China Series E: Technological Sciences*, *52*(8), 2161–2166. doi:10.100711431-009-0165-6

Gao, Y. (2017). Influences of institutional differences on Chinese enterprises' Investment on countries in "The Belt and Road" Strategy - Based on regulatory effects of ethnic Chinese in host countries. *Modern Economy*, *8*(4), 551–556. doi:10.4236/me.2017.84042

Goodall, K., Li, N., & Warner, M. (2007). Expatriate Managers in China: The Influence of Chinese Culture on Cross-Cultural Management. *Journal of General Management*, *12*(4).

Hall, P. A., & Soskice, D. (2001). *Varieties of capitalism: The Institutional Foundations of Comparative Advantage*. Oxford, UK: Oxford University Press. doi:10.1093/0199247757.001.0001

Han, D. (2017). Malaysia welcomes 'One Belt, One Road' But Keeps China at Arm's Length. *World Politics*. Available from http://www.worldpolitics.com/trend-lines/22091/malaysia-welcomes-one-belt-one-road-but-keeps-china-at-arm-s-length

Hanif, L. (2017). China, Malaysia exchange 9 MOUs, agreements. *News of Asia*. Available from http://newsofasia.net/china-malaysia-exchange-9-mous-agreements

He, Mao, Chen, & Yang. (2006). The Mode Share Model of the High-speed Passenger Railway Line and Its Application. *Journal of the China Railway Society, 2006*(3), 18-21.

He, M.-C., Zhang, J.-B., Zhang, Y.-F., & Tian, B. (2015). Strategy of "one Belt and one Road" confronted with barriers and countermeasures. *Journal of Xinjiang Normal University*, *36*(3), 36–45.

Herrero, A. G., & Xu, J. (2017). China's Belt and Road Initiative: Can Europe Expect Trade Gains? *China & World Economy*, *25*(6), 84–99. doi:10.1111/cwe.12222

Hilpert, H. G. (2011). *China's trade policy*. SWP Research Paper.

Hitt, M. A., & Ireland, R. D. (1985). Corporate distinctive competence, strategy, industry and performance. *Strategic Management Journal*, *6*(3), 273–293. doi:10.1002mj.4250060307

Hofstede Insights. (2018). *Compare Countries*. Available from https://www.hofstede-insights.com/product/compare-countries/

Hofstede, G. (2010). *What about China?* Available from https://geert-hofstede.com/china.html

Hofstede, G. (2010). *What about Malaysia?* Available from https://geert-hofstede.com/malaysia.html

Hofstede, G. (2001). *Culture's Consequences: Comparing Values, Behaviors, Institutions, and Organizations across Nations* (2nd ed.). Thousand Oaks, CA: Sage Publications.

Hofstede, G. (2007). Asian Management in the 21st Century. *Asia Pacific Journal of Management*, *24*(4), 411–420. doi:10.100710490-007-9049-0

Hofstede, G., & Hofstede, G. (2005). *Culture and Organizations: Software of the Mind*. New York: McGraw-Hill.

Hofstede, G., Hofstede, G. J., & Minkov, M. (2010). *Cultures and Organizations: Software of the Mind* (3rd ed.). New York: McGraw-Hill USA.

Hong, W. (2016). Strategic Collaboration between "Belt and Road" and Intellectual Property Rights. *Frontline*, (10), 70.

Hong, W. (2016). The Cooperation between the Belt and Road Initiative and Strategic of Protection Intellectual Property. *Front Journal*, *10*, 20.

Hu. (2017). *China's Patent Applications to "The Belt and Road" Related Countries Show A Favorable Growth Trend.* Academic Press.

Huang, J. (2017) China. In Foreign Investment Regulatıon Review (pp. 54-66). UN: Law Business Research.

Huang, H.-T. (2015). "The Belt and Road" Initiative: The nature of interaction and the building of trust. *Tianjin Social Sciences*, *6*, 87–92.

Huang, L. Y., Zhen, S. F., & Wang, J. (2018). Research on the Win-Win Corporation Mechanism between Multi-national Corporation and Host Country under the Background of One Belt and One Road: Based on the Perspective of Corporate Social Responsibility. *Management Review*, *30*(2), 172–182.

Ignatius, D. (2017). The new silk road: Is there a plan for Malaysia? *Free Malaysia Today*. Available from http://www.freemalaysiatoday.com/category/opinion/2017/05/29/the-new-silk-road-is-there-a-plan-for-malaysia

Islam, D. M. Z., Dinwoodie, J., & Roe, M. (2005). Towards supply chain integration through multimodal transport in developing economies: The case of Bangladesh. *Maritime Economics & Logistics*, *7*(4), 382–399. doi:10.1057/palgrave.mel.9100144

Jennings, R. (2017). Malaysia buying Chinese ships to protect its waters from China. *VOA*. Available from https://www.voanews.com/a/malaysia-buying-chinese-ships-to-protect-waters-from-china-others/3780026.html

Jiang. (2017, Mary 15). Tourism cooperation and resonation with "The Belt and Road" initiative. *Chinese Tourism News*.

Jiangbo. (2013). Research on historical and cultural name of Phoenix, cultural tourism product planning. *Tourism Overview*, *9*, 170-180.

Jiang, Y. (2011). Rethinking the Beijing Consensus: How China responds to crises. *The Pacific Review*, *24*(3), 337–356. doi:10.1080/09512748.2011.577234

Jinchen, T. (2016). *One Belt and One Road': Connecting China and the world.* Global Infrastructure Initiative website. HKTDC Research, The Belt and Road Initiative. Retrieved September 21, 2018, from http://china-trade-research.hktdc.com/business-news/article/The-Belt-and-Road-Initiative/The-Belt-and-Road-Initiative/obor/en/1/1X000000/1X0A36B7.htm

John, T. (2017). Malaysia One of the Greatest Beneficiaries of OBOR. *New Straits Times*. Available from https://www.nst.com.my/opinion/columnists/2017/05/239626/malaysia-one-greatest-beneficiaries-obor

Jun, L. (2012). *Research on Model of Freight Transportation Mode Choice Based on Behaviour Analysis*. Wuhan, China: Wuhan University of Technology.

Kirshner, J. (2017). Bölgesel hegemonya ve bir RMB bölgesinin doğuşu. In E. Helleiner & J. Kirshner (Eds.), Yeni Çin Seddi: Çin'in uluslararası para ilişkilerinde güç ve siyaset (pp. 173-192). İstanbul: Koç Üniversitesi Yayınları.

Kowalski, P. (2010). China and India: A tale of two trade integration approaches. In B. Eichengreen, P. Gupta, & R. Kumar (Eds.), Emerging giants: China and India in the World Economy (pp. 184-224). Oxford, UK: Oxford Scholarship.

Kroeber, A. R. (2016). *China's economy: What everyone needs to know*. Oxford, UK: Oxford University Press.

Lall, S., & Albaladejo, M. (2004). China's competitive performance: A threat to East Asian manufactured exports? *World Development*, *32*(9), 1441–1466. doi:10.1016/j.worlddev.2004.03.006

Lardy, N. (2012). *Sustaining China's economic growth after the Global Financial Crisis*. Retrieved from https://www.frbsf.org/economic-research/files/Lardy.pdf

Layne, C. (2018). The US–Chinese power shift and the end of the Pax Americana. *International Affairs*, *94*(1), 89–111. doi:10.1093/ia/iix249

Lee, K., Jee, M., & Eun, J. (2011). Assessing China's economic catch-up at the firm level and beyond: Washington Consensus, East Asian Consensus and the Beijing Model. *Industry and Innovation*, *18*(5), 487–507. doi:10.1080/13662716.2011.583463

Lee, P. T. W., Hu, Z. H., Lee, S. J., Choi, K. S., & Shin, S. H. (2018). Research trends and agenda on the Belt and Road (B&R) initiative with a focus on maritime transport. *Maritime Policy & Management*, *45*(3), 282–300. doi:10.1080/03088839.2017.1400189

Leer, Y. V. D., & Yau, J. (2016). China's New Silk Route - The Long and Winding Road. *PwC*. Available from http://www.pwc.com/gx/en/issues/high-growth-markets/publications/china-new-silk-route.html

Lehmann, J. P., Buche, I., & Perrinjaquet, M. (2016). One Belt – One Road: China's re-Engineering of the Global Business Environment. *IMD*. Retrieved from https://www.imd.org/research/insightsimd/one-belt-one-road-chinas-re-engineering-of-the-global-business-environment

Li, M. (2015). *China's "one belt, one road" initiative: New round of opening up*. Academic Press.

Li. (2008). *Intellectual Property Law*. Beijing: Law Press China.

Lin, J. Y., & Wang, Y. (2015). *China's contribution to development cooperation: Ideas, opportunities and finances*. Working Papers P119. FERDI. Retrieved from http://www.ferdi.fr/sites/www.ferdi.fr/files/publication/fichiers/wp119_lin-wang_paper_for_ferdi_web_1.pdf

Lin, B., & Xu, L. (2015). Energy conservation of electrolytic aluminum industry in China. *Renewable & Sustainable Energy Reviews*, *43*, 676–686. doi:10.1016/j.rser.2014.11.021

Liu, M. K. (2016). *The challenges and opportunities of China's new Silk Road*. Available from https://www.weeconomic.org/2016/01/the-challenges-and-opportunities-of-china-s-new-silk-road

Liu, W. D. (2015). Scientific understanding of the Belt and Road Initiative of China and related research themes. *Progress in Geography*, *34*(5), 538–544.

Liu, W., & Dunford, M. (2016). Inclusive globalization: Unpacking China's Belt and Road Initiative. *Area Development and Policy*, *1*(3), 323–340. doi:10.1080/23792949.2016.1232598

Liu, W., Shi, H. B., Zhang, Z., Tsai, S. B., Zhai, Y., Chen, Q., & Wang, J. (2018). The Development Evaluation of Economic Zones in China. *International Journal of Environmental Research and Public Health*, *15*(1), 56. doi:10.3390/ijerph15010056 PMID:29301304

Liu, W., Wei, Q., Huang, S. Q., & Tsai, S. B. (2017). Doing good again? A multilevel institutional perspective on corporate environmental responsibility and philanthropic strategy. *International Journal of Environmental Research and Public Health*, *14*(10), 1283. doi:10.3390/ijerph14101283 PMID:29064451

Liu, X., Zhang, K., Chen, B., Zhou, J., & Miao, L. (2018). Analysis of logistics service supply chain for the One Belt and One Road initiative of China. *Transportation Research Part E, Logistics and Transportation Review*.

Li, X. Y. (2015). Relations to be prioritized in China's "Belt and Road Initiative". *International Economic Review*, *1*, 54–63.

Lo, C. (2015). China's Silk Road Strategy. *Inter Economics*, *29*(4), 54.

Lu. (2013). *Dictionary of Management*. Shanghai: Lexicographical Publishing House.

Luo. (2018). The Belt and Road Initiative and China's Strategic Vision. *Yunmeng Journal*, (4), 63.

Magri, P. (2018). Introduction. In A. Amighini & P. Magri (Eds.), *China Champion of (Which) Globalisation* (pp. 7–12). Milano, İtaly: ISPI.

Malaysia External Trade Development Corporation. (2018). *Tapping Business Opportunities along the Silk Route*. Available from http://www.matrade.gov.my/en/about-matrade/media/press-releases/4296-tapping-business-opportunities-along-the-silk-route

Malaysiakini. (2017). *Malaysia Inks Second Phase Deals on ECRL and Malacca-Pengerang Pipeline*. Available from https://www.malaysiakini.com/news/382127

Maneschi, A. (2004). The true meaning of David Ricardo's four magic numbers. *Journal of International Economics*, *62*(2), 433–443. doi:10.1016/S0022-1996(03)00008-4

Martin, M. F. (2012). *China's banking system: Issues for congress*. Retrieved from https://fas.org/sgp/crs/row/R42380.pdf

May, C., & Nölke, A. (2014). Capitalism in large emerging economies and the new global trade order. In D. Desse (Ed.), *Handbook of the International Political Economy of Trade*. Cheltenham, UK: Edward Elgar. doi:10.4337/9781781954997.00028

Mcgregor, R. (2006). The trillion dollar question: China is grappling with how to deploy its foreign exchange riches. *Financial Times*, 25.

McNally, C. A. (2013b). How emerging forms of capitalism are changing the global economic order. *East-West Center*, (107), 1-8. Retrieved from https://www.eastwestcenter.org/sites/default/files/private/api107.pdf

McNally, C. (2012). Sino-Capitalism: China's reemergence and the international political economy. *World Politics*, *64*(4), 741–776. doi:10.1017/S0043887112000202

McNally, C. A. (2013a). The Challenge of refurbished state capitalism: Implications for the global political economic order. *Recht and Management*, *6*, 33–48.

McNally, C. A. (2013c). Refurbishing state capitalism: A policy analysis of efforts to rebalance China's political economy. *Journal of Current Chinese Affairs*, *42*(4), 45–71. doi:10.1177/186810261304200403

McNally, C. A. (2015). The political economic logic of RMB Internationalization: A study in Sino-capitalism. *International Politics*, *52*(6), 704–723. doi:10.1057/ip.2015.15

Minghong, Y. (2017). Understanding the One Belt One Road Initiative: China's perspective. In B. K. Sharma & D. N. D. Kundu (Eds.), *China's One Belt One Road: Initiative, Challenges and Prospects* (pp. 7–26). Vij Books.

Ministry of International Trade and Industry Malaysia. (2017). *Halal Industry Development Corporation Signs MoU with Weifang Sime Darby Port Co., Ltd China to Develop 1B1R Halal Infrastructure*. Available from http://www.miti.gov.my/index.php/pages/view/4239

Ministry of International Trade and Industry Malaysia. (2017). *MITI Report 2017*. Author.

Mongolian Tourism Association. (n.d.). Retrieved from http://www.travelmongolia.org/index.php?do=cat&category=1

Mustafic, A. (2017). China's One Belt, One Road and energy security initiatives: A plan to conquer the world? *Sarajevo Journal of Social Sciences - Inquiry*, *2*(2), 153-190.

Nataraj, G., & Sekhani, R. (2016). *China's One Belt One Road initiative: Analysis from an Indian perspective (HKTDC Research).* Retrieved from http://china-trade-research.hktdc.com/business-news/article/The-Belt-and-Road-Initiative/"China'sOne-Belt-One-Road-Initiative"--Analysis-from-an-Indian Perspective/obor/en/1/1X000000/1X0A5J3C.htm

Naughton, B. (2010). China's distinctive system: Can it be a model for others? *Journal of Contemporary China*, *19*(65), 437–460. doi:10.1080/10670561003666079

New Sarawak Tribune. (2017). *CM Witnesses Exchange of MOU of Methanol Plant*. Available from https://www.newsarawaktribune.com.my/news/cm-witnesses-exchange-of-mou-for-methanol-plan

Nölke, A., & Claar, S. (2013). Varieties of capitalism in emerging countries. *Transformation*, *81/82*(1), 33–54. doi:10.1353/trn.2013.0001

Nölke, A., Ten Brink, T., Claar, T., & May, C. (2015). Domestic structures, foreign economic policies and global economic order: Implications from the rise of large emerging economies. *European Journal of International Relations*, *21*(3), 538–567. doi:10.1177/1354066114553682

Nölke, A., & Vliegenthart, A. (2009). Enlarging the varieties of capitalism: The emergence of dependent market economies is East Central Europe. *World Politics*, *61*(4), 670–702. doi:10.1017/S0043887109990098

Pan. (2015). On the Protection Model of Intellectual Property Internationalization and China's Coping Strategies. *Law Review*, (1), 159.

Pandit, S. D., & Basu, R. (2014). Connectivity, Development and Regional Integration: The Case of Indo-Myanmar Kaladan Project. *IUP Journal of International Relations*, *8*(3), 25–39.

Parameswaran, P. (2017). The real trouble with China's Belt and Road. *The Diplomat*. Available from http://thediplomat.com/2017/05/the-real-trouble-with-chinas-belt-and-road

Pencea, S. (2017). A Look Into the Complexities of the One Belt, One Road Strategy. *Global Economic Observer*, *5*(1), 142–158.

Perlez, J. (2014). U.S. opposing China's answer to World Bank. *The New York Times*. Retrieved from https://www.nytimes.com/2014/10/10/world/asia/chinas-plan-for-regional-development-bank-runs-into-us-opposition.html

Peters, B. G. (1998). *Comparative politics: Theory and methods*. NYU Press. doi:10.1007/978-1-349-26926-6

Pitlo, L. B. (2016). China-Southeast Asia connectivity: Opportunities and challenges for the Maritime Silk Road. *China US Focus*. Available from http://www.chinausfocus.com/foreign-policy/china-southeast-asia-connectivity-opportunities-and-challenges-for-the-maritime-silk-road

Pontusson, J. (2005). Varieties and commonalities of capitalism. In D. Coates (Ed.), Varieties of capitalism, varieties of approaches (pp. 163-188). Palgrave Macmillian. doi:10.1057/9780230522725_9

Prasad, E. S. (2016). *China`s economy and financial markets: Reforms and markets, U.S–China economic and security review commission, Hearing on China`s 13th Five Year Plan*. Retrieved from https://www.brookings.edu/wp-content/uploads/2016/07/USCESRCTestimony27Apr16.pdf

Qu & Zhang (2011). Research on Administrative Protection of Intellectual Property Rights. *Political and Legal Studies*, (3), 57.

Quigley, J. (1989). Socialist Law and the Civil Law Tradition. *The American Journal of Comparative Law*, *37*(4), 781.

Ramo, J. C. (2004). *The Beijing Consensus*. The Foreign Policy Centre. Retrieved from http://www.chinaelections.org/uploadfile/200909/20090918021638239.pdf

Reuters. (2014a). *Alibaba's Yuebao Dents Chinese Banks' Profitability*. Available from http://www.reuters.com/article/china-banks-idUSL2N0MG0BV20140320

Reuters. (2014b). *China Banks Strike Back against Threat from Internet Finance*. Available from http://uk.reuters.com/article/uk-china-banks-online-idUKBREA1M12I20140223

Reuters. (2017a). *AirAsia to Launch New Chinese Low Cost Carrier*. Available from http://www.reuters.com/article/us-airasia-china-idUSKCN18A0TL

Reuters. (2017b). *China loosens some license requirements for foreign banks*. Available from http://www.reuters.com/article/us-china-banking-regulations-idUSKBN16O0BS?il=0

Rodrik, D. (2013). *The new mercantilist challenge*. Project Syndicate. Retrieved from http://www.fabricedefever.com/pdf/Rodrik%20%20The%20new%20mercantilist%20 challenge.pdf

Ruffin, R. (2002). David Ricardo's discovery of comparative advantage. *History of Political Economy*, *34*(4), 727–748. doi:10.1215/00182702-34-4-727

Schmidt, V. A. (2009). Putting the political back into political economy. *World Politics*, 1–28.

Schuler, D. A. (1996). Corporate political strategy and foreign competition: The case of the steel industry. *Academy of Management Journal*, *39*(3), 720–737.

Selat, A. M. (1987). *Malaysia's China policy: the bilateral relationship (Master's thesis)*. Australian National University.

Şenses, F., Öniş, Z., & Bakır, C. (2013). *Ülke deneyimleri ışığında küresel kriz ve yeni ekonomik düzen*. İstanbul: İletişim Yayınları.

Sheu, J. B., & Kundu, T. (2017). Forecasting time-varying logistics distribution flows in the One Belt-One Road strategic context. *Transportation Research Part E, Logistics and Transportation Review*.

Sophie, Q. (2017). *One Belt One Road in Malaysia*. Retrieved from https://www.aspistrategist.org.au/one-belt-one-road-malaysia-chinas-strategic-enabler

Stalk, G., Evans, P., & Shulman, L. E. (1992). Competing on capabilities: The new rules of corporate strategy. *Harvard Business Review*, *70*(2), 57–69. PMID:10117369

State Intellectual Property Office: Main Statistical Data Report on China's patent intensive industries. (2015). State Intellectual Property Office: A review of Intensive Intellectual Property Industries and Its Economical Performance in the European Union.

State Intellectual Property Office: Statistics on Patent of Countries along "The Belt and Road. (2018). Patent Statistics Bulletin, 2018(1).

Stephen, M., & Parizek, M. (2015). *New pressures on the WTO: The Rise of illiberal trading states*. Retrieved from https://statecapitalist.wordpress.com/2015/01/15/stephen-parizek-new-pressures-on-the-wto-the-rise-of-illiberal-trading-states/

Su, H. (2015). A study on the transfer of China's manufacturing under "the Belt and Road" Initiative. *International Trade*, *3*, 18–21.

Sumathy, P. (2017). China's One Belt One Road Initiatives: Strengthening Economic Linkage for Mutual Benefits. *New Straits Times.* Available from https://www.nst.com.my/opinion/columnists/2017/05/235414/chinas-one-belt-one-road-initiative-strengthening-economic

Swaine, M. D. (2015). Chinese views and commentary on the 'One Belt, One Road'initiative. *China Leadership Monitor*, *47*(2), 3.

Tang, S., Liu, D., & Xie, X. (2017). The Analysis of the "One Belt and One Road" for the game between China and the United States. In *Proceedings of the 3rd International Conference on Social Science and Management*. DEStech Publications, Inc.

Tang, J. (2018). *Competitiveness of Container Rail-road Intermodal Transport and Its Improving Strategies in China*. Beijing, China: Beijing Jiaotong University.

Ten Brink, T. (2014). The challenges of China's non-liberal capitalism for the liberal global economic order. *Harvard Asia Quarterly*, *16*(2), 36-44.

The Economist. (2017). *What is China's Belt and Road Initiative?* Available from https://www.economist.com/blogs/economist-explains/2017/05/economist-explains-11

The National Development and Reform Commission. the Ministry of Foreign Affairs, & the Ministry of Commerce. (n.d.). *Vision and Alignment to Promote the Construction of the Silk Road Economic Belt and the 21st Century Maritime Silk Road*. Retrieved from http://www.xinhuanet.com/finance/2015-03/28/c_1114793986.htm

The Star. (2016). *MayBank's ShenZhen Branch Opens*. Author.

The Star. (2017a). *OBOR lights the way to China*. Retrieved from http://www.thestar.com.my/business/business-news/2017/04/10/obor-lights-the-way-to-china

The Star. (2017b). *Prospering with Belt and Road*. Available from http://www.thestar.com.my/news/nation/2017/05/21/prospering-with-belt-and-road-malaysia-is-one-of-64-countries-to-reap-the-benefits-of-chinas-initiat

The Star. (2017c). *Robotic City among RM31bil worth of Deals Signed*. Available from http://www.thestar.com.my/news/nation/2017/05/15/robotic-city-among-rm31bil-worth-of-deals-signed

The Star. (2017d). *RM 55bil East Coast Rail Kicks Off*. Available from http://www.thestar.com.my/business/business-news/2017/03/29/east-coast-rail-kicks-off

The Star. (2017e). *Titijaya to tie up with CREC in RM575mil Sabah property project*. Available from http://www.thestar.com.my/business/business-news/2017/05/15/titijaya-to-tie-up-with-crec-in-rm575mil-sabah-property-project

The Star. (2017f). *Why Malaysia Supports China's Belt and Road*. Available from http://www.thestar.com.my/news/nation/2017/05/12/why-malaysia-supports-china-belt-and-road

The Star. (2018). *Dr Mahathir Calls for China's Help with Fiscal Problems*. Available from https://www.thestar.com.my/news/nation/2018/08/20/dr-mahathir-calls-for-china-help-with-fiscal-problems/#lmwA3d8Kyzfc5APk.99

The Straight Times. (2017). *East Coast Rail Link: Malaysia Touts Rail Trade Route as Rival to Singapore*. Available from https://www.straitstimes.com/asia/se-asia/east-coast-rail-link-malaysia-touts-rail-trade-route-as-rival-to-singapore

Tiezzi, S. (2018). Free trade with Chinese characteristics. In A. Amighini & P. Magri (Eds.), *China Champion of (Which) Globalisation* (pp. 39–60). Milano, İtaly: ISPI.

Timmer, H., Bussolo, M., Gould, D. M., Letelier, R. A., Nguyen, T. C., Panterov, G. L., . . . Sanchez, C. (2016). The impact of China on Europe and Central Asia. Europe and Central Asia economic update. Washington, DC: World Bank Group.

Turker, D. (2009). Measuring Corporate Social Responsibility: A Scale Development Study. *Journal of Business Ethics*, *85*(4), 411–427. doi:10.100710551-008-9780-6

United Nations. (2017). *Sustainable development goals*. Available from http://www.un.org/sustainabledevelopment/sustainable-development-goals

USTR. (2017). *Announces Initiation of Section 301 Investigation of China*. Retrieved from https://ustr.gov/about-us/policy-offices/press-office/press-releases/2017/august/ustr-announces-initiation-section

Veras, E. Z. (2016). Cultural Differences between Countries: The Brazilian and the Chinese Ways of Doing Business. *Journal on Innovation and Sustainability*, *2*(2), 77–83.

Wang, H. (2017). Küresel dengesizlikler ve döviz kuru silahının gücünün sınırları. In E. Helleiner & J. Kirshner (Eds.), Yeni Çin Seddi: Çin'in Uluslararası Para İlişkilerinde Güç ve Siyaset (pp. 97-106). İstanbul: Koç Üniversitesi Yayınları.

Wang, H., Liu, W., Zhu, M., & Wang, Q. (2018). Embrace or Not? An Empirical Study of the Impact of Globalization on the Country's Sustainability in the Case of NAFTA. *Sustainability*, *10*(10), 3436. doi:10.3390u10103436

Wang, Q. Y. (2008). *Corporate social responsibility of Multinational Enterprises.* China Economic Publishing House.

Wei, L. Q., Chiang, F. T., & Wu, L. Z. (2012). Developing and utilizing network resources: Roles of political skill. *Journal of Management Studies, 49*(2), 381–402. doi:10.1111/j.1467-6486.2010.00987.x

Weiss, M. A. (2017). Asian Infrastructure Investment Bank (AIIB) (Congressional Research Service No. 7–5700). Washington, DC: Government Printing Service.

Wei, Z., Jian, W., & Zhu, L. (2015). Reliability Analysis of Railway Container Transport Time. *Journal of the China Railway Society, 37*(11), 10–15.

Wen, Junrong, & Wei. (2014, June 30). New Silk Road: Through Common Prosperity. *The People's Daily.*

Wijeratne, D., Yau, J., Wong, G., Rathbone, M., Neu, B. L., & Lau, S. (2017). Repaving the ancient Silk Routes. *PwC.* Available from https://www.pwc.com/gx/en/issues/high-growth-markets/publications/repaving-the-ancient-silk-routes.html

Witt, M. A. (2010). *China: What variety of capitalism?* INSEAD Working Paper No. 2010/88/EPS. Retrieved from https://ssrn.com/abstract=1695940

Wolf, M. (2014). *The shifts and the shocks: What we have learned-and have still to learn-from the financial crisis.* Penguin Books.

Wu, H. (2009). Evaluation and Reflection on China's Intellectual Property Legal System Construction. *Chinese Law,* (1), 57.

Wu, H. (2016). "One Belt and One Road" Strategic Conception and Intellectual Property Protection. The Rule of Law Society, (5), 11.

Wu, H., & Futao, L. (2013). The Concept and Policy of China's Intellectual Property Judicial Protection. Contemporary Law, (6), 42.

Wu, Z. (2013). *Legal concept.* Beijing: Law Press China.

Xie. (2008). Study on the development and sustainable development of tourism resources of nomadic culture. *Heilongjiang History, 24,* 89-90.

Xin, J. (2017). Malaysia fast and firm to grasp Belt and Road opportunities. *CGTN.* Retrieved from https://news.cgtn.com/news/3d41444e34557a4d/share_p.html

Xu, G. D., Ao, H., & She, Y. G. (2012). Current status and development trend of aluminum industry in world and strategy suggestions in China under background of sustainable development. *Chin J Nonferrous Met, 22*(7), 2040–2050.

Yağcı, M. (2016). A Beijing Consensus in the making: The rise of Chinese initiatives in the international political economy and implications for developing countries. *Perceptions: Journal of International Affairs*, *21*(2), 29–56.

Yang, D., Pan, K., & Wang, S. (2017). On service network improvement for shipping lines under the one belt one road initiative of China. *Transportation Research Part E, Logistics and Transportation Review*.

Yang, F.-H., & Yan, C.-F. (2015). A study on the implementation mechanism of Chinese direct investment under "the Belt and Road" Initiative. *Theoretical Investigation*, *5*, 80–83.

Yao, D., & Whalley, J. (2016). The China (Shanghai) Pilot Free Trade Zone: Background, Developments and Preliminary Assessment of Initial Impacts. *World Economy*, *39*(1), 2–15. doi:10.1111/twec.12364

Yi & Li. (2018). The United States Launched 301 Investigation into China and China's Countermeasures. *Journal of Northwest University (Philosophy and Social Sciences Edition)*, (1), 65-81.

Ying, W. A. N. G., Dan, H. A. O., Hai-ying, L. I., Xiao-jie, Y. A. N., & Huan-dong, W. A. N. G. (2014). Research on Share Rate of Passenger Flow in Railway Transportation Corridor Based on Matching between Supply and Demand. *Journal of the China Railway Society*, *36*(12), 1–5.

Yin, R. K. (2009). *Case study research: Design and methods (applied social research methods)*. London: Sage.

Yuan. (2014). National Strategy Analysis of the Belt and Road Initiative. *Theoretical Monthly*, *11*, 6.

Yuan, J. F. (1990). Corporate social responsibility. *Maritime Press*, *1990*, 46–52.

Yu, H. (2017). Motivation behind China's 'One Belt, One Road' Initiatives and Establishment of the Asian Infrastructure Investment Bank. *Journal of Contemporary China*, *26*(105), 353–368. doi:10.1080/10670564.2016.1245894

Yu, Z. (1991). *Law Dictionary*. Beijing: China University of Political Science & Law Press.

Zahra, S. A. (1996). Technology strategy and new venture performance: A study of corporate-sponsored and independent biotechnology ventures. *Journal of Business Venturing*, *11*(4), 289–321. doi:10.1016/0883-9026(95)00128-X

Zeng, Q., Wang, G. W., Qu, C., & Li, K. X. (2017). Impact of the Carat Canal on the evolution of hub ports under China's Belt and Road initiative. *Transportation Research Part E, Logistics and Transportation Review*.

Ze, W. (2006). *Association of Southeast Asian Nations*. Beijing: China Legal Publishing House.

Zhang, C., Gao, X., & Cao, H. (2015). Research on the Path of China's Overseas Intellectual Property Protection under the Background of the Belt and Road Initiative. Science Management Research, (5), 7.

Zhang, Gao, & Cao. (2015). Research on China's Overseas Intellectual Property Protection under the Background of "The Belt and Road". *Scientific Management Research*, (5), 5-9.

Zhang, Z., Wang, L., & Shan, L. (2015). Intellectual Property Strategy under the "One Belt, One Road" Strategic Concept. Chinese Inventions and Patents, (6), 111.

Zhang, Z.G., Liang, Z. G., & Liang, K. G. (2012). Research on Corporate Social Responsibility from the Stakeholder Perspective. *China Soft Science, 2012*(2), 139-146.

Zhang. (2016). Obstacles, Predicament and Reform Prospects in the Transformation and Upgrading of China's Industrial Structure. *Journal of Renmin University of China*, (5), 29-37

Zhang, F. (2015). China as a global Force. *Asia & the Pacific Policy Studies*, *3*(1), 120–128. doi:10.1002/app5.115

Zhang, Z. Y. (2016). *''The Blet And Road" and construction of Chinese "Going Global" coporate social responsibility and soft power*. Social Sciences Academic Press.

Zhang, Z., Wang, L., & Shan, L. (2015). Intellectual Property ProtectionStrategy under the Concept of "The Belt and Road". *China Invention & Patent*, *c*(06), 107–112.

Zhang, Z., Wang, L., & Shan, L. (2015). Strategic of Protection Intellectual Property under the Belt and Road Initiative. *Chinese Invention and Patent*, *6*, 30.

Zhao, Huang, & Zhang. (2002). *Management of tourist attractions*. Nanjing: Nankai University Press.

Zheng, S. (2003). *Intellectual Property Law*. Beijing: Law Press China.

Zheng, Z. (2018). *Empirical Study of Coal Transportation on Multimodal Transport Network in China*. Beijing, China: Beijing Jiaotong University.

Газрын.Засгийн (1998). оны 192-р тогтоолоор “Аялал жуулчлалын бодлого зохицуулах Үндэсний Зөвлөл”-ийг байгуулж, дүрмийг нь баталжээ.

Мөнх-ЭрдэнэБ. (n.d.). *Монгол улсад аялж буй гадаадын жуулчдын зардлын тү.вэр судалгаа*. Retrieved from www.mongolbank.mn

Related References

To continue our tradition of advancing information science and technology research, we have compiled a list of recommended IGI Global readings. These references will provide additional information and guidance to further enrich your knowledge and assist you with your own research and future publications.

Abtahi, M. S., Behboudi, L., & Hasanabad, H. M. (2017). Factors Affecting Internet Advertising Adoption in Ad Agencies. *International Journal of Innovation in the Digital Economy*, *8*(4), 18–29. doi:10.4018/IJIDE.2017100102

Agrawal, S. (2017). The Impact of Emerging Technologies and Social Media on Different Business(es): Marketing and Management. In O. Rishi & A. Sharma (Eds.), *Maximizing Business Performance and Efficiency Through Intelligent Systems* (pp. 37–49). Hershey, PA: IGI Global. doi:10.4018/978-1-5225-2234-8.ch002

Alnoukari, M., Razouk, R., & Hanano, A. (2016). BSC-SI: A Framework for Integrating Strategic Intelligence in Corporate Strategic Management. *International Journal of Social and Organizational Dynamics in IT*, *5*(2), 1–14. doi:10.4018/IJSODIT.2016070101

Alnoukari, M., Razouk, R., & Hanano, A. (2016). BSC-SI, A Framework for Integrating Strategic Intelligence in Corporate Strategic Management. *International Journal of Strategic Information Technology and Applications*, *7*(1), 32–44. doi:10.4018/IJSITA.2016010103

Altındağ, E. (2016). Current Approaches in Change Management. In A. Goksoy (Ed.), *Organizational Change Management Strategies in Modern Business* (pp. 24–51). Hershey, PA: IGI Global. doi:10.4018/978-1-4666-9533-7.ch002

Alvarez-Dionisi, L. E., Turner, R., & Mittra, M. (2016). Global Project Management Trends. *International Journal of Information Technology Project Management*, *7*(3), 54–73. doi:10.4018/IJITPM.2016070104

Anantharaman, R. N., Rajeswari, K. S., Angusamy, A., & Kuppusamy, J. (2017). Role of Self-Efficacy and Collective Efficacy as Moderators of Occupational Stress Among Software Development Professionals. *International Journal of Human Capital and Information Technology Professionals*, *8*(2), 45–58. doi:10.4018/IJHCITP.2017040103

Aninze, F., El-Gohary, H., & Hussain, J. (2018). The Role of Microfinance to Empower Women: The Case of Developing Countries. *International Journal of Customer Relationship Marketing and Management*, *9*(1), 54–78. doi:10.4018/IJCRMM.2018010104

Arsenijević, O. M., Orčić, D., & Kastratović, E. (2017). Development of an Optimization Tool for Intangibles in SMEs: A Case Study from Serbia with a Pilot Research in the Prestige by Milka Company. In M. Vemić (Ed.), *Optimal Management Strategies in Small and Medium Enterprises* (pp. 320–347). Hershey, PA: IGI Global. doi:10.4018/978-1-5225-1949-2.ch015

Aryanto, V. D., Wismantoro, Y., & Widyatmoko, K. (2018). Implementing Eco-Innovation by Utilizing the Internet to Enhance Firm's Marketing Performance: Study of Green Batik Small and Medium Enterprises in Indonesia. *International Journal of E-Business Research*, *14*(1), 21–36. doi:10.4018/IJEBR.2018010102

Atiku, S. O., & Fields, Z. (2017). Multicultural Orientations for 21st Century Global Leadership. In N. Baporikar (Ed.), *Management Education for Global Leadership* (pp. 28–51). Hershey, PA: IGI Global. doi:10.4018/978-1-5225-1013-0.ch002

Atiku, S. O., & Fields, Z. (2018). Organisational Learning Dimensions and Talent Retention Strategies for the Service Industries. In N. Baporikar (Ed.), *Global Practices in Knowledge Management for Societal and Organizational Development* (pp. 358–381). Hershey, PA: IGI Global. doi:10.4018/978-1-5225-3009-1.ch017

Ávila, L., & Teixeira, L. (2018). The Main Concepts Behind the Dematerialization of Business Processes. In M. Khosrow-Pour, D.B.A. (Ed.), Encyclopedia of Information Science and Technology, Fourth Edition (pp. 888-898). Hershey, PA: IGI Global. doi:10.4018/978-1-5225-2255-3.ch076

Bartens, Y., Chunpir, H. I., Schulte, F., & Voß, S. (2017). Business/IT Alignment in Two-Sided Markets: A COBIT 5 Analysis for Media Streaming Business Models. In S. De Haes & W. Van Grembergen (Eds.), *Strategic IT Governance and Alignment in Business Settings* (pp. 82–111). Hershey, PA: IGI Global. doi:10.4018/978-1-5225-0861-8.ch004

Bashayreh, A. M. (2018). Organizational Culture and Organizational Performance. In W. Lee & F. Sabetzadeh (Eds.), *Contemporary Knowledge and Systems Science* (pp. 50–69). Hershey, PA: IGI Global. doi:10.4018/978-1-5225-5655-8.ch003

Bedford, D. A. (2018). Sustainable Knowledge Management Strategies: Aligning Business Capabilities and Knowledge Management Goals. In N. Baporikar (Ed.), *Global Practices in Knowledge Management for Societal and Organizational Development* (pp. 46–73). Hershey, PA: IGI Global. doi:10.4018/978-1-5225-3009-1.ch003

Benmoussa, F., Nakara, W. A., & Jaouen, A. (2016). The Use of Social Media by SMEs in the Tourism Industry. In I. Lee (Ed.), *Encyclopedia of E-Commerce Development, Implementation, and Management* (pp. 2159–2170). Hershey, PA: IGI Global. doi:10.4018/978-1-4666-9787-4.ch155

Berger, R. (2016). Indigenous Management and Bottom of Pyramid Countries: The Role of National Institutions. In U. Aung & P. Ordoñez de Pablos (Eds.), *Managerial Strategies and Practice in the Asian Business Sector* (pp. 107–123). Hershey, PA: IGI Global. doi:10.4018/978-1-4666-9758-4.ch007

Bharwani, S., & Musunuri, D. (2018). Reflection as a Process From Theory to Practice. In M. Khosrow-Pour, D.B.A. (Ed.), Encyclopedia of Information Science and Technology, Fourth Edition (pp. 1529-1539). Hershey, PA: IGI Global. doi:10.4018/978-1-5225-2255-3.ch132

Bhatt, G. D., Wang, Z., & Rodger, J. A. (2017). Information Systems Capabilities and Their Effects on Competitive Advantages: A Study of Chinese Companies. *Information Resources Management Journal*, *30*(3), 41–57. doi:10.4018/IRMJ.2017070103

Bhushan, M., & Yadav, A. (2017). Concept of Cloud Computing in ESB. In R. Bhadoria, N. Chaudhari, G. Tomar, & S. Singh (Eds.), *Exploring Enterprise Service Bus in the Service-Oriented Architecture Paradigm* (pp. 116–127). Hershey, PA: IGI Global. doi:10.4018/978-1-5225-2157-0.ch008

Bhushan, S. (2017). System Dynamics Base-Model of Humanitarian Supply Chain (HSCM) in Disaster Prone Eco-Communities of India: A Discussion on Simulation and Scenario Results. *International Journal of System Dynamics Applications*, *6*(3), 20–37. doi:10.4018/IJSDA.2017070102

Biswas, A., & De, A. K. (2017). On Development of a Fuzzy Stochastic Programming Model with Its Application to Business Management. In S. Trivedi, S. Dey, A. Kumar, & T. Panda (Eds.), *Handbook of Research on Advanced Data Mining Techniques and Applications for Business Intelligence* (pp. 353–378). Hershey, PA: IGI Global. doi:10.4018/978-1-5225-2031-3.ch021

Bücker, J., & Ernste, K. (2018). Use of Brand Heroes in Strategic Reputation Management: The Case of Bacardi, Adidas, and Daimler. In A. Erdemir (Ed.), *Reputation Management Techniques in Public Relations* (pp. 126–150). Hershey, PA: IGI Global. doi:10.4018/978-1-5225-3619-2.ch007

Bureš, V. (2018). Industry 4.0 From the Systems Engineering Perspective: Alternative Holistic Framework Development. In R. Brunet-Thornton & F. Martinez (Eds.), *Analyzing the Impacts of Industry 4.0 in Modern Business Environments* (pp. 199–223). Hershey, PA: IGI Global. doi:10.4018/978-1-5225-3468-6.ch011

Buzady, Z. (2017). Resolving the Magic Cube of Effective Case Teaching: Benchmarking Case Teaching Practices in Emerging Markets – Insights from the Central European University Business School, Hungary. In D. Latusek (Ed.), *Case Studies as a Teaching Tool in Management Education* (pp. 79–103). Hershey, PA: IGI Global. doi:10.4018/978-1-5225-0770-3.ch005

Campatelli, G., Richter, A., & Stocker, A. (2016). Participative Knowledge Management to Empower Manufacturing Workers. *International Journal of Knowledge Management*, *12*(4), 37–50. doi:10.4018/IJKM.2016100103

Căpusneanu, S., & Topor, D. I. (2018). Business Ethics and Cost Management in SMEs: Theories of Business Ethics and Cost Management Ethos. In I. Oncioiu (Ed.), *Ethics and Decision-Making for Sustainable Business Practices* (pp. 109–127). Hershey, PA: IGI Global. doi:10.4018/978-1-5225-3773-1.ch007

Carneiro, A. (2016). Maturity in Health Organization Information Systems: Metrics and Privacy Perspectives. *International Journal of Privacy and Health Information Management*, *4*(2), 1–18. doi:10.4018/IJPHIM.2016070101

Chan, R. L., Mo, P. L., & Moon, K. K. (2018). Strategic and Tactical Measures in Managing Enterprise Risks: A Study of the Textile and Apparel Industry. In K. Strang, M. Korstanje, & N. Vajjhala (Eds.), *Research, Practices, and Innovations in Global Risk and Contingency Management* (pp. 1–19). Hershey, PA: IGI Global. doi:10.4018/978-1-5225-4754-9.ch001

Chandan, H. C. (2016). Motivations and Challenges of Female Entrepreneurship in Developed and Developing Economies. In N. Baporikar (Ed.), *Handbook of Research on Entrepreneurship in the Contemporary Knowledge-Based Global Economy* (pp. 260–286). Hershey, PA: IGI Global. doi:10.4018/978-1-4666-8798-1.ch012

Charlier, S. D., Burke-Smalley, L. A., & Fisher, S. L. (2018). Undergraduate Programs in the U.S: A Contextual and Content-Based Analysis. In J. Mendy (Ed.), *Teaching Human Resources and Organizational Behavior at the College Level* (pp. 26–57). Hershey, PA: IGI Global. doi:10.4018/978-1-5225-2820-3.ch002

Chaudhuri, S. (2016). Application of Web-Based Geographical Information System (GIS) in E-Business. In U. Panwar, R. Kumar, & N. Ray (Eds.), *Handbook of Research on Promotional Strategies and Consumer Influence in the Service Sector* (pp. 389–405). Hershey, PA: IGI Global. doi:10.4018/978-1-5225-0143-5.ch023

Choudhuri, P. S. (2016). An Empirical Study on the Quality of Services Offered by the Private Life Insurers in Burdwan. In U. Panwar, R. Kumar, & N. Ray (Eds.), *Handbook of Research on Promotional Strategies and Consumer Influence in the Service Sector* (pp. 31–55). Hershey, PA: IGI Global. doi:10.4018/978-1-5225-0143-5.ch002

Dahlberg, T., Kivijärvi, H., & Saarinen, T. (2017). IT Investment Consistency and Other Factors Influencing the Success of IT Performance. In S. De Haes & W. Van Grembergen (Eds.), *Strategic IT Governance and Alignment in Business Settings* (pp. 176–208). Hershey, PA: IGI Global. doi:10.4018/978-1-5225-0861-8.ch007

Damnjanović, A. M. (2017). Knowledge Management Optimization through IT and E-Business Utilization: A Qualitative Study on Serbian SMEs. In M. Vemić (Ed.), *Optimal Management Strategies in Small and Medium Enterprises* (pp. 249–267). Hershey, PA: IGI Global. doi:10.4018/978-1-5225-1949-2.ch012

Daneshpour, H. (2017). Integrating Sustainable Development into Project Portfolio Management through Application of Open Innovation. In M. Vemić (Ed.), *Optimal Management Strategies in Small and Medium Enterprises* (pp. 370–387). Hershey, PA: IGI Global. doi:10.4018/978-1-5225-1949-2.ch017

Daniel, A. D., & Reis de Castro, V. (2018). Entrepreneurship Education: How to Measure the Impact on Nascent Entrepreneurs. In A. Carrizo Moreira, J. Guilherme Leitão Dantas, & F. Manuel Valente (Eds.), *Nascent Entrepreneurship and Successful New Venture Creation* (pp. 85–110). Hershey, PA: IGI Global. doi:10.4018/978-1-5225-2936-1.ch004

David, F., van der Sijde, P., & van den Besselaar, P. (2016). Enterpreneurial Incentives, Obstacles, and Management in University-Business Co-Operation: The Case of Indonesia. In J. Saiz-Álvarez (Ed.), *Handbook of Research on Social Entrepreneurship and Solidarity Economics* (pp. 499–518). Hershey, PA: IGI Global. doi:10.4018/978-1-5225-0097-1.ch024

David, R., Swami, B. N., & Tangirala, S. (2018). Ethics Impact on Knowledge Management in Organizational Development: A Case Study. In N. Baporikar (Ed.), *Global Practices in Knowledge Management for Societal and Organizational Development* (pp. 19–45). Hershey, PA: IGI Global. doi:10.4018/978-1-5225-3009-1.ch002

Delias, P., & Lakiotaki, K. (2018). Discovering Process Horizontal Boundaries to Facilitate Process Comprehension. *International Journal of Operations Research and Information Systems*, *9*(2), 1–31. doi:10.4018/IJORIS.2018040101

Denholm, J., & Lee-Davies, L. (2018). Success Factors for Games in Business and Project Management. In *Enhancing Education and Training Initiatives Through Serious Games* (pp. 34–68). Hershey, PA: IGI Global. doi:10.4018/978-1-5225-3689-5.ch002

Deshpande, M. (2017). Best Practices in Management Institutions for Global Leadership: Policy Aspects. In N. Baporikar (Ed.), *Management Education for Global Leadership* (pp. 1–27). Hershey, PA: IGI Global. doi:10.4018/978-1-5225-1013-0.ch001

Deshpande, M. (2018). Policy Perspectives for SMEs Knowledge Management. In N. Baporikar (Ed.), *Knowledge Integration Strategies for Entrepreneurship and Sustainability* (pp. 23–46). Hershey, PA: IGI Global. doi:10.4018/978-1-5225-5115-7.ch002

Dezdar, S. (2017). ERP Implementation Projects in Asian Countries: A Comparative Study on Iran and China. *International Journal of Information Technology Project Management*, *8*(3), 52–68. doi:10.4018/IJITPM.2017070104

Domingos, D., Martinho, R., & Varajão, J. (2016). Controlled Flexibility in Healthcare Processes: A BPMN-Extension Approach. In M. Cruz-Cunha, I. Miranda, R. Martinho, & R. Rijo (Eds.), *Encyclopedia of E-Health and Telemedicine* (pp. 521–535). Hershey, PA: IGI Global. doi:10.4018/978-1-4666-9978-6.ch040

Domingos, D., Respício, A., & Martinho, R. (2017). Reliability of IoT-Aware BPMN Healthcare Processes. In C. Reis & M. Maximiano (Eds.), *Internet of Things and Advanced Application in Healthcare* (pp. 214–248). Hershey, PA: IGI Global. doi:10.4018/978-1-5225-1820-4.ch008

Dosumu, O., Hussain, J., & El-Gohary, H. (2017). An Exploratory Study of the Impact of Government Policies on the Development of Small and Medium Enterprises in Developing Countries: The Case of Nigeria. *International Journal of Customer Relationship Marketing and Management*, *8*(4), 51–62. doi:10.4018/IJCRMM.2017100104

Durst, S., Bruns, G., & Edvardsson, I. R. (2017). Retaining Knowledge in Smaller Building and Construction Firms. *International Journal of Knowledge and Systems Science*, *8*(3), 1–12. doi:10.4018/IJKSS.2017070101

Edvardsson, I. R., & Durst, S. (2017). Outsourcing, Knowledge, and Learning: A Critical Review. *International Journal of Knowledge-Based Organizations*, *7*(2), 13–26. doi:10.4018/IJKBO.2017040102

Edwards, J. S. (2018). Integrating Knowledge Management and Business Processes. In M. Khosrow-Pour, D.B.A. (Ed.), Encyclopedia of Information Science and Technology, Fourth Edition (pp. 5046-5055). Hershey, PA: IGI Global. doi:10.4018/978-1-5225-2255-3.ch437

Ejiogu, A. O. (2018). Economics of Farm Management. In *Agricultural Finance and Opportunities for Investment and Expansion* (pp. 56–72). Hershey, PA: IGI Global. doi:10.4018/978-1-5225-3059-6.ch003

Ekanem, I., & Abiade, G. E. (2018). Factors Influencing the Use of E-Commerce by Small Enterprises in Nigeria. *International Journal of ICT Research in Africa and the Middle East*, *7*(1), 37–53. doi:10.4018/IJICTRAME.2018010103

Ekanem, I., & Alrossais, L. A. (2017). Succession Challenges Facing Family Businesses in Saudi Arabia. In P. Zgheib (Ed.), *Entrepreneurship and Business Innovation in the Middle East* (pp. 122–146). Hershey, PA: IGI Global. doi:10.4018/978-1-5225-2066-5.ch007

El Faquih, L., & Fredj, M. (2017). Ontology-Based Framework for Quality in Configurable Process Models. *Journal of Electronic Commerce in Organizations, 15*(2), 48–60. doi:10.4018/JECO.2017040104

El-Gohary, H., & El-Gohary, Z. (2016). An Attempt to Explore Electronic Marketing Adoption and Implementation Aspects in Developing Countries: The Case of Egypt. *International Journal of Customer Relationship Marketing and Management, 7*(4), 1–26. doi:10.4018/IJCRMM.2016100101

Entico, G. J. (2016). Knowledge Management and the Medical Health Librarians: A Perception Study. In J. Yap, M. Perez, M. Ayson, & G. Entico (Eds.), *Special Library Administration, Standardization and Technological Integration* (pp. 52–77). Hershey, PA: IGI Global. doi:10.4018/978-1-4666-9542-9.ch003

Faisal, M. N., & Talib, F. (2017). Building Ambidextrous Supply Chains in SMEs: How to Tackle the Barriers? *International Journal of Information Systems and Supply Chain Management, 10*(4), 80–100. doi:10.4018/IJISSCM.2017100105

Fernandes, T. M., Gomes, J., & Romão, M. (2017). Investments in E-Government: A Benefit Management Case Study. *International Journal of Electronic Government Research, 13*(3), 1–17. doi:10.4018/IJEGR.2017070101

Fouda, F. A. (2016). A Suggested Curriculum in Career Education to Develop Business Secondary Schools Students' Career Knowledge Management Domains and Professional Thinking. *International Journal of Technology Diffusion, 7*(2), 42–62. doi:10.4018/IJTD.2016040103

Gallardo-Vázquez, D., & Pajuelo-Moreno, M. L. (2016). How Spanish Universities are Promoting Entrepreneurship through Your Own Lines of Teaching and Research? In L. Carvalho (Ed.), *Handbook of Research on Entrepreneurial Success and its Impact on Regional Development* (pp. 431–454). Hershey, PA: IGI Global. doi:10.4018/978-1-4666-9567-2.ch019

Gao, S. S., Oreal, S., & Zhang, J. (2018). Contemporary Financial Risk Management Perceptions and Practices of Small-Sized Chinese Businesses. In I. Management Association (Ed.), Global Business Expansion: Concepts, Methodologies, Tools, and Applications (pp. 917-931). Hershey, PA: IGI Global. doi:10.4018/978-1-5225-5481-3.ch041

Garg, R., & Berning, S. C. (2017). Indigenous Chinese Management Philosophies: Key Concepts and Relevance for Modern Chinese Firms. In B. Christiansen & G. Koc (Eds.), *Transcontinental Strategies for Industrial Development and Economic Growth* (pp. 43–57). Hershey, PA: IGI Global. doi:10.4018/978-1-5225-2160-0.ch003

Gencer, Y. G. (2017). Supply Chain Management in Retailing Business. In U. Akkucuk (Ed.), *Ethics and Sustainability in Global Supply Chain Management* (pp. 197–210). Hershey, PA: IGI Global. doi:10.4018/978-1-5225-2036-8.ch011

Giacosa, E. (2016). Innovation in Luxury Fashion Businesses as a Means for the Regional Development. In L. Carvalho (Ed.), *Handbook of Research on Entrepreneurial Success and its Impact on Regional Development* (pp. 206–222). Hershey, PA: IGI Global. doi:10.4018/978-1-4666-9567-2.ch010

Giacosa, E. (2018). The Increasing of the Regional Development Thanks to the Luxury Business Innovation. In L. Carvalho (Ed.), *Handbook of Research on Entrepreneurial Ecosystems and Social Dynamics in a Globalized World* (pp. 260–273). Hershey, PA: IGI Global. doi:10.4018/978-1-5225-3525-6.ch011

Gianni, M., & Gotzamani, K. (2016). Integrated Management Systems and Information Management Systems: Common Threads. In P. Papajorgji, F. Pinet, A. Guimarães, & J. Papathanasiou (Eds.), *Automated Enterprise Systems for Maximizing Business Performance* (pp. 195–214). Hershey, PA: IGI Global. doi:10.4018/978-1-4666-8841-4.ch011

Gianni, M., Gotzamani, K., & Linden, I. (2016). How a BI-wise Responsible Integrated Management System May Support Food Traceability. *International Journal of Decision Support System Technology*, *8*(2), 1–17. doi:10.4018/IJDSST.2016040101

Glykas, M., & George, J. (2017). Quality and Process Management Systems in the UAE Maritime Industry. *International Journal of Productivity Management and Assessment Technologies*, *5*(1), 20–39. doi:10.4018/IJPMAT.2017010102

Glykas, M., Valiris, G., Kokkinaki, A., & Koutsoukou, Z. (2018). Banking Business Process Management Implementation. *International Journal of Productivity Management and Assessment Technologies*, *6*(1), 50–69. doi:10.4018/IJPMAT.2018010104

Gomes, J., & Romão, M. (2017). The Balanced Scorecard: Keeping Updated and Aligned with Today's Business Trends. *International Journal of Productivity Management and Assessment Technologies*, *5*(2), 1–15. doi:10.4018/IJPMAT.2017070101

Gomes, J., & Romão, M. (2017). Aligning Information Systems and Technology with Benefit Management and Balanced Scorecard. In S. De Haes & W. Van Grembergen (Eds.), *Strategic IT Governance and Alignment in Business Settings* (pp. 112–131). Hershey, PA: IGI Global. doi:10.4018/978-1-5225-0861-8.ch005

Grefen, P., & Turetken, O. (2017). Advanced Business Process Management in Networked E-Business Scenarios. *International Journal of E-Business Research*, *13*(4), 70–104. doi:10.4018/IJEBR.2017100105

Haider, A., & Saetang, S. (2017). Strategic IT Alignment in Service Sector. In S. Rozenes & Y. Cohen (Eds.), *Handbook of Research on Strategic Alliances and Value Co-Creation in the Service Industry* (pp. 231–258). Hershey, PA: IGI Global. doi:10.4018/978-1-5225-2084-9.ch012

Haider, A., & Tang, S. S. (2016). Maximising Value Through IT and Business Alignment: A Case of IT Governance Institutionalisation at a Thai Bank. *International Journal of Technology Diffusion*, *7*(3), 33–58. doi:10.4018/IJTD.2016070104

Hajilari, A. B., Ghadaksaz, M., & Fasghandis, G. S. (2017). Assessing Organizational Readiness for Implementing ERP System Using Fuzzy Expert System Approach. *International Journal of Enterprise Information Systems*, *13*(1), 67–85. doi:10.4018/IJEIS.2017010105

Haldorai, A., Ramu, A., & Murugan, S. (2018). Social Aware Cognitive Radio Networks: Effectiveness of Social Networks as a Strategic Tool for Organizational Business Management. In H. Bansal, G. Shrivastava, G. Nguyen, & L. Stanciu (Eds.), *Social Network Analytics for Contemporary Business Organizations* (pp. 188–202). Hershey, PA: IGI Global. doi:10.4018/978-1-5225-5097-6.ch010

Hall, O. P. Jr. (2017). Social Media Driven Management Education. *International Journal of Knowledge-Based Organizations*, *7*(2), 43–59. doi:10.4018/IJKBO.2017040104

Hanifah, H., Halim, H. A., Ahmad, N. H., & Vafaei-Zadeh, A. (2017). Innovation Culture as a Mediator Between Specific Human Capital and Innovation Performance Among Bumiputera SMEs in Malaysia. In N. Ahmad, T. Ramayah, H. Halim, & S. Rahman (Eds.), *Handbook of Research on Small and Medium Enterprises in Developing Countries* (pp. 261–279). Hershey, PA: IGI Global. doi:10.4018/978-1-5225-2165-5.ch012

Hartlieb, S., & Silvius, G. (2017). Handling Uncertainty in Project Management and Business Development: Similarities and Differences. In Y. Raydugin (Ed.), *Handbook of Research on Leveraging Risk and Uncertainties for Effective Project Management* (pp. 337–362). Hershey, PA: IGI Global. doi:10.4018/978-1-5225-1790-0.ch016

Hass, K. B. (2017). Living on the Edge: Managing Project Complexity. In Y. Raydugin (Ed.), *Handbook of Research on Leveraging Risk and Uncertainties for Effective Project Management* (pp. 177–201). Hershey, PA: IGI Global. doi:10.4018/978-1-5225-1790-0.ch009

Hassan, A., & Privitera, D. S. (2016). Google AdSense as a Mobile Technology in Education. In J. Holland (Ed.), *Wearable Technology and Mobile Innovations for Next-Generation Education* (pp. 200–223). Hershey, PA: IGI Global. doi:10.4018/978-1-5225-0069-8.ch011

Hassan, A., & Rahimi, R. (2016). Consuming "Innovation" in Tourism: Augmented Reality as an Innovation Tool in Digital Tourism Marketing. In N. Pappas & I. Bregoli (Eds.), *Global Dynamics in Travel, Tourism, and Hospitality* (pp. 130–147). Hershey, PA: IGI Global. doi:10.4018/978-1-5225-0201-2.ch008

Hawking, P., & Carmine Sellitto, C. (2017). Developing an Effective Strategy for Organizational Business Intelligence. In M. Tavana (Ed.), *Enterprise Information Systems and the Digitalization of Business Functions* (pp. 222–237). Hershey, PA: IGI Global. doi:10.4018/978-1-5225-2382-6.ch010

Hawking, P., & Sellitto, C. (2017). A Fast-Moving Consumer Goods Company and Business Intelligence Strategy Development. *International Journal of Enterprise Information Systems, 13*(2), 22–33. doi:10.4018/IJEIS.2017040102

Hawking, P., & Sellitto, C. (2017). Business Intelligence Strategy: Two Case Studies. *International Journal of Business Intelligence Research, 8*(2), 17–30. doi:10.4018/IJBIR.2017070102

Haynes, J. D., Arockiasamy, S., Al Rashdi, M., & Al Rashdi, S. (2016). Business and E Business Strategies for Coopetition and Thematic Management as a Sustained Basis for Ethics and Social Responsibility in Emerging Markets. In M. Al-Shammari & H. Masri (Eds.), *Ethical and Social Perspectives on Global Business Interaction in Emerging Markets* (pp. 25–39). Hershey, PA: IGI Global. doi:10.4018/978-1-4666-9864-2.ch002

Hee, W. J., Jalleh, G., Lai, H., & Lin, C. (2017). E-Commerce and IT Projects: Evaluation and Management Issues in Australian and Taiwanese Hospitals. *International Journal of Public Health Management and Ethics, 2*(1), 69–90. doi:10.4018/IJPHME.2017010104

Hernandez, A. A. (2018). Exploring the Factors to Green IT Adoption of SMEs in the Philippines. *Journal of Cases on Information Technology*, *20*(2), 49–66. doi:10.4018/JCIT.2018040104

Hernandez, A. A., & Ona, S. E. (2016). Green IT Adoption: Lessons from the Philippines Business Process Outsourcing Industry. *International Journal of Social Ecology and Sustainable Development*, *7*(1), 1–34. doi:10.4018/IJSESD.2016010101

Hollman, A., Bickford, S., & Hollman, T. (2017). Cyber InSecurity: A Post-Mortem Attempt to Assess Cyber Problems from IT and Business Management Perspectives. *Journal of Cases on Information Technology*, *19*(3), 42–70. doi:10.4018/JCIT.2017070104

Igbinakhase, I. (2017). Responsible and Sustainable Management Practices in Developing and Developed Business Environments. In Z. Fields (Ed.), *Collective Creativity for Responsible and Sustainable Business Practice* (pp. 180–207). Hershey, PA: IGI Global. doi:10.4018/978-1-5225-1823-5.ch010

Ilahi, L., Ghannouchi, S. A., & Martinho, R. (2016). A Business Process Management Approach to Home Healthcare Processes: On the Gap between Intention and Reality. In M. Cruz-Cunha, I. Miranda, R. Martinho, & R. Rijo (Eds.), *Encyclopedia of E-Health and Telemedicine* (pp. 439–457). Hershey, PA: IGI Global. doi:10.4018/978-1-4666-9978-6.ch035

Iwata, J. J., & Hoskins, R. G. (2017). Managing Indigenous Knowledge in Tanzania: A Business Perspective. In P. Jain & N. Mnjama (Eds.), *Managing Knowledge Resources and Records in Modern Organizations* (pp. 198–214). Hershey, PA: IGI Global. doi:10.4018/978-1-5225-1965-2.ch012

Jabeen, F., Ahmad, S. Z., & Alkaabi, S. (2016). The Internationalization Decision-Making of United Arab Emirates Family Businesses. In N. Zakaria, A. Abdul-Talib, & N. Osman (Eds.), *Handbook of Research on Impacts of International Business and Political Affairs on the Global Economy* (pp. 1–22). Hershey, PA: IGI Global. doi:10.4018/978-1-4666-9806-2.ch001

Jain, P. (2017). Ethical and Legal Issues in Knowledge Management Life-Cycle in Business. In P. Jain & N. Mnjama (Eds.), *Managing Knowledge Resources and Records in Modern Organizations* (pp. 82–101). Hershey, PA: IGI Global. doi:10.4018/978-1-5225-1965-2.ch006

Jamali, D., Abdallah, H., & Matar, F. (2016). Opportunities and Challenges for CSR Mainstreaming in Business Schools. *International Journal of Technology and Educational Marketing*, *6*(2), 1–29. doi:10.4018/IJTEM.2016070101

James, S., & Hauli, E. (2017). Holistic Management Education at Tanzanian Rural Development Planning Institute. In N. Baporikar (Ed.), *Management Education for Global Leadership* (pp. 112–136). Hershey, PA: IGI Global. doi:10.4018/978-1-5225-1013-0.ch006

Janošková, M., Csikósová, A., & Čulková, K. (2018). Measurement of Company Performance as Part of Its Strategic Management. In R. Leon (Ed.), *Managerial Strategies for Business Sustainability During Turbulent Times* (pp. 309–335). Hershey, PA: IGI Global. doi:10.4018/978-1-5225-2716-9.ch017

Jean-Vasile, A., & Alecu, A. (2017). Theoretical and Practical Approaches in Understanding the Influences of Cost-Productivity-Profit Trinomial in Contemporary Enterprises. In A. Jean Vasile & D. Nicolò (Eds.), *Sustainable Entrepreneurship and Investments in the Green Economy* (pp. 28–62). Hershey, PA: IGI Global. doi:10.4018/978-1-5225-2075-7.ch002

Jha, D. G. (2016). Preparing for Information Technology Driven Changes. In S. Tiwari & L. Nafees (Eds.), *Innovative Management Education Pedagogies for Preparing Next-Generation Leaders* (pp. 258–274). Hershey, PA: IGI Global. doi:10.4018/978-1-4666-9691-4.ch015

Joia, L. A., & Correia, J. C. (2018). CIO Competencies From the IT Professional Perspective: Insights From Brazil. *Journal of Global Information Management*, *26*(2), 74–103. doi:10.4018/JGIM.2018040104

Juma, A., & Mzera, N. (2017). Knowledge Management and Records Management and Competitive Advantage in Business. In P. Jain & N. Mnjama (Eds.), *Managing Knowledge Resources and Records in Modern Organizations* (pp. 15–28). Hershey, PA: IGI Global. doi:10.4018/978-1-5225-1965-2.ch002

K., I., & A, V. (2018). Monitoring and Auditing in the Cloud. In K. Munir (Ed.), *Cloud Computing Technologies for Green Enterprises* (pp. 318-350). Hershey, PA: IGI Global. doi:10.4018/978-1-5225-3038-1.ch013

Kabra, G., Ghosh, V., & Ramesh, A. (2018). Enterprise Integrated Business Process Management and Business Intelligence Framework for Business Process Sustainability. In A. Paul, D. Bhattacharyya, & S. Anand (Eds.), *Green Initiatives for Business Sustainability and Value Creation* (pp. 228–238). Hershey, PA: IGI Global. doi:10.4018/978-1-5225-2662-9.ch010

Kaoud, M. (2017). Investigation of Customer Knowledge Management: A Case Study Research. *International Journal of Service Science, Management, Engineering, and Technology*, *8*(2), 12–22. doi:10.4018/IJSSMET.2017040102

Kara, M. E., & Fırat, S. Ü. (2016). Sustainability, Risk, and Business Intelligence in Supply Chains. In M. Erdoğdu, T. Arun, & I. Ahmad (Eds.), *Handbook of Research on Green Economic Development Initiatives and Strategies* (pp. 501–538). Hershey, PA: IGI Global. doi:10.4018/978-1-5225-0440-5.ch022

Katuu, S. (2018). A Comparative Assessment of Enterprise Content Management Maturity Models. In N. Gwangwava & M. Mutingi (Eds.), *E-Manufacturing and E-Service Strategies in Contemporary Organizations* (pp. 93–118). Hershey, PA: IGI Global. doi:10.4018/978-1-5225-3628-4.ch005

Khan, M. A. (2016). MNEs Management Strategies in Developing Countries: Establishing the Context. In M. Khan (Ed.), *Multinational Enterprise Management Strategies in Developing Countries* (pp. 1–33). Hershey, PA: IGI Global. doi:10.4018/978-1-5225-0276-0.ch001

Khan, M. A. (2016). Operational Approaches in Organizational Structure: A Case for MNEs in Developing Countries. In M. Khan (Ed.), *Multinational Enterprise Management Strategies in Developing Countries* (pp. 129–151). Hershey, PA: IGI Global. doi:10.4018/978-1-5225-0276-0.ch007

Kinnunen, S., Ylä-Kujala, A., Marttonen-Arola, S., Kärri, T., & Baglee, D. (2018). Internet of Things in Asset Management: Insights from Industrial Professionals and Academia. *International Journal of Service Science, Management, Engineering, and Technology*, *9*(2), 104–119. doi:10.4018/IJSSMET.2018040105

Klein, A. Z., Sabino de Freitas, A., Machado, L., Freitas, J. C. Jr, Graziola, P. G. Jr, & Schlemmer, E. (2017). Virtual Worlds Applications for Management Education. In L. Tomei (Ed.), *Exploring the New Era of Technology-Infused Education* (pp. 279–299). Hershey, PA: IGI Global. doi:10.4018/978-1-5225-1709-2.ch017

Kożuch, B., & Jabłoński, A. (2017). Adopting the Concept of Business Models in Public Management. In M. Lewandowski & B. Kożuch (Eds.), *Public Sector Entrepreneurship and the Integration of Innovative Business Models* (pp. 10–46). Hershey, PA: IGI Global. doi:10.4018/978-1-5225-2215-7.ch002

Kumar, J., Adhikary, A., & Jha, A. (2017). Small Active Investors' Perceptions and Preferences Towards Tax Saving Mutual Fund Schemes in Eastern India: An Empirical Note. *International Journal of Asian Business and Information Management*, *8*(2), 35–45. doi:10.4018/IJABIM.2017040103

Lassoued, Y., Bouzguenda, L., & Mahmoud, T. (2016). Context-Aware Business Process Versions Management. *International Journal of e-Collaboration*, *12*(3), 7–33. doi:10.4018/IJeC.2016070102

Lavassani, K. M., & Movahedi, B. (2017). Applications Driven Information Systems: Beyond Networks toward Business Ecosystems. *International Journal of Innovation in the Digital Economy*, *8*(1), 61–75. doi:10.4018/IJIDE.2017010104

Lazzareschi, V. H., & Brito, M. S. (2017). Strategic Information Management: Proposal of Business Project Model. In G. Jamil, A. Soares, & C. Pessoa (Eds.), *Handbook of Research on Information Management for Effective Logistics and Supply Chains* (pp. 59–88). Hershey, PA: IGI Global. doi:10.4018/978-1-5225-0973-8.ch004

Lederer, M., Kurz, M., & Lazarov, P. (2017). Usage and Suitability of Methods for Strategic Business Process Initiatives: A Multi Case Study Research. *International Journal of Productivity Management and Assessment Technologies*, *5*(1), 40–51. doi:10.4018/IJPMAT.2017010103

Lee, I. (2017). A Social Enterprise Business Model and a Case Study of Pacific Community Ventures (PCV). In V. Potocan, M. Ünğan, & Z. Nedelko (Eds.), *Handbook of Research on Managerial Solutions in Non-Profit Organizations* (pp. 182–204). Hershey, PA: IGI Global. doi:10.4018/978-1-5225-0731-4.ch009

Lee, L. J., & Leu, J. (2016). Exploring the Effectiveness of IT Application and Value Method in the Innovation Performance of Enterprise. *International Journal of Enterprise Information Systems*, *12*(2), 47–65. doi:10.4018/IJEIS.2016040104

Lee, Y. (2016). Alignment Effect of Entrepreneurial Orientation and Marketing Orientation on Firm Performance. *International Journal of Customer Relationship Marketing and Management*, *7*(4), 58–69. doi:10.4018/IJCRMM.2016100104

Leon, L. A., Seal, K. C., Przasnyski, Z. H., & Wiedenman, I. (2017). Skills and Competencies Required for Jobs in Business Analytics: A Content Analysis of Job Advertisements Using Text Mining. *International Journal of Business Intelligence Research*, *8*(1), 1–25. doi:10.4018/IJBIR.2017010101

Leu, J., Lee, L. J., & Krischke, A. (2016). Value Engineering-Based Method for Implementing the ISO14001 System in the Green Supply Chains. *International Journal of Strategic Decision Sciences*, *7*(4), 1–20. doi:10.4018/IJSDS.2016100101

Levy, C. L., & Elias, N. I. (2017). SOHO Users' Perceptions of Reliability and Continuity of Cloud-Based Services. In M. Moore (Ed.), *Cybersecurity Breaches and Issues Surrounding Online Threat Protection* (pp. 248–287). Hershey, PA: IGI Global. doi:10.4018/978-1-5225-1941-6.ch011

Levy, M. (2018). Change Management Serving Knowledge Management and Organizational Development: Reflections and Review. In N. Baporikar (Ed.), *Global Practices in Knowledge Management for Societal and Organizational Development* (pp. 256–270). Hershey, PA: IGI Global. doi:10.4018/978-1-5225-3009-1.ch012

Lewandowski, M. (2017). Public Organizations and Business Model Innovation: The Role of Public Service Design. In M. Lewandowski & B. Kożuch (Eds.), *Public Sector Entrepreneurship and the Integration of Innovative Business Models* (pp. 47–72). Hershey, PA: IGI Global. doi:10.4018/978-1-5225-2215-7.ch003

Lhannaoui, H., Kabbaj, M. I., & Bakkoury, Z. (2017). A Survey of Risk-Aware Business Process Modelling. *International Journal of Risk and Contingency Management*, *6*(3), 14–26. doi:10.4018/IJRCM.2017070102

Li, J., Sun, W., Jiang, W., Yang, H., & Zhang, L. (2017). How the Nature of Exogenous Shocks and Crises Impact Company Performance?: The Effects of Industry Characteristics. *International Journal of Risk and Contingency Management*, *6*(4), 40–55. doi:10.4018/IJRCM.2017100103

Lu, C., & Liu, S. (2016). Cultural Tourism O2O Business Model Innovation-A Case Study of CTrip. *Journal of Electronic Commerce in Organizations*, *14*(2), 16–31. doi:10.4018/JECO.2016040102

Machen, B., Hosseini, M. R., Wood, A., & Bakhshi, J. (2016). An Investigation into using SAP-PS as a Multidimensional Project Control System (MPCS). *International Journal of Enterprise Information Systems*, *12*(2), 66–81. doi:10.4018/IJEIS.2016040105

Malega, P. (2017). Small and Medium Enterprises in the Slovak Republic: Status and Competitiveness of SMEs in the Global Markets and Possibilities of Optimization. In M. Vemić (Ed.), *Optimal Management Strategies in Small and Medium Enterprises* (pp. 102–124). Hershey, PA: IGI Global. doi:10.4018/978-1-5225-1949-2.ch006

Malewska, K. M. (2017). Intuition in Decision-Making on the Example of a Non-Profit Organization. In V. Potocan, M. Üngan, & Z. Nedelko (Eds.), *Handbook of Research on Managerial Solutions in Non-Profit Organizations* (pp. 378–399). Hershey, PA: IGI Global. doi:10.4018/978-1-5225-0731-4.ch018

Maroofi, F. (2017). Entrepreneurial Orientation and Organizational Learning Ability Analysis for Innovation and Firm Performance. In N. Baporikar (Ed.), *Innovation and Shifting Perspectives in Management Education* (pp. 144–165). Hershey, PA: IGI Global. doi:10.4018/978-1-5225-1019-2.ch007

Martins, P. V., & Zacarias, M. (2017). A Web-based Tool for Business Process Improvement. *International Journal of Web Portals*, *9*(2), 68–84. doi:10.4018/IJWP.2017070104

Matthies, B., & Coners, A. (2017). Exploring the Conceptual Nature of e-Business Projects. *Journal of Electronic Commerce in Organizations*, *15*(3), 33–63. doi:10.4018/JECO.2017070103

McKee, J. (2018). Architecture as a Tool to Solve Business Planning Problems. In M. Khosrow-Pour, D.B.A. (Ed.), Encyclopedia of Information Science and Technology, Fourth Edition (pp. 573-586). Hershey, PA: IGI Global. doi:10.4018/978-1-5225-2255-3.ch050

McMurray, A. J., Cross, J., & Caponecchia, C. (2018). The Risk Management Profession in Australia: Business Continuity Plan Practices. In N. Bajgoric (Ed.), *Always-On Enterprise Information Systems for Modern Organizations* (pp. 112–129). Hershey, PA: IGI Global. doi:10.4018/978-1-5225-3704-5.ch006

Meddah, I. H., & Belkadi, K. (2018). Mining Patterns Using Business Process Management. In R. Hamou (Ed.), *Handbook of Research on Biomimicry in Information Retrieval and Knowledge Management* (pp. 78–89). Hershey, PA: IGI Global. doi:10.4018/978-1-5225-3004-6.ch005

Mendes, L. (2017). TQM and Knowledge Management: An Integrated Approach Towards Tacit Knowledge Management. In D. Jaziri-Bouagina & G. Jamil (Eds.), *Handbook of Research on Tacit Knowledge Management for Organizational Success* (pp. 236–263). Hershey, PA: IGI Global. doi:10.4018/978-1-5225-2394-9.ch009

Mnjama, N. M. (2017). Preservation of Recorded Information in Public and Private Sector Organizations. In P. Jain & N. Mnjama (Eds.), *Managing Knowledge Resources and Records in Modern Organizations* (pp. 149–167). Hershey, PA: IGI Global. doi:10.4018/978-1-5225-1965-2.ch009

Mokoqama, M., & Fields, Z. (2017). Principles of Responsible Management Education (PRME): Call for Responsible Management Education. In Z. Fields (Ed.), *Collective Creativity for Responsible and Sustainable Business Practice* (pp. 229–241). Hershey, PA: IGI Global. doi:10.4018/978-1-5225-1823-5.ch012

Muniapan, B. (2017). Philosophy and Management: The Relevance of Vedanta in Management. In P. Ordóñez de Pablos (Ed.), *Managerial Strategies and Solutions for Business Success in Asia* (pp. 124–139). Hershey, PA: IGI Global. doi:10.4018/978-1-5225-1886-0.ch007

Muniapan, B., Gregory, M. L., & Ling, L. A. (2016). Marketing Education in Sarawak: Looking at It from the Employers' Viewpoint. In B. Smith & A. Porath (Eds.), *Global Perspectives on Contemporary Marketing Education* (pp. 112–130). Hershey, PA: IGI Global. doi:10.4018/978-1-4666-9784-3.ch008

Murad, S. E., & Dowaji, S. (2017). Using Value-Based Approach for Managing Cloud-Based Services. In A. Turuk, B. Sahoo, & S. Addya (Eds.), *Resource Management and Efficiency in Cloud Computing Environments* (pp. 33–60). Hershey, PA: IGI Global. doi:10.4018/978-1-5225-1721-4.ch002

Mutahar, A. M., Daud, N. M., Thurasamy, R., Isaac, O., & Abdulsalam, R. (2018). The Mediating of Perceived Usefulness and Perceived Ease of Use: The Case of Mobile Banking in Yemen. *International Journal of Technology Diffusion*, *9*(2), 21–40. doi:10.4018/IJTD.2018040102

Naidoo, V. (2017). E-Learning and Management Education at African Universities. In N. Baporikar (Ed.), *Management Education for Global Leadership* (pp. 181–201). Hershey, PA: IGI Global. doi:10.4018/978-1-5225-1013-0.ch009

Naidoo, V., & Igbinakhase, I. (2018). Opportunities and Challenges of Knowledge Retention in SMEs. In N. Baporikar (Ed.), *Knowledge Integration Strategies for Entrepreneurship and Sustainability* (pp. 70–94). Hershey, PA: IGI Global. doi:10.4018/978-1-5225-5115-7.ch004

Nayak, S., & Prabhu, N. (2017). Paradigm Shift in Management Education: Need for a Cross Functional Perspective. In N. Baporikar (Ed.), *Management Education for Global Leadership* (pp. 241–255). Hershey, PA: IGI Global. doi:10.4018/978-1-5225-1013-0.ch012

Ndede-Amadi, A. A. (2016). Student Interest in the IS Specialization as Predictor of the Success Potential of New Information Systems Programmes within the Schools of Business in Kenyan Public Universities. *International Journal of Information Systems and Social Change*, *7*(2), 63–79. doi:10.4018/IJISSC.2016040104

Nedelko, Z., & Potocan, V. (2016). Management Practices for Processes Optimization: Case of Slovenia. In G. Alor-Hernández, C. Sánchez-Ramírez, & J. García-Alcaraz (Eds.), *Handbook of Research on Managerial Strategies for Achieving Optimal Performance in Industrial Processes* (pp. 545–561). Hershey, PA: IGI Global. doi:10.4018/978-1-5225-0130-5.ch025

Nedelko, Z., & Potocan, V. (2017). Management Solutions in Non-Profit Organizations: Case of Slovenia. In V. Potocan, M. Üngan, & Z. Nedelko (Eds.), *Handbook of Research on Managerial Solutions in Non-Profit Organizations* (pp. 1–22). Hershey, PA: IGI Global. doi:10.4018/978-1-5225-0731-4.ch001

Nedelko, Z., & Potocan, V. (2017). Priority of Management Tools Utilization among Managers: International Comparison. In V. Wang (Ed.), *Encyclopedia of Strategic Leadership and Management* (pp. 1083–1094). Hershey, PA: IGI Global. doi:10.4018/978-1-5225-1049-9.ch075

Nedelko, Z., Raudeliūnienė, J., & Črešnar, R. (2018). Knowledge Dynamics in Supply Chain Management. In N. Baporikar (Ed.), *Knowledge Integration Strategies for Entrepreneurship and Sustainability* (pp. 150–166). Hershey, PA: IGI Global. doi:10.4018/978-1-5225-5115-7.ch008

Nguyen, H. T., & Hipsher, S. A. (2018). Innovation and Creativity Used by Private Sector Firms in a Resources-Constrained Environment. In S. Hipsher (Ed.), *Examining the Private Sector's Role in Wealth Creation and Poverty Reduction* (pp. 219–238). Hershey, PA: IGI Global. doi:10.4018/978-1-5225-3117-3.ch010

Nycz, M., & Pólkowski, Z. (2016). Business Intelligence as a Modern IT Supporting Management of Local Government Units in Poland. *International Journal of Knowledge and Systems Science*, *7*(4), 1–18. doi:10.4018/IJKSS.2016100101

Obaji, N. O., Senin, A. A., & Olugu, M. U. (2016). Supportive Government Policy as a Mechanism for Business Incubation Performance in Nigeria. *International Journal of Information Systems and Social Change*, *7*(4), 52–66. doi:10.4018/IJISSC.2016100103

Obicci, P. A. (2017). Risk Sharing in a Partnership. In *Risk Management Strategies in Public-Private Partnerships* (pp. 115–152). Hershey, PA: IGI Global. doi:10.4018/978-1-5225-2503-5.ch004

Obidallah, W. J., & Raahemi, B. (2017). Managing Changes in Service Oriented Virtual Organizations: A Structural and Procedural Framework to Facilitate the Process of Change. *Journal of Electronic Commerce in Organizations*, *15*(1), 59–83. doi:10.4018/JECO.2017010104

Ojasalo, J., & Ojasalo, K. (2016). Service Logic Business Model Canvas for Lean Development of SMEs and Start-Ups. In N. Baporikar (Ed.), *Handbook of Research on Entrepreneurship in the Contemporary Knowledge-Based Global Economy* (pp. 217–243). Hershey, PA: IGI Global. doi:10.4018/978-1-4666-8798-1.ch010

Ojo, O. (2017). Impact of Innovation on the Entrepreneurial Success in Selected Business Enterprises in South-West Nigeria. *International Journal of Innovation in the Digital Economy*, *8*(2), 29–38. doi:10.4018/IJIDE.2017040103

Okdinawati, L., Simatupang, T. M., & Sunitiyoso, Y. (2017). Multi-Agent Reinforcement Learning for Value Co-Creation of Collaborative Transportation Management (CTM). *International Journal of Information Systems and Supply Chain Management*, *10*(3), 84–95. doi:10.4018/IJISSCM.2017070105

Ortner, E., Mevius, M., Wiedmann, P., & Kurz, F. (2016). Design of Interactional Decision Support Applications for E-Participation in Smart Cities. *International Journal of Electronic Government Research*, *12*(2), 18–38. doi:10.4018/IJEGR.2016040102

Pal, K. (2018). Building High Quality Big Data-Based Applications in Supply Chains. In A. Kumar & S. Saurav (Eds.), *Supply Chain Management Strategies and Risk Assessment in Retail Environments* (pp. 1–24). Hershey, PA: IGI Global. doi:10.4018/978-1-5225-3056-5.ch001

Palos-Sanchez, P. R., & Correia, M. B. (2018). Perspectives of the Adoption of Cloud Computing in the Tourism Sector. In J. Rodrigues, C. Ramos, P. Cardoso, & C. Henriques (Eds.), *Handbook of Research on Technological Developments for Cultural Heritage and eTourism Applications* (pp. 377–400). Hershey, PA: IGI Global. doi:10.4018/978-1-5225-2927-9.ch018

Parry, V. K., & Lind, M. L. (2016). Alignment of Business Strategy and Information Technology Considering Information Technology Governance, Project Portfolio Control, and Risk Management. *International Journal of Information Technology Project Management*, *7*(4), 21–37. doi:10.4018/IJITPM.2016100102

Pashkova, N., Trujillo-Barrera, A., Apostolakis, G., Van Dijk, G., Drakos, P. D., & Baourakis, G. (2016). Business Management Models of Microfinance Institutions (MFIs) in Africa: A Study into Their Enabling Environments. *International Journal of Food and Beverage Manufacturing and Business Models*, *1*(2), 63–82. doi:10.4018/IJFBMBM.2016070105

Patiño, B. E. (2017). New Generation Management by Convergence and Individual Identity: A Systemic and Human-Oriented Approach. In N. Baporikar (Ed.), *Innovation and Shifting Perspectives in Management Education* (pp. 119–143). Hershey, PA: IGI Global. doi:10.4018/978-1-5225-1019-2.ch006

Pawliczek, A., & Rössler, M. (2017). Knowledge of Management Tools and Systems in SMEs: Knowledge Transfer in Management. In A. Bencsik (Ed.), *Knowledge Management Initiatives and Strategies in Small and Medium Enterprises* (pp. 180–203). Hershey, PA: IGI Global. doi:10.4018/978-1-5225-1642-2.ch009

Pejic-Bach, M., Omazic, M. A., Aleksic, A., & Zoroja, J. (2018). Knowledge-Based Decision Making: A Multi-Case Analysis. In R. Leon (Ed.), *Managerial Strategies for Business Sustainability During Turbulent Times* (pp. 160–184). Hershey, PA: IGI Global. doi:10.4018/978-1-5225-2716-9.ch009

Perano, M., Hysa, X., & Calabrese, M. (2018). Strategic Planning, Cultural Context, and Business Continuity Management: Business Cases in the City of Shkoder. In A. Presenza & L. Sheehan (Eds.), *Geopolitics and Strategic Management in the Global Economy* (pp. 57–77). Hershey, PA: IGI Global. doi:10.4018/978-1-5225-2673-5.ch004

Pereira, R., Mira da Silva, M., & Lapão, L. V. (2017). IT Governance Maturity Patterns in Portuguese Healthcare. In S. De Haes & W. Van Grembergen (Eds.), *Strategic IT Governance and Alignment in Business Settings* (pp. 24–52). Hershey, PA: IGI Global. doi:10.4018/978-1-5225-0861-8.ch002

Perez-Uribe, R., & Ocampo-Guzman, D. (2016). Conflict within Colombian Family Owned SMEs: An Explosive Blend between Feelings and Business. In J. Saiz-Álvarez (Ed.), *Handbook of Research on Social Entrepreneurship and Solidarity Economics* (pp. 329–354). Hershey, PA: IGI Global. doi:10.4018/978-1-5225-0097-1.ch017

Pérez-Uribe, R. I., Torres, D. A., Jurado, S. P., & Prada, D. M. (2018). Cloud Tools for the Development of Project Management in SMEs. In R. Perez-Uribe, C. Salcedo-Perez, & D. Ocampo-Guzman (Eds.), *Handbook of Research on Intrapreneurship and Organizational Sustainability in SMEs* (pp. 95–120). Hershey, PA: IGI Global. doi:10.4018/978-1-5225-3543-0.ch005

Petrisor, I., & Cozmiuc, D. (2017). Global Supply Chain Management Organization at Siemens in the Advent of Industry 4.0. In L. Saglietto & C. Cezanne (Eds.), *Global Intermediation and Logistics Service Providers* (pp. 123–142). Hershey, PA: IGI Global. doi:10.4018/978-1-5225-2133-4.ch007

Pierce, J. M., Velliaris, D. M., & Edwards, J. (2017). A Living Case Study: A Journey Not a Destination. In N. Silton (Ed.), *Exploring the Benefits of Creativity in Education, Media, and the Arts* (pp. 158–178). Hershey, PA: IGI Global. doi:10.4018/978-1-5225-0504-4.ch008

Radosavljevic, M., & Andjelkovic, A. (2017). Multi-Criteria Decision Making Approach for Choosing Business Process for the Improvement: Upgrading of the Six Sigma Methodology. In J. Stanković, P. Delias, S. Marinković, & S. Rochhia (Eds.), *Tools and Techniques for Economic Decision Analysis* (pp. 225–247). Hershey, PA: IGI Global. doi:10.4018/978-1-5225-0959-2.ch011

Radovic, V. M. (2017). Corporate Sustainability and Responsibility and Disaster Risk Reduction: A Serbian Overview. In M. Camilleri (Ed.), *CSR 2.0 and the New Era of Corporate Citizenship* (pp. 147–164). Hershey, PA: IGI Global. doi:10.4018/978-1-5225-1842-6.ch008

Raghunath, K. M., Devi, S. L., & Patro, C. S. (2018). Impact of Risk Assessment Models on Risk Factors: A Holistic Outlook. In K. Strang, M. Korstanje, & N. Vajjhala (Eds.), *Research, Practices, and Innovations in Global Risk and Contingency Management* (pp. 134–153). Hershey, PA: IGI Global. doi:10.4018/978-1-5225-4754-9.ch008

Raman, A., & Goyal, D. P. (2017). Extending IMPLEMENT Framework for Enterprise Information Systems Implementation to Information System Innovation. In M. Tavana (Ed.), *Enterprise Information Systems and the Digitalization of Business Functions* (pp. 137–177). Hershey, PA: IGI Global. doi:10.4018/978-1-5225-2382-6.ch007

Rao, Y., & Zhang, Y. (2017). The Construction and Development of Academic Library Digital Special Subject Databases. In L. Ruan, Q. Zhu, & Y. Ye (Eds.), *Academic Library Development and Administration in China* (pp. 163–183). Hershey, PA: IGI Global. doi:10.4018/978-1-5225-0550-1.ch010

Ravasan, A. Z., Mohammadi, M. M., & Hamidi, H. (2018). An Investigation Into the Critical Success Factors of Implementing Information Technology Service Management Frameworks. In K. Jakobs (Ed.), *Corporate and Global Standardization Initiatives in Contemporary Society* (pp. 200–218). Hershey, PA: IGI Global. doi:10.4018/978-1-5225-5320-5.ch009

Renna, P., Izzo, C., & Romaniello, T. (2016). The Business Process Management Systems to Support Continuous Improvements. In W. Nuninger & J. Châtelet (Eds.), *Handbook of Research on Quality Assurance and Value Management in Higher Education* (pp. 237–256). Hershey, PA: IGI Global. doi:10.4018/978-1-5225-0024-7.ch009

Rezaie, S., Mirabedini, S. J., & Abtahi, A. (2018). Designing a Model for Implementation of Business Intelligence in the Banking Industry. *International Journal of Enterprise Information Systems*, *14*(1), 77–103. doi:10.4018/IJEIS.2018010105

Riccò, R. (2016). Diversity Management: Bringing Equality, Equity, and Inclusion in the Workplace. In J. Prescott (Ed.), *Handbook of Research on Race, Gender, and the Fight for Equality* (pp. 335–359). Hershey, PA: IGI Global. doi:10.4018/978-1-5225-0047-6.ch015

Romano, L., Grimaldi, R., & Colasuonno, F. S. (2017). Demand Management as a Success Factor in Project Portfolio Management. In L. Romano (Ed.), *Project Portfolio Management Strategies for Effective Organizational Operations* (pp. 202–219). Hershey, PA: IGI Global. doi:10.4018/978-1-5225-2151-8.ch008

Rostek, K. B. (2016). Risk Management: Role and Importance in Business Organization. In D. Jakóbczak (Ed.), *Analyzing Risk through Probabilistic Modeling in Operations Research* (pp. 149–178). Hershey, PA: IGI Global. doi:10.4018/978-1-4666-9458-3.ch007

Rouhani, S., & Savoji, S. R. (2016). A Success Assessment Model for BI Tools Implementation: An Empirical Study of Banking Industry. *International Journal of Business Intelligence Research, 7*(1), 25–44. doi:10.4018/IJBIR.2016010103

Ruan, Z. (2016). A Corpus-Based Functional Analysis of Complex Nominal Groups in Written Business Discourse: The Case of "Business". *International Journal of Computer-Assisted Language Learning and Teaching, 6*(2), 74–90. doi:10.4018/IJCALLT.2016040105

Ruhi, U. (2018). Towards an Interdisciplinary Socio-Technical Definition of Virtual Communities. In M. Khosrow-Pour, D.B.A. (Ed.), Encyclopedia of Information Science and Technology, Fourth Edition (pp. 4278-4295). Hershey, PA: IGI Global. doi:10.4018/978-1-5225-2255-3.ch371

Ryan, J., Doster, B., Daily, S., & Lewis, C. (2016). A Case Study Perspective for Balanced Perioperative Workflow Achievement through Data-Driven Process Improvement. *International Journal of Healthcare Information Systems and Informatics, 11*(3), 19–41. doi:10.4018/IJHISI.2016070102

Safari, M. R., & Jiang, Q. (2018). The Theory and Practice of IT Governance Maturity and Strategies Alignment: Evidence From Banking Industry. *Journal of Global Information Management, 26*(2), 127–146. doi:10.4018/JGIM.2018040106

Sahoo, J., Pati, B., & Mohanty, B. (2017). Knowledge Management as an Academic Discipline: An Assessment. In B. Gunjal (Ed.), *Managing Knowledge and Scholarly Assets in Academic Libraries* (pp. 99–126). Hershey, PA: IGI Global. doi:10.4018/978-1-5225-1741-2.ch005

Saini, D. (2017). Relevance of Teaching Values and Ethics in Management Education. In N. Baporikar (Ed.), *Management Education for Global Leadership* (pp. 90–111). Hershey, PA: IGI Global. doi:10.4018/978-1-5225-1013-0.ch005

Sambhanthan, A. (2017). Assessing and Benchmarking Sustainability in Organisations: An Integrated Conceptual Model. *International Journal of Systems and Service-Oriented Engineering*, *7*(4), 22–43. doi:10.4018/IJSSOE.2017100102

Sambhanthan, A., & Potdar, V. (2017). A Study of the Parameters Impacting Sustainability in Information Technology Organizations. *International Journal of Knowledge-Based Organizations*, *7*(3), 27–39. doi:10.4018/IJKBO.2017070103

Sánchez-Fernández, M. D., & Manríquez, M. R. (2018). The Entrepreneurial Spirit Based on Social Values: The Digital Generation. In P. Isaias & L. Carvalho (Eds.), *User Innovation and the Entrepreneurship Phenomenon in the Digital Economy* (pp. 173–193). Hershey, PA: IGI Global. doi:10.4018/978-1-5225-2826-5.ch009

Sanchez-Ruiz, L., & Blanco, B. (2017). Process Management for SMEs: Barriers, Enablers, and Benefits. In M. Vemić (Ed.), *Optimal Management Strategies in Small and Medium Enterprises* (pp. 293–319). Hershey, PA: IGI Global. doi:10.4018/978-1-5225-1949-2.ch014

Sanz, L. F., Gómez-Pérez, J., & Castillo-Martinez, A. (2018). Analysis of the European ICT Competence Frameworks. In V. Ahuja & S. Rathore (Eds.), *Multidisciplinary Perspectives on Human Capital and Information Technology Professionals* (pp. 225–245). Hershey, PA: IGI Global. doi:10.4018/978-1-5225-5297-0.ch012

Sarvepalli, A., & Godin, J. (2017). Business Process Management in the Classroom. *Journal of Cases on Information Technology*, *19*(2), 17–28. doi:10.4018/JCIT.2017040102

Satpathy, B., & Muniapan, B. (2016). Ancient Wisdom for Transformational Leadership and Its Insights from the Bhagavad-Gita. In U. Aung & P. Ordoñez de Pablos (Eds.), *Managerial Strategies and Practice in the Asian Business Sector* (pp. 1–10). Hershey, PA: IGI Global. doi:10.4018/978-1-4666-9758-4.ch001

Saygili, E. E., Ozturkoglu, Y., & Kocakulah, M. C. (2017). End Users' Perceptions of Critical Success Factors in ERP Applications. *International Journal of Enterprise Information Systems*, *13*(4), 58–75. doi:10.4018/IJEIS.2017100104

Saygili, E. E., & Saygili, A. T. (2017). Contemporary Issues in Enterprise Information Systems: A Critical Review of CSFs in ERP Implementations. In M. Tavana (Ed.), *Enterprise Information Systems and the Digitalization of Business Functions* (pp. 120–136). Hershey, PA: IGI Global. doi:10.4018/978-1-5225-2382-6.ch006

Seidenstricker, S., & Antonino, A. (2018). Business Model Innovation-Oriented Technology Management for Emergent Technologies. In M. Khosrow-Pour, D.B.A. (Ed.), Encyclopedia of Information Science and Technology, Fourth Edition (pp. 4560-4569). Hershey, PA: IGI Global. doi:10.4018/978-1-5225-2255-3.ch396

Senaratne, S., & Gunarathne, A. D. (2017). Excellence Perspective for Management Education from a Global Accountants' Hub in Asia. In N. Baporikar (Ed.), *Management Education for Global Leadership* (pp. 158–180). Hershey, PA: IGI Global. doi:10.4018/978-1-5225-1013-0.ch008

Sensuse, D. I., & Cahyaningsih, E. (2018). Knowledge Management Models: A Summative Review. *International Journal of Information Systems in the Service Sector*, *10*(1), 71–100. doi:10.4018/IJISSS.2018010105

Sensuse, D. I., Wibowo, W. C., & Cahyaningsih, E. (2016). Indonesian Government Knowledge Management Model: A Theoretical Model. *Information Resources Management Journal*, *29*(1), 91–108. doi:10.4018/irmj.2016010106

Seth, M., Goyal, D., & Kiran, R. (2017). Diminution of Impediments in Implementation of Supply Chain Management Information System for Enhancing its Effectiveness in Indian Automobile Industry. *Journal of Global Information Management*, *25*(3), 1–20. doi:10.4018/JGIM.2017070101

Seyal, A. H., & Rahman, M. N. (2017). Investigating Impact of Inter-Organizational Factors in Measuring ERP Systems Success: Bruneian Perspectives. In M. Tavana (Ed.), *Enterprise Information Systems and the Digitalization of Business Functions* (pp. 178–204). Hershey, PA: IGI Global. doi:10.4018/978-1-5225-2382-6.ch008

Shaikh, A. A., & Karjaluoto, H. (2016). On Some Misconceptions Concerning Digital Banking and Alternative Delivery Channels. *International Journal of E-Business Research*, *12*(3), 1–16. doi:10.4018/IJEBR.2016070101

Shams, S. M. (2016). Stakeholder Relationship Management in Online Business and Competitive Value Propositions: Evidence from the Sports Industry. *International Journal of Online Marketing*, *6*(2), 1–17. doi:10.4018/IJOM.2016040101

Shamsuzzoha, A. (2016). Management of Risk and Resilience within Collaborative Business Network. In R. Addo-Tenkorang, J. Kantola, P. Helo, & A. Shamsuzzoha (Eds.), *Supply Chain Strategies and the Engineer-to-Order Approach* (pp. 143–159). Hershey, PA: IGI Global. doi:10.4018/978-1-5225-0021-6.ch008

Shaqrah, A. A. (2018). Analyzing Business Intelligence Systems Based on 7s Model of McKinsey. *International Journal of Business Intelligence Research*, *9*(1), 53–63. doi:10.4018/IJBIR.2018010104

Sharma, A. J. (2017). Enhancing Sustainability through Experiential Learning in Management Education. In N. Baporikar (Ed.), *Management Education for Global Leadership* (pp. 256–274). Hershey, PA: IGI Global. doi:10.4018/978-1-5225-1013-0.ch013

Shetty, K. P. (2017). Responsible Global Leadership: Ethical Challenges in Management Education. In N. Baporikar (Ed.), *Innovation and Shifting Perspectives in Management Education* (pp. 194–223). Hershey, PA: IGI Global. doi:10.4018/978-1-5225-1019-2.ch009

Sinthupundaja, J., & Kohda, Y. (2017). Effects of Corporate Social Responsibility and Creating Shared Value on Sustainability. *International Journal of Sustainable Entrepreneurship and Corporate Social Responsibility*, *2*(1), 27–38. doi:10.4018/IJSECSR.2017010103

Škarica, I., & Hrgović, A. V. (2018). Implementation of Total Quality Management Principles in Public Health Institutes in the Republic of Croatia. *International Journal of Productivity Management and Assessment Technologies*, *6*(1), 1–16. doi:10.4018/IJPMAT.2018010101

Smuts, H., Kotzé, P., Van der Merwe, A., & Loock, M. (2017). Framework for Managing Shared Knowledge in an Information Systems Outsourcing Context. *International Journal of Knowledge Management*, *13*(4), 1–30. doi:10.4018/IJKM.2017100101

Soares, E. R., & Zaidan, F. H. (2016). Information Architecture and Business Modeling in Modern Organizations of Information Technology: Professional Career Plan in Organizations IT. In G. Jamil, J. Poças Rascão, F. Ribeiro, & A. Malheiro da Silva (Eds.), *Handbook of Research on Information Architecture and Management in Modern Organizations* (pp. 439–457). Hershey, PA: IGI Global. doi:10.4018/978-1-4666-8637-3.ch020

Sousa, M. J., Cruz, R., Dias, I., & Caracol, C. (2017). Information Management Systems in the Supply Chain. In G. Jamil, A. Soares, & C. Pessoa (Eds.), *Handbook of Research on Information Management for Effective Logistics and Supply Chains* (pp. 469–485). Hershey, PA: IGI Global. doi:10.4018/978-1-5225-0973-8.ch025

Spremic, M., Turulja, L., & Bajgoric, N. (2018). Two Approaches in Assessing Business Continuity Management Attitudes in the Organizational Context. In N. Bajgoric (Ed.), *Always-On Enterprise Information Systems for Modern Organizations* (pp. 159–183). Hershey, PA: IGI Global. doi:10.4018/978-1-5225-3704-5.ch008

Steenkamp, A. L. (2018). Some Insights in Computer Science and Information Technology. In *Examining the Changing Role of Supervision in Doctoral Research Projects: Emerging Research and Opportunities* (pp. 113–133). Hershey, PA: IGI Global. doi:10.4018/978-1-5225-2610-0.ch005

Studdard, N., Dawson, M., Burton, S. L., Jackson, N., Leonard, B., Quisenberry, W., & Rahim, E. (2016). Nurturing Social Entrepreneurship and Building Social Entrepreneurial Self-Efficacy: Focusing on Primary and Secondary Schooling to Develop Future Social Entrepreneurs. In Z. Fields (Ed.), *Incorporating Business Models and Strategies into Social Entrepreneurship* (pp. 154–175). Hershey, PA: IGI Global. doi:10.4018/978-1-4666-8748-6.ch010

Sun, Z. (2016). A Framework for Developing Management Intelligent Systems. *International Journal of Systems and Service-Oriented Engineering*, *6*(1), 37–53. doi:10.4018/IJSSOE.2016010103

Swami, B., & Mphele, G. T. (2016). Problems Preventing Growth of Small Entrepreneurs: A Case Study of a Few Small Entrepreneurs in Botswana Sub-Urban Areas. In N. Baporikar (Ed.), *Handbook of Research on Entrepreneurship in the Contemporary Knowledge-Based Global Economy* (pp. 479–508). Hershey, PA: IGI Global. doi:10.4018/978-1-4666-8798-1.ch020

Tabach, A., & Croteau, A. (2017). Configurations of Information Technology Governance Practices and Business Unit Performance. *International Journal of IT/Business Alignment and Governance*, *8*(2), 1–27. doi:10.4018/IJITBAG.2017070101

Talaue, G. M., & Iqbal, T. (2017). Assessment of e-Business Mode of Selected Private Universities in the Philippines and Pakistan. *International Journal of Online Marketing*, *7*(4), 63–77. doi:10.4018/IJOM.2017100105

Tam, G. C. (2017). Project Manager Sustainability Competence. In *Managerial Strategies and Green Solutions for Project Sustainability* (pp. 178–207). Hershey, PA: IGI Global. doi:10.4018/978-1-5225-2371-0.ch008

Tambo, T. (2018). Fashion Retail Innovation: About Context, Antecedents, and Outcome in Technological Change Projects. In I. Management Association (Ed.), Fashion and Textiles: Breakthroughs in Research and Practice (pp. 233-260). Hershey, PA: IGI Global. doi:10.4018/978-1-5225-3432-7.ch010

Tambo, T., & Mikkelsen, O. E. (2016). Fashion Supply Chain Optimization: Linking Make-to-Order Purchasing and B2B E-Commerce. In S. Joshi & R. Joshi (Eds.), *Designing and Implementing Global Supply Chain Management* (pp. 1–21). Hershey, PA: IGI Global. doi:10.4018/978-1-4666-9720-1.ch001

Tandon, K. (2016). Innovative Andragogy: The Paradigm Shift to Heutagogy. In S. Tiwari & L. Nafees (Eds.), *Innovative Management Education Pedagogies for Preparing Next-Generation Leaders* (pp. 238–257). Hershey, PA: IGI Global. doi:10.4018/978-1-4666-9691-4.ch014

Tantau, A. D., & Frăţilă, L. C. (2018). Information and Management System for Renewable Energy Business. In *Entrepreneurship and Business Development in the Renewable Energy Sector* (pp. 200–244). Hershey, PA: IGI Global. doi:10.4018/978-1-5225-3625-3.ch006

Teixeira, N., Pardal, P. N., & Rafael, B. G. (2018). Internationalization, Financial Performance, and Organizational Challenges: A Success Case in Portugal. In L. Carvalho (Ed.), *Handbook of Research on Entrepreneurial Ecosystems and Social Dynamics in a Globalized World* (pp. 379–423). Hershey, PA: IGI Global. doi:10.4018/978-1-5225-3525-6.ch017

Trad, A., & Kalpić, D. (2016). The E-Business Transformation Framework for E-Commerce Architecture-Modeling Projects. In I. Lee (Ed.), *Encyclopedia of E-Commerce Development, Implementation, and Management* (pp. 733–753). Hershey, PA: IGI Global. doi:10.4018/978-1-4666-9787-4.ch052

Trad, A., & Kalpić, D. (2016). The E-Business Transformation Framework for E-Commerce Control and Monitoring Pattern. In I. Lee (Ed.), *Encyclopedia of E-Commerce Development, Implementation, and Management* (pp. 754–777). Hershey, PA: IGI Global. doi:10.4018/978-1-4666-9787-4.ch053

Trad, A., & Kalpić, D. (2018). The Business Transformation Framework, Agile Project and Change Management. In M. Khosrow-Pour, D.B.A. (Ed.), Encyclopedia of Information Science and Technology, Fourth Edition (pp. 620-635). Hershey, PA: IGI Global. doi:10.4018/978-1-5225-2255-3.ch054

Trad, A., & Kalpić, D. (2018). The Business Transformation and Enterprise Architecture Framework: The Financial Engineering E-Risk Management and E-Law Integration. In B. Sergi, F. Fidanoski, M. Ziolo, & V. Naumovski (Eds.), *Regaining Global Stability After the Financial Crisis* (pp. 46–65). Hershey, PA: IGI Global. doi:10.4018/978-1-5225-4026-7.ch003

Turulja, L., & Bajgoric, N. (2018). Business Continuity and Information Systems: A Systematic Literature Review. In N. Bajgoric (Ed.), *Always-On Enterprise Information Systems for Modern Organizations* (pp. 60–87). Hershey, PA: IGI Global. doi:10.4018/978-1-5225-3704-5.ch004 van Wessel, R. M., de Vries, H. J., & Ribbers, P. M. (2016). Business Benefits through Company IT Standardization. In K. Jakobs (Ed.), *Effective Standardization Management in Corporate Settings* (pp. 34–53). Hershey, PA: IGI Global. doi:10.4018/978-1-4666-9737-9.ch003

Vargas-Hernández, J. G. (2017). Professional Integrity in Business Management Education. In N. Baporikar (Ed.), *Management Education for Global Leadership* (pp. 70–89). Hershey, PA: IGI Global. doi:10.4018/978-1-5225-1013-0.ch004

Vasista, T. G., & AlAbdullatif, A. M. (2017). Role of Electronic Customer Relationship Management in Demand Chain Management: A Predictive Analytic Approach. *International Journal of Information Systems and Supply Chain Management, 10*(1), 53–67. doi:10.4018/IJISSCM.2017010104

Vergidis, K. (2016). Rediscovering Business Processes: Definitions, Patterns, and Modelling Approaches. In P. Papajorgji, F. Pinet, A. Guimarães, & J. Papathanasiou (Eds.), *Automated Enterprise Systems for Maximizing Business Performance* (pp. 97–122). Hershey, PA: IGI Global. doi:10.4018/978-1-4666-8841-4.ch007

Vieru, D., & Bourdeau, S. (2017). Survival in the Digital Era: A Digital Competence-Based Multi-Case Study in the Canadian SME Clothing Industry. *International Journal of Social and Organizational Dynamics in IT, 6*(1), 17–34. doi:10.4018/IJSODIT.2017010102

Vijayan, G., & Kamarulzaman, N. H. (2017). An Introduction to Sustainable Supply Chain Management and Business Implications. In M. Khan, M. Hussain, & M. Ajmal (Eds.), *Green Supply Chain Management for Sustainable Business Practice* (pp. 27–50). Hershey, PA: IGI Global. doi:10.4018/978-1-5225-0635-5.ch002

Vlachvei, A., & Notta, O. (2017). Firm Competitiveness: Theories, Evidence, and Measurement. In A. Vlachvei, O. Notta, K. Karantininis, & N. Tsounis (Eds.), *Factors Affecting Firm Competitiveness and Performance in the Modern Business World* (pp. 1–42). Hershey, PA: IGI Global. doi:10.4018/978-1-5225-0843-4.ch001

von Rosing, M., Fullington, N., & Walker, J. (2016). Using the Business Ontology and Enterprise Standards to Transform Three Leading Organizations. *International Journal of Conceptual Structures and Smart Applications, 4*(1), 71–99. doi:10.4018/IJCSSA.2016010104

von Rosing, M., & von Scheel, H. (2016). Using the Business Ontology to Develop Enterprise Standards. *International Journal of Conceptual Structures and Smart Applications, 4*(1), 48–70. doi:10.4018/IJCSSA.2016010103

Walczak, S. (2016). Artificial Neural Networks and other AI Applications for Business Management Decision Support. *International Journal of Sociotechnology and Knowledge Development*, *8*(4), 1–20. doi:10.4018/IJSKD.2016100101

Wamba, S. F., Akter, S., Kang, H., Bhattacharya, M., & Upal, M. (2016). The Primer of Social Media Analytics. *Journal of Organizational and End User Computing*, *28*(2), 1–12. doi:10.4018/JOEUC.2016040101

Wang, C., Schofield, M., Li, X., & Ou, X. (2017). Do Chinese Students in Public and Private Higher Education Institutes Perform at Different Level in One of the Leadership Skills: Critical Thinking?: An Exploratory Comparison. In V. Wang (Ed.), *Encyclopedia of Strategic Leadership and Management* (pp. 160–181). Hershey, PA: IGI Global. doi:10.4018/978-1-5225-1049-9.ch013

Wang, F., Raisinghani, M. S., Mora, M., & Wang, X. (2016). Strategic E-Business Management through a Balanced Scored Card Approach. In I. Lee (Ed.), *Encyclopedia of E-Commerce Development, Implementation, and Management* (pp. 361–386). Hershey, PA: IGI Global. doi:10.4018/978-1-4666-9787-4.ch027

Wang, J. (2017). Multi-Agent based Production Management Decision System Modelling for the Textile Enterprise. *Journal of Global Information Management*, *25*(4), 1–15. doi:10.4018/JGIM.2017100101

Wiedemann, A., & Gewald, H. (2017). Examining Cross-Domain Alignment: The Correlation of Business Strategy, IT Management, and IT Business Value. *International Journal of IT/Business Alignment and Governance*, *8*(1), 17–31. doi:10.4018/IJITBAG.2017010102

Wolf, R., & Thiel, M. (2018). Advancing Global Business Ethics in China: Reducing Poverty Through Human and Social Welfare. In S. Hipsher (Ed.), *Examining the Private Sector's Role in Wealth Creation and Poverty Reduction* (pp. 67–84). Hershey, PA: IGI Global. doi:10.4018/978-1-5225-3117-3.ch004

Wu, J., Ding, F., Xu, M., Mo, Z., & Jin, A. (2016). Investigating the Determinants of Decision-Making on Adoption of Public Cloud Computing in E-government. *Journal of Global Information Management*, *24*(3), 71–89. doi:10.4018/JGIM.2016070104

Xu, L., & de Vrieze, P. (2016). Building Situational Applications for Virtual Enterprises. In I. Lee (Ed.), *Encyclopedia of E-Commerce Development, Implementation, and Management* (pp. 715–724). Hershey, PA: IGI Global. doi:10.4018/978-1-4666-9787-4.ch050

Yablonsky, S. (2018). Innovation Platforms: Data and Analytics Platforms. In *Multi-Sided Platforms (MSPs) and Sharing Strategies in the Digital Economy: Emerging Research and Opportunities* (pp. 72–95). Hershey, PA: IGI Global. doi:10.4018/978-1-5225-5457-8.ch003

Yusoff, A., Ahmad, N. H., & Halim, H. A. (2017). Agropreneurship among Gen Y in Malaysia: The Role of Academic Institutions. In N. Ahmad, T. Ramayah, H. Halim, & S. Rahman (Eds.), *Handbook of Research on Small and Medium Enterprises in Developing Countries* (pp. 23–47). Hershey, PA: IGI Global. doi:10.4018/978-1-5225-2165-5.ch002

Zanin, F., Comuzzi, E., & Costantini, A. (2018). The Effect of Business Strategy and Stock Market Listing on the Use of Risk Assessment Tools. In *Management Control Systems in Complex Settings: Emerging Research and Opportunities* (pp. 145–168). Hershey, PA: IGI Global. doi:10.4018/978-1-5225-3987-2.ch007

Zgheib, P. W. (2017). Corporate Innovation and Intrapreneurship in the Middle East. In P. Zgheib (Ed.), *Entrepreneurship and Business Innovation in the Middle East* (pp. 37–56). Hershey, PA: IGI Global. doi:10.4018/978-1-5225-2066-5.ch003

About the Contributors

Wei Liu is presently the PhD scholar of the University of Sydney. His current research interests include nonmarket strategy in emerging economies, corporate sustainable strategy, regional studies, and strategic management in the Chinese context. He has published several papers in refereed journals and presented numerous papers at top-tier international business conferences. He also served as the reviewer in many journals and conferences. He has won two National Social Science Foundation of China Grant which supports his research on the Belt and Road Initiative. He is also funded by the University of Sydney China Studies Centre Research Support Grants.

Zhe Zhang is a current PhD candidate in the Sydney School of Architecture, Design and Planning, The University of Sydney. He currently focuses his research interests on the governance of city-regions and the mechanisms of regional planning. Zhe holds a Bachelor of Architecture from Henan University, Kaifeng and Master in Architecture from South China University of Technology, Guangzhou. Before joining the University of Sydney, he has worked in various projects related to architectural designing such as protection and renewal planning of traditional villages, modern buildings design with Lingnan characteristics, renovation of traditional dwellings and planning on the historical blocks and streets. Also, Zhe has participated the joint research on Heritage Architecture of Guangdong Province and research on Vocabulary with Lingnan Characteristics, which is funded by Chinese National Natural Science Foundation Projects. Previous projects experience has ignited Zhe's interests on urban planning. So in doctoral research, Zhe explores the recent emergence of transformed forms and mechanisms of urban planning under the context of regional development of China's city-regions.

Sang-Bing Tsai is currently a Professor at University of Electronic Science and Technology of China Zhongshan Institute, Capital University of Economics and Business and Wuyi University. He is both Technology Management and Business Management PhD. He has published many research articles in SCI / SSCI journals, including International Journal of Production Research, International Journal of

Web Services Research, Advances in Mechanical Engineering, IEEE Transactions on Systems Man Cybernetics-Systems, Plos One, Environment and Planning B-Planning & Design, Sustainability, Renewable & Sustainable Energy Reviews,...etc. His recent research interests in Computer Science, Information Management, Big Data, Sustainability, Green Operation and Applied Mathematics. He has well over 100 published peer-reviewed journal articles. Dr. Tsai is will be the Co-Editor-in-Chief for the Journal of Organizational and End User Computing. He is currently the Associate Editor for Journal of Global Information Management, and Associate Editor for International Journal of Digital Crime and Forensics, as well as serving on the editorial boards of 10 other journals.

* * *

Bahar Baysal Kar is currently an assistant professor at the Department of Economics at Kırklareli University in Turkey. She received his Ph.D. degree in Economics from Uludag University in Turkey. She received his MBA and a bachelor's degree from Uludag University. Her research interest in comparative political economy, international political economy, economic thought, economic systems, the political economy of the Turkey, economics and ethics, economic development. Specifically, varieties of capitalism, the future of global capitalism and the implications of global financial crisis for the future of new world order are her recent research themes. She has published many academic papers.

Jian-Yu Chen is the PhD scholar of Graduate School of International Studies at Dong-A University in South Korea. He earned a Master's degree in business administration and Management from Pusan National University in 2016. His research interests include corporate social responsibility and international business. He is funded by the BK21 PLUS (Brain Korea 21 Program for Leading Universities & Students) from 2017 to 2019.

Ying Chen is currently a master researcher in English Education at the University of Malaya.

Teo Poh Chuin is a Senior Lecturer from Faculty of Accountancy, Finance and Business at Tunku Abdul Rahman University College, Kuala Lumpur, Malaysia. She is an independent researcher who is actively involved in research projects and publication. Her research interest is in international marketing and international business. She is experienced in teaching students from different origin countries at postgraduate and undergraduate levels.

Taha Egri holds a PhD. degree in Economics from Istanbul University, Turkey. He was a visiting scholar at George Mason University between 2014 and 2016. He is currently working as an assistant professor at Kırklareli University, where his primary fields of interest include institutional economics, political economy of the Middle East, military-economy relations and Islamic Economics. Egri has published several articles on macroeconomic issues and middle east economies and has edited two books on Islamic Economics. He is also a member of the editorial board of two peer-reviewed journal namely, "the Journal of Human and Society" and "Turkish Journal of Islamic Economics".

Ge Han has a PhD from City University of Macau and is a research assistant of Macau "One Belt. One Road" Research Center.

Maoxiang Lang, Ph.D., School of Traffic and Transportation, Beijing Jiaotong University, Professor, doctoral tutor, deputy director of Logistics Engineering Department, special researcher of China logistics society. He is mainly engaged in the field of transportation logistics management, modern freight transport technology and management, transportation marketing management. He published more than 90 articles in journal papers and conference papers.

Fuda Li is currently a PhD student at the City University of Macau. Before that, he has received his bachelor's degree at the Hunan University in 2013 and master degree at the Lanzhou University in 2016.

Shiqi Li is a doctor in the School of Traffic and Transportation, Beijing Jiatong University.

Xinyao Li is a research student in Northeast Electric Power University.

Yu Xueqiao received his M.S. degree in engineering from Northeast Forestry University in Harbin, China. He is currently a Ph.D candidate in Beijing Jiaotong University. His research interest is mainly in the area of Multi-modal Transportation and Logistic Management. He has done a lot of in-depth research in these areas and published a related paper.

Wang Yanling received her Ph.D in Transportation from Beijing Jiaotong University in Beijing, China. She is currently an associate professor in Beijing City University. Her research interest is mainly in the area of Traffic and Transportation. She has published more than a dozen research papers in academic Journals in the above research area and has participated in several conferences.

Xiao Yu received his Ph.D in China academy of railway sciences, Beijing, China. He is currently an associate research fellow in China academy of railway sciences. His research interest is mainly in the area of Signal and Communication. He has published several research papers in academic Journals in the above research area and has participated in several conferences.

Yong Zhang is currently a postgraduate student at the University of Macau, majoring in international law.

Linling Zhong is a graduated postgraduate student and received her master degree in Interpreting and Translation, Mandarin and English from University of Nottingham Ningbo China (UNNC). She has published an academic paper titled Analysis on Translation of Children's Literature from the Perspective of Functional Equivalence Theory Based on Tale in Orange in CPCI-SSH. Her research interests in translation, teaching English to speakers of other languages and children's literature.

Ping Zhou is a Director of the Macau "One Belt One Road" Research Centre, and the Associate Professor majoring in National Institute of Portuguese Studies at the City University of Macau. He also serves as the Visiting Professor at the Peking University.

Index

Ensure Quality Research is Introduced to the Academic Community

Become an IGI Global Reviewer for Authored Book Projects

The overall success of an authored book project is dependent on quality and timely reviews.

In this competitive age of scholarly publishing, constructive and timely feedback significantly expedites the turnaround time of manuscripts from submission to acceptance, allowing the publication and discovery of forward-thinking research at a much more expeditious rate. Several IGI Global authored book projects are currently seeking highly qualified experts in the field to fill vacancies on their respective editorial review boards:

Applications may be sent to:
development@igi-global.com

Applicants must have a doctorate (or an equivalent degree) as well as publishing and reviewing experience. Reviewers are asked to write reviews in a timely, collegial, and constructive manner. All reviewers will begin their role on an ad-hoc basis for a period of one year, and upon successful completion of this term can be considered for full editorial review board status, with the potential for a subsequent promotion to Associate Editor.

If you have a colleague that may be interested in this opportunity, we encourage you to share this information with them.

www.ingramcontent.com/pod-product-compliance
Lightning Source LLC
LaVergne TN
LVHW081328300926
849161LV00008B/1913